Social Work Practice with Transgender and Gender Expansive Youth

This fully revised third edition explores the childhood and adolescent experiences of transgender persons, providing foundational knowledge for social workers and related professions about working with trans and gender expansive youth.

Organized through the lens of four distinct forms of knowledge – knowledge of lived expertise, community-based knowledge, practice knowledge, and knowledge obtained through formal/traditional education – this text balances discussion of theory with a range of rich personal narratives and case studies. Updates and additions reflect recent changes to the WPATH guidelines and the NASW Code of Ethics, include brand new material examining the origins of gender identity and non-binary identities, explore intersectional identities, and offer expanded content considering trauma-informed interventions and ethical issues. Each featuring at least one trans or gender expansive author, chapters present concrete and practical recommendations to encourage competent and positive practice.

With a focus on both macro and micro social work practice, this book will be a valuable resource to any social service practitioners working with children or adolescents.

Jama Shelton, PhD, MSW, associate professor, Silberman School of Social Work; associate director, Silberman Center for Sexuality and Gender; has worked with queer and trans youth for 20 years.

Gerald P. Mallon, DSW, LCSW, is associate dean of research and scholarship and Julia Lathrop Professor of Child Welfare, and has been a child welfare practitioner, advocate, educator, and researcher for more than 45 years.

"This book turns much of what we have been taught to be the 'evidence base' about transgender and gender diverse youth on its head, sharing the lived experiences of these individuals and connecting it to a social work context. It contains a delightful buffet of interviews, case studies, research, and more, allowing the reader to more deeply understand the diverse and nuanced needs of this population, while also centering their successes and resilience. An absolute must read for any youth centered practitioners, educators, and researchers."

— **Shanna K. Kattari, PhD, MEd, CSE,** *assistant professor,*
University of Michigan School of Social Work and
Department of Women's and Gender Studies

"Understanding the unique strengths, resiliencies, and resourcefulness of transgender and gender expansive youth is critical for all social workers. This volume expertly captures the joy and exceptionalism of transgender and gender expansive youth from the lived experiences of those whose knowledge matters most. While the challenges of thriving within a context of oppressive structures are not ignored, these structures are used to contextualize the strength and resilience that result from the joy of authenticity in the midst of these challenges."

— **Alan Detlaff,** *dean and Maconda Brown O'Connor Endowed Dean's Chair,*
University of Houston Graduate College of Social Work

"This is a thoughtful book of collective wisdom that will profoundly shape the way that we practice and teach social work, ultimately saving lives. One of the most compelling points of the book is the clear delineation of core principles of the book and the way that this is operationalized through a collection of chapters that feature voices of transgender and gender expansive youth, as well as social work practitioners, and researchers. This book provides a compelling and holistic approach to practice with the population and fills a major gap in the social work practice literature. I will certainly use it in my LGBTQIA+ issues in social welfare course, in my work with youth, and to inform my research."

— **Maurice N. Gattis, PhD,** *associate professor,*
Virginia Commonwealth University School of Social Work

Social Work Practice with Transgender and Gender Expansive Youth

Third Edition

Edited by Jama Shelton and Gerald P. Mallon

Routledge
Taylor & Francis Group

NEW YORK AND LONDON

Third edition published 2022
by Routledge
605 Third Avenue, New York, NY 10158

and by Routledge
2 Park Square, Milton Park, Abingdon, Oxon, OX14 4RN

Routledge is an imprint of the Taylor & Francis Group, an informa business

© 2022 Taylor & Francis

The right of Jama Shelton and Gerald P. Mallon to be identified as
the authors of the editorial material, and of the authors for their
individual chapters, has been asserted in accordance with sections 77
and 78 of the Copyright, Designs and Patents Act 1988.

First edition published by Routledge 2000
Second edition published by Routledge 2009

Library of Congress Cataloging-in-Publication Data
Names: Shelton, Jama, editor. | Mallon, Gerald P., editor.
Title: Social work practice with transgender and gender expansive
youth / edited by Jama Shelton and Gerald P. Mallon.
Description: 3rd Edition. | New York: Routledge, 2021. | Revised
edition of Social work practice with transgender and gender variant
youth, 2009. | Includes bibliographical references and index.
Identifiers: LCCN 2021007958 (print) | LCCN 2021007959 (ebook) |
ISBN 9780367277499 (hardback) | ISBN 9780367277482 (paperback)
| ISBN 9780429297687 (ebook)
Subjects: LCSH: Transgender youth--Psychology. | Transgender
youth--Mental health services. | Gender-nonconforming youth. |
Social work with gender-nonconforming youth. | Social work with
transgender youth. | Transgender people--Services for--United States.
Classification: LCC HQ77.9.S64 2021 (print) | LCC HQ77.9 (ebook)
| DDC 362.7/850973--dc23
LC record available at https://lccn.loc.gov/2021007958
LC ebook record available at https://lccn.loc.gov/2021007959

ISBN: 978-0-367-27749-9 (hbk)
ISBN: 978-0-367-27748-2 (pbk)
ISBN: 978-0-429-29768-7 (ebk)

DOI: 10.4324/9780429297687

Typeset in Baskerville
by MPS Limited, Dehradun

This book is dedicated to all of the trans and gender expansive youth who are brilliantly and boldly living their lives. We see you and we all have a lot to learn from you.

Contents

Contributors

Leah Abay, LMSW (all pronouns), Leah is an LMSW currently working with individuals experiencing homelessness at Women In Need in Brooklyn, NY. Leah graduated from New York University with a master in social work in May of 2020 where she served LGBTQIA folks of all ages through direct practice, community organizing, and advocacy work.

Kelly Ancharski, MSW (they/them), Kelly is a recent master of social work graduate from New York University and currently works at McSilver Institute for Poverty Policy and Research. Kelly is dedicated to centering trans+, queer, and anti-racist grassroots activism, community organizing, and youth development in their research, direct practice, and advocacy.

Finn Brigham, MA (he/his), Finn is the director of Project Management at Callen-Lorde Community Health Center, the largest LGBT health center in the world. Finn has been published in the *Journal of Gay and Lesbian Mental Health* and has presented on LGB and transgender health issues across the country, including at The White House. He has a master's of non-profit management from The New School in New York City and is a frequent media spokesperson on transgender issues for outlets such as VICE, NY1, NBC, and BET, among others.

SJ Dodd, PhD (she/her), SJ is an associate professor at the Silberman School of Social Work, Hunter College, CUNY, and the CUNY Graduate Center. She is also founding director of the Silberman Center for Sexuality and Gender (SCSG). Dr. Dodd's latest book projects include *Sex-Positive Social Work* (CUP, 2020) and the *Routledge Handbook of Social Work and Sexualities* (due out early in 2021). Please see www.https://silbermanscsg.com

Marc Dones (they/them), Marc is a social scientist, entrepreneur, and policy strategist with 10+ years of experience in reimagining public systems to support historically marginalized communities. Dones has written or contributed to multiple book chapters, essays, and articles. They hold a degree in psychiatric anthropology from New York University.

Maggie Dunleavy (they/them), Maggie is a MSW candidate at Silberman School of Social Work. They are interested in research and clinical work that supports and honors the courage, creativity, and power of trans people and communities.

Kristian M. Gambardella, MSW (he/him), Kristian earned his MSW at Silberman School of Social Work at Hunter College and participated in an advanced year-long educational program developed by the National Child Traumatic Stress Network in child and adolescent trauma. He entered the field of social work with a passion for supporting gender-expansive youth and has worked in a variety of capacities with this population from camp counselor to research study coordinator.

Twiggy Pucci Garçon (she/her and they/them), Since finding support in the ballroom community 16 years ago, Twiggy leverages every opportunity to generate conversations around equity for LGBTQ+ people. Twiggy currently serves as chief program officer of Cyndi Lauper's True Colors United, working for more than half a decade in the fight and protection of rights for young people with lived experiences of homelessness. She has collaborated with artists, filmmakers, academics and policymakers to increase visibility of both creative and sociopolitical agendas. Twiggy is currently working on FX's POSE as a Consultant and as a runway choreographer and is producing the upcoming documentary "The Legend of Dorian Corey".

Aiyanna Horton (she/her), Aiyanna joined Advocates for Richmond Youth in 2014. She is passionate about working collaboratively with her peers to ensure that the needs of LGBTQ youth are included in decision making about youth homelessness. Previously, Aiyanna has done work in Richmond to develop LGBTQ-affirming sex education materials for community-based health organizations. She was also selected as a True Fellow with the True Colors Fund in 2016.

Ryan Karnoski, LCSW (he/him), Ryan is a licensed clinical social worker with a background in clinical mental health and child and family welfare services. Ryan received his bachelor of arts and master of social work degrees from the University of Washington, Seattle, and is currently a doctoral student at the University of California, Berkeley. Ryan is passionate about building a safer, healthier, and happier future for trans young people.

Aaron Kemmerer (he/him), Aaron is a doctoral student at Virginia Commonwealth University's School of Social Work. He joined Advocates for Richmond Youth in 2015. His research focuses on economic justice and housing stability for LGBTQ+ people. He is passionate about trans liberation in the U.S. South and beyond.

Bec Sokha Keo, MSW (they/them), Bec is a second-generation Cambodian-American who was born and raised on the land of the Karankawa, Coahuitecan, Atakapa-Ishak, and Sana tribes (also known as Houston, Texas). They are a child and grandchild of refugees who survived the Cambodian genocide along with racism, classism, and white supremacy in the United States. A first generation college graduate and current doctoral candidate at the University of Houston Graduate College of Social Work, their work currently focuses on community, research, and public impact activities with community-based organizations led by and serving people living with HIV/AIDS.

M. Killian Kinney, MSW (they/them), M. Killian Kinney is a doctoral candidate and associate faculty at Indiana University School of Social Work. Mx. Kinney is a queer, white, currently able-bodied, neuro-diverse, nonbinary person. Their community-driven research explores health equity, identity development, and well-being among transgender and nonbinary individuals and communities. Please see www.KillianKinney.com

Jonathan Lykes, MSW (he/they/she), Jonathan is a Black queer artist, activist, and academic. His interdisciplinary approach to art, activism, and anti-oppression work, merges policy change, artistic expression, and activism. Combining these forms of social transformation—and harnessing their synergy—Jonathan works to create awareness, promote personal healing, surmount institutional barriers, and generate systemic change. Jonathan's current position as founder/executive director of Liberation House merges his multidisciplinary artistic background with public policy reform, community engagement, and systems change work to teach liberation praxis by pushing the revolutionary edge of radical transformative movement work.

Finneran K. Muzzey, MA (they/them), Finneran is a doctoral candidate in the Department of Human Development and Family Studies at Michigan State University. They conduct research with queer populations, examining the influence of interpersonal relationships on sexual development and mental health outcomes. They are also a statistician and examine the ethics of conducting research with socially vulnerable populations.

Ryan Papciak, LCSW (he/him), Ryan is a licensed clinical social worker and second-year doctoral student at Barry University in Miami, Florida. Ryan has a background in utilizing the Functional Family Therapy model to work with the juvenile justice population. For his dissertation, Ryan is studying the relationship between gender dysphoria and trauma in the transgender community.

Anthony Ritosa (he/him), Anthony is a MSW candidate at Silberman School of Social Work. He is interested in international social work and learning new languages as new ways of connecting and understanding the great diversity of human experience.

Meghan Romanelli, PhD, LCSW (she/they/Meghan), Meghan is an assistant professor at the University of Washington School of Social Work. Meghan's research aims to understand and address the multisystemic factors that lead to mental health disparities among queer and trans+ communities, with a focus on the role of service access and treatment engagement.

Valentín Sierra, MSW (Yoeme), Valentín is an Indigenous social worker dedicated to promoting the holistic well-being of Native and Indigenous young people. Valentín's work primarily focuses on eliminating mental health disparities, particularly suicide and depression, through culturally grounded practices and interventions. Valentín graduated with highest honors from the University of California, Davis, with a bachelor of arts degree in Native American studies. Valentín also holds a master of social welfare degree from the University of California, Berkeley, where they are currently completing their PhD. Valentín is an associate clinical social worker in the state of California.

Oliver Stabbe (they/them), Oliver is a public health advocate and researcher committed to social equity by addressing social determinants of health for marginalized populations, with a particular focus on LGBTQ and disability communities. Oliver received their bachelor of arts degree from the University of Rochester and is currently a masters in public health candidate at UC Berkeley.

Justice Valentine (xe/xem), Justice has been involved in organizing and activism in the South since 2016. Xe joined Advocates for Richmond Youth in 2018. Justice is a passionate researcher who pushes our team to think about the intersections between movements.

Liliana Valvano (she/her), Liliana Valvano is a queer and autistic MSW student at Silberman School for Social Work whose background is in ethnic studies and autistic/disability justice community organizing. Her work focuses on the importance of deconstructing the medical model which pathologizes autism, and instead, accepting autistic people without forcing them to assimilate to non-autistic standards in order to be valued.

Alex Wagaman, PhD (she/her), Alex is an associate professor in the School of Social Work at Virginia Commonwealth University. She has been working with Advocates for Richmond Youth and the movement to end youth homelessness since 2014. Alex is passionate about creating and supporting spaces where youth and young adults are leading for change.

Liam Waller, BSW (he/him), Liam is a trans and queer social worker pursuing his MSW at Appalachian State University. Liam is passionate about social-justice-centered work and is the founder of an organization called Radical Kindred that supports rural LGBTQ+ folks in Boone, NC. He is currently in practicum in a clinical mental health setting.

Hez Wollin, LCSW (they/them), Hez is a trans clinical social worker living and working on Chechenyo Ohlone Land (San Francisco Bay Area). They are passionate about many different aspects of trans mental health, including perinatal and postpartum work. In their spare time, they enjoy making pottery and riding bikes. Please see www.hezwellness.com

About the Editors

Jama Shelton, PhD, is associate professor at the Silberman Social Work at Hunter College in New York City and associate director of the Silberman Center for Sexuality and Gender.

Dr. Shelton has worked with queer and trans youth for 20 years. Prior to joining Silberman, Dr. Shelton was the deputy executive director of True Colors United, a leading organization in the national movement to address youth homelessness. Their scholarship focuses LGBTQ+ youth homelessness and addressing structural barriers rooted in cis/heterosexism.

Dr. Shelton earned their PhD in Social Welfare at the CUNY Graduate Center in New York City and their MSW at the NYU Silver School of Social Work in New York City.

Correspondence may be sent to them via email at: jshelton@hunter.cuny.edu

Gerald P. Mallon, DSW, is the Julia Lathrop Professor of Child Welfare and associate dean of scholarship and research at the Silberman Social Work at Hunter College in New York City.

For more than 45 years, Dr. Mallon has been a child welfare practitioner, advocate, and researcher. He is the author or editor of twenty-eight books, and numerous peer-reviewed publications in professional journals. Dr. Mallon also serves as the senior editor of the peer-reviewed journal *Child Welfare*.

Dr. Mallon earned his doctorate in social welfare from the City University of New York at Hunter College, holds an MSW from Fordham University, and a BSW from Dominican College.

Dr. Mallon has lectured extensively in the United States, and internationally in Argentina, Australia, Canada, Chile, Cuba, Hong Kong, Indonesia, India, Ireland, Israel, Mexico, Norway, Singapore, the Netherlands, and the United Kingdom.

Correspondence may be sent to them via email at: gmallon@hunter.cuny.edu.

Foreword

When the world collapses, state violence intensifies, systems supposed to "help" and "protect" assume cis/hetero-normative bodies, when white supremacy soars through the veins of "social services" – who picks up the pieces? It's social workers, nurses, teachers … You are of course first responders, often without a guidebook to help navigate the radically transformative landscape of human needs/desires/identities and social movements.

But you wander alone, in the dark – no longer.

Social Work Practice with Transgender and Gender Expansive Youth, is a fierce, gentle, and user-friendly guidebook/manifesto designed to "be of use" as we all struggle with questions about how to stand beside and accompany bold and daring, quiet and withdrawn, powerful and terrified transgender and gender expansive youth; as we all worry we have been carried unwittingly across the porous lines between advocacy and neo-liberal complicity; as we begin, in our hearts and nightmares, to question the colonizing and transphobic history and design of social work practice. This volume will accompany readers, unapologetically and yet without judgment, as we explore and resist how white supremacy, cis-heterosexism, classism, transphobia, and xenophobia over-determine our practice. These essays are infused with rich understandings of intersectionality and anti-racist principles; the writers contest gender/sexuality binaries and refuse to romance families; these essays reject deficit perspectives and challenge heteronormativity. These chapters animate assets and organizing by and for transgender and gender expansive youth.

The essays in this volume are crafted to provoke a liberatory imagination for social work practice so we might honor the gifts of transgender and gender expansive youth whom we accompany, address the wounds of structural and intimate violence they endure, and support in awe the brilliance of youth activism, creativity, and youth-led movements for transjustice. Bravo to the co-editors, the authors, and the young transgender and gender expansive folks whose lives and desires dance on the pages of this volume.

Michelle Fine, distinguished professor of Critical Psychology
Urban Education and Social Welfare
The Graduate Center, CUNY

Acknowledgments

Thank you to all who contributed to and otherwise supported this book. The fact that we were collectively able to make this happen during a global pandemic, increased violence against Black Americans, and a chaotic presidential election year speaks to the importance of this text and your commitment to the well-being of trans and gender expansive youth.

We acknowledge those trans and gender expansive people who came before us, whose work and lives made it possible for us to publish a book like this and to imagine a world in which we are all celebrated.

Introduction

Jama Shelton and Gerald P. Mallon

History of This Text

The original idea for writing this book (first titled: *Social Services with Transgendered (sic) Youth*) came from discussions I had with Dr. Ray Berger, who was the editor of *The Journal of Gay and Lesbian Social Services* at the time this was first published in 1999. Now retired, Dr. Berger was a wonderful person to work with. His tireless quest to help practitioners and scholars to think about and write about LGBTQ persons allowed me and many others to write articles and edit special issue journals that speak to the needs of persons whose voices have been marginalized.

In 2008, the second edition of this book was expanded and published as *Social Work Practice with Transgender and Gender Variant Youth*, with many of the original contributors writing chapters, and several new authors writing additional chapters.

In 2021, the third edition of this book is published as *Social Work Practice with Transgender and Gender Expansive Youth* with all new contributors, almost all of whom are people who identify as trans or gender expansive. In initially putting this third edition together, I invited my wonderful colleague, Dr. Jama Shelton to join me as co-editor. However, it became very apparent to me almost immediately that Jama was the true expert in this area and my knowledge about editing a book about trans and gender expansive youth was quickly coming to an end. As one ages, I think it is important for one to know when it is time to hand off the baton, as it were, to one who is much more knowledgeable and skilled. As such, Jama and I flipped roles and they became the first author and I took on the role as the second author. Dr. Jama Shelton is an extraordinary scholar and an absolutely delightful person to work with. Their knowledge of trans young people and their scholarship in this area makes them one of the leading scholars in the international arena on these issues. Although I have been very happy to be a part of this new publication, it is Jama who deserves all the credit for the final product. I am happy to step off to the side, proud of what began 22 years ago when there were no books about trans youth and delighted to

DOI: 10.4324/9780429297687-101

follow their lead. Thank you, Jama, for being such a great colleague, a wonderful collaborator, and an extraordinary person. – Gerald P. Mallon

Core Organizing Principles of This Edition

Knowledge produced *about* trans and gender expansive (TGE) people should be produced *by* and *with* TGE people. Though this concept may seem obvious regarding knowledge production about any community, it is not always enacted in practice. There are many scholars who have contributed valuable research to guide social work practice with TGE youth. We acknowledge their contributions, and are proud to be able to highlight the work of TGE authors in this book. Each chapter in this text includes at least one TGE author.

Lived expertise is as valuable as formal education. This one can sometimes be controversial. While social workers may believe this in theory, it can be challenging to implement in practice and can cause discomfort particularly among those who have received years and years of formal education. We work so hard to get our degrees! It is true. And it is also true that one can research and read about a particular experience for years and not understand what it is fundamentally like to live that experience every single day. You will notice that some contributors have formal degrees and some do not. You can find that information in the section about contributors, but will not see that information listed with the chapters themselves. This book also includes several conversational style chapters with individuals who possess lived expertise and whose knowledge and willingness to share their expertise is invaluable.

Social workers need to interrogate the ways the profession is complicit in maintaining the status quo. As discussed in chapter 2, societal systems were set up to produce certain outcomes. Most organizing systems in our country were constructed on racist, patriarchal, cis/heterosexist principles, limiting the ability of Black people, TGE people, disabled people, people who are unstably housed, and people living in poverty to succeed. This is not to say that these groups of people cannot succeed – it is to say that in order to do so, certain groups of people must work twice as hard, often for twice as long, to achieve the same outcomes as members of privileged groups within our society.

Literature documenting the pervasive marginalization of and disparities faced by TGE people must be contextualized within the larger macro context and also be accompanied by literature that highlights the strength and resourcefulness, resistance and survival strategies, and the joy of being one's authentic self in community. It is true that TGE people and communities experience health and economic disparities compared to the general population. However, it is imperative that literature documenting risks and disparities be contextualized within the oppressive social structures TGE people navigate daily. There is nothing inherently *at risk* about a TGE individual. To focus solely on individual or community-level disparities reinforces the individualization of social problems, is reductive, and ignores the remarkable ability of TGE people to survive and thrive despite oppressive structural barriers.

Gratitude and Joy

Co-editing this book is not something that I take lightly. The fact that my voice, and the voices of people like me, are on every single page of this book is something that brings me immeasurable joy. This is something I do not take for granted. It has become very evident in the past few years that there is still some question about the right of trans and gender expansive people to even exist in the eyes of our government, as well as in the eyes of many individual people that we may be interacting with on a daily basis. Consider that for a second. Really take that in. What is it like to know that the people you encounter in your daily interactions – at the grocery store, at the doctor's office, maybe even within your family – don't actually believe that who you are is valid. Damn. That's a lot, right? If you are a social worker, it is your ethical imperative to change this. Some people view expansive possibilities of gender as a threat. What is so threatening about living an authentic life, having your basic needs met, and experiencing joy?

This work has brought me so much joy. My friends and family have said throughout the process of making this book – you're *still* working? Because the idea of work has become so intertwined with obligation, stress, perhaps boredom and resentment, I don't know how to respond to this question. That is not what characterizes this work. This work, for me, is creation. It is about expanding possibilities and celebrating the brilliance of human variation. It is, in my wildest dreams, about contributing to a movement that recognizes and values the voices and experiences of any individual who does not neatly fit into the limited ideas of who and what we are supposed to be.

I am grateful to those who have endlessly supported me and fostered the development of my own voice. I'd like to give a specific shout out to Gary Mallon, SJ Dodd, Mary Cavanaugh, Mary McKay, Anna Ortega-Williams, Alex Wagaman, Stephen Russell, Alan Detlaff, Gregory Lewis, Sandy Silverman, Peggy Morton, Kim Bender, Pam Scheffer, Jerry Peterson, Marc Dones, Alice Tutt, Robyn Maguire, Gigi Glynn, and Glennda Testone, who have each been invaluable resources to me at various moments throughout this journey.

1 Socio-Structural Context of Trans and Gender Expansive Youth

Bec Sokha Keo

Introduction

The mental and physical health profiles of transgender and gender expansive (TGE) youth must be contextualized in the social, structural, and political circumstances in which TGE youth are situated. Individuals whose gender is assigned coercively at birth, including transgender, nonbinary, and gender-queer people, are disproportionately burdened by trauma related to inter-personal, self-directed, and collective violence (Richmond, Burnes, & Carroll, 2012). For example, in the largest known community based survey of nearly 28,000 TGE people in the United States, nearly half experienced verbal harassment and/or physical assault (48%) as well was nearly half who ex-perienced sexual assault in their lifetime (47%) (James & Herman, 2017). In addition, the survey found a 40% suicide rate among the population, an es-timate nine times higher than the overall US suicide rate. Finally, historical collective violence such as traumas experienced in public and within institu-tions (such as health care, education, law enforcement, and politics) spans across generations but is only recently becoming more known (Asakura, 2017; Richmond et al., 2012).

While there have been great advances in informing the public on diverse gender experiences, many of these efforts further marginalized genderqueer and nonbinary identities (Beemyn, 2015). For example, unique gender ex-periences of genderqueer and nonbinary people are often excluded from transgender rights movements (Beemyn, 2015). In addition, genderqueer and nonbinary individuals remain largely absent from research (Darwin, 2017), which has almost exclusively focused on binary gender identities (Budge, Rossman, & Howard, 2014). Furthermore, in instances when research studies offer gender options beyond the binary, genderqueer and nonbinary parti-cipants are often grouped with binary transgender participants in a broad sexual and gender diverse category or grouped with binary transgender participants in explicitly gender diverse studies. This aggregated approach to inquiry limits the generalizability of findings and neglects experiences of genderqueer and nonbinary communities who face unique socio-structural challenges rooted in binarism. To better understand the research landscape of

DOI: 10.4324/9780429297687-1

genderqueer and nonbinary communities in the United States, this paper will apply dimensions of the Gender Minority Stress and Resilience framework (Hendricks & Testa, 2012; Testa, Habarth, Peta, Balsam, & Bockting, 2015) for organizing the review of literature on stressors, resilience, and the physical and mental health outcomes encountered by genderqueer and nonbinary communities. Implications for gender affirming social work research, practice provision, and policy with genderqueer and nonbinary communities are discussed. Guided by an Intersectional (Crenshaw, 1989) and Gender Minority Stress and Resilience (Hendricks & Testa, 2012) frameworks, this chapter will provide information about trauma and resilience among TGE youth and discuss implications for affirmative social work practice, research, and policy with TGE youth.

Intersectional and Gender Minority Stress, Resilience Frameworks

Intersectionality is a framework coined by Kimberle Crenshaw, a Black feminist scholar (Crenshaw, 1989). This framework recognizes the interconnectedness of systems of oppression (e.g., racism, classism, ableism, heterosexism, and xenophobia) and how these systems work simultaneously to privilege or disadvantage certain groups of people (Crenshaw, 2017). Furthermore, the systems of oppression are enacted interpersonally, institutionally, and politically. The oppressions are known to contribute to economic, health and housing adversities disproportionately impacting individuals who belong to historically socially stigmatized groups, such as Black women of transgender experience, Latinx gender non-conforming people, and gender expansive youth who are Black, Indigenous, and people of color (BIPOC).

Another and less studied system that is harmful to TGE youth is binarism. Binarism is a set of attitudes, beliefs and actions that classify ideas, objects or systems (such as gender, race, sexual orientation or political ideology) into two, often opposing, categories (Alizai, Doneys, & Doane, 2017; He, 2014). Known as a colonial mechanism to establish hierarchies and dominance within racial, gender, sexual, and other social groups, binarism acts as a system of oppression akin to racism, classism, cissexism, and heterosexism (Alizai et al., 2017; Hinchy, 2017). Many cultures have traditionally recognized genders that transcend a binary gender understanding – for example, fa'affafine in Samoa or and bissu, calalai, and calabai in Indonesia. However, colonial rule's enforcement of capitalist, patriarchal, heterosexist, and binarist values have led to interpersonal, structural and political violence plaguing sexually diverse and gender expansive communities across the world (Ali, Keo, & Chaudhuri, 2020).

In the United States, gender expansive people (including genderqueer and nonbinary people) make up over one-third of the population of individuals whose gender differs than assumed at birth (James & Herman, 2017).

Despite this significant representation of gender expansive people within trans communities in the United States (James & Herman, 2017; Meerwijk & Sevelius, 2017; Puckett, Cleary, Rossman, Mustanski, & Newcomb, 2018; Tebbe & Moradi, 2016), institutions such as language, media, mass incarceration, health, and education, systematically stigmatize or erase TGE communities by adopting binary gender norms (Baptista & de Loureiro Himmel, 2016; Beemyn, 2015; Factor & Rothblum, 2008; Kattari, Walls, & Speer, 2017; Pemberton, 2013; Richmond et al., 2012). This restrictive approach ignores unique experiences of gender expansive people and regularly reinforces barriers to mental health, physical health, and well-being among the population (Bith-Melander et al., 2010; Warren, Smalley, & Barefoot, 2016).

Gender Minority Stress and Resilience

The Gender Minority Stress and Resilience Model (GMSRM; Testa et al., 2015) is an extension of Meyer's (1995) minority stress model and assesses distal stress, proximal stress, and resilience as well as their influence on mental and physical health outcomes experienced by TGE people. Testa and colleagues conceptualize TGE distal (i.e., external) stressors as mistreatment such as discrimination, rejection, non-affirmation, and violence in response to one's gender identity or expression. Proximal (i.e., internal) stressors include internalized transphobia, expectations of rejection, discrimination, violence, or non-affirmation, as well as nondisclosure. Connectedness with TGE community and pride regarding TGE identity are considered resilience and protective factors within this framework.

Distal Stressors

TGE youth face alarming rates of interpersonal and institutional violence and exclusion from peers, family members, community, and institutions (e.g., educational, medical, religious), with higher rates among TGE youth who are nonbinary, BIPOC, or disabled (Keener, 2015). In a study of over 1,000 TGE and cisgender gay, lesbian, bisexual, and queer adolescents, higher rates of multi-traumas were reported among gender expansive individuals assigned male at birth (71.5%) and gender expansive individuals assigned female at birth (49.5%) compared to cisgender gay, bisexual, or queer young men (33.0%) (Sterzing, Ratliff, Gartner, McGeough, & Johnson, 2017). In addition, scholars have identified higher stress related to racism and transphobia among gender expansive people of color compared to their white counterparts (Kattari, Walls, Whitfield, et al., 2017). Furthermore, TGE individuals with disabilities face disability-related discrimination when accessing health, mental health, drug treatment, and crisis services (Kattari et al., 2017).

More generally, TGE young people encounter a lack of TGE affirming care from providers often leading to being referred out or being denied care (Puckett et al., 2018). As a result of routine enforcement of transphobia and a binary gender system, many TGE must use the gender assumed at birth when interacting socially and navigating institutions (Richards et al., 2016). Given the pervasive adoption of binarism across social, structural, and institutional systems, gender expansive individuals in particular often feel isolated and unwelcome in social service environments (Ansara, 2015). In addition to facing rejection within service systems, TGE individuals also encounter stressors as a result of gendered facilities such as restrooms and changing rooms. For example, a study exploring identity development, disclosure, and community relationship revealed that most (89%) gender expansive individuals experience discomfort when having to choose a gendered toilet (Factor & Rothblum, 2008).

Proximal Stressors

In Testa and colleague's (2015) model, proximal stressors, such as internalized anti-TGE attitudes, negative expectations, and nondisclosure also have a critical role in mental and physical health outcomes of TGE communities (Testa et al., 2015). Although proximal stressors among TGE communities are less studied compared to distal stressors, researchers are beginning to examine internalized factors within TGE groups. For example, Factor and Rothblum (2008) found that genderqueer individuals were least likely to disclose their gender identity with primary health providers compared to transwomen and transmen. This difference may be due to the unique impact of binarism and transphobia on nonbinary communities compared to transgender women and men.

Resilience and Protective Factors

Community connectedness has been identified as a resilience indicator among TGE individuals (Budge et al., 2014; Hendricks & Testa, 2012; Moody & Smith, 2013). For example, Testa and colleagues establish the protective role of relationships with other TGE people against adverse mental and physical health outcomes among TGE individuals. In addition, affirming relationships with individuals outside of one's community, such as those between TGE and LGBQ communities enhance wellness of TGE individuals (Factor & Rothblum, 2008). Tebbe and Moradi (2016) also found that social support from friends was a protective factor against suicide among TGE individuals. Further exploration of interpersonal and structural affirmation, their role in building resilience, and how they may protect against mental, physical, and economic challenges is needed.

Researchers suggest that psychosocial profiles within the TGE community are diverse. For example, Warren and colleagues (2016) found that gender expansive individuals, in particular genderqueer and nonbinary people, experience different mental health challenges compared to transgender women and men. In addition, Nadal (2018) proposed microaggressions unique to gender expansive communities including: presumption of the gender binary, incorrect gender pronouns, and misidentification or incorrect categorization. In a study explicitly examining gender expansive individuals' coping, psychological distress, and mental health, researchers identified greater levels of psychological distress (i.e., depression (53%) and anxiety (39%) among their sample compared to the general population (Budge et al., 2014). When considering intersecting identities such as gender and sexuality, gender expansive individuals, who also identified as queer reported levels of non-suicidal self-injury (51.6%) that were higher than the average for their entire TGE sample (Reisner & Juntunen, 2015). In addition, Budge and colleagues (2014) found that gender expansive and trans men of color faced economic hardships despite high levels of education. Budge and colleagues (2014) also asserted that gender expansive people may feel more anxiety that manifests as hypervigilance, given the restrictively gendered environments these groups must face regularly. Finally, fear and anxiety were reported to interfere with pursing necessary health care, thus reinforcing health inequities among this population (Puckett et al., 2018).

Implications

Research

Despite the notable research contributions made around TGE youth scholarship, there is much more to be known regarding TGE youth health and wellness. It is important that research about TGE youth is led by TGE youth. In addition TGE youth scholars of color should be prioritized. In this effort, social workers may engage in community based participatory action research, linking research to social action led by the community of focus. One example is Asakura and colleagues' (2020) art-based participatory action research with TGE youth. In their study, a collaboration between researchers and TGE youth resulted in a deconstruction of perceptions around TGE youth vulnerability and resilience. The youth utilized art to counter normative discourses around vulnerability and resilience, engage in self-reflection and expression, develop space for queer and TGE youth activism. The project concluded with a week-long art exhibit showcasing the TGE youth artists' work. May the wisdom and insight of TGE youth guide the research narratives about TGE youth.

Policy

Likewise, involve TGE youth in policy efforts. Given the intersectional oppressions confronting compounding stigmatized groups, social workers may collaborate with, for example BIPOC TGE homeless youth activists, to ensure access to racial and TGE affirming housing, education, social services as well as emotional, behavioral, and physical care services. In addition, social workers may work with TGE youth and policy makers to reallocate resources to facilitate TGE youth power and cross-movement solidarity. In addition, social workers and TGE youth of color may work together to advance policy agendas set forth by the Black Lives Matter Movement. Such policy efforts include divestment in oppressive systems that disproportionately entangle TGE youth of color (e.g., the prison industrial complex and child welfare system). Instead, communities may prioritize investment in BIPOC TGE youth grassroots movements.

Practice

Finally, social workers may apply both intersectional and minority stress frameworks in clinical practice with TGE youth. In addition to recognizing TGE-related traumas that TGE youth face, social workers may work with youth to identify and work through interpersonal and institutional violence based in compounding oppressions such as racism, ableism, and binarism. Social workers can work with T/GE youth to: (1) identify the sources of hurt in their lives; (2) enhance their emotional and intellectual capacity; (3) find and build life-affirming community; and (4) engage in T/GE youth-led socio-political movements.

Case Study

A social worker in a predominantly white community based organization that serves LGBTQ communities coordinates a drop in program for TGE youth. A newer participant (they/them pronouns), who is Black and nonbinary enters the program after school one afternoon in distress. The participant discloses abuse by peers in school due to their race, gender identity, and expression. They shared that teachers have witnessed the abuse and have not intervened. Instead, the teachers blame the Black nonbinary TGE youth scholar for their "choices" and "lack of professionalism." In addition, the participant, a student at a public high school, believes they have been denied multiple internships due to their gender identity and expression. While their parents and church community are supportive and affirming of their gender identity and expression, the student's resources and support system are limited. There are no state, local, or school district protections inclusive of gender identity and gender expression. In fact, there have been recent efforts to pass anti-TGE legislation at city, state, and federal levels, which aim to sanction discrimination and limit access to healthcare, housing, and education for TGE individuals.

Reflection Questions:

1. What are the structural issues at play?
2. How do you see binarism showing up in the participant's encounters with their classmates and teachers? Racism?
3. How can you imagine engaging the young person and their support network in change efforts?

Land Acknowledgment

We wish to recognize the land of the Karankawa, Coahuiltecan, Atakapa-Ishak, and Sana upon which this writing is produced. Our intention is to honor these tribes by knowing the land of the native people on which we settle and learning to act in solidarity with them.

References

Ali, S., Keo, B. S., & Chaudhuri, S. (2020). Critically understanding South Asian sexual health: A call for a holistic and sex positive approach. *International Journal of Sexual Health, 32*(3), 177–187.

Alizai, A., Doneys, P., & Doane, D. L. (2017). Impact of gender binarism on Hijras' life course and their access to fundamental human rights in Pakistan. *Journal of Homosexuality, 64*(9), 1214–1240.

Ansara, Y. G. (2015). Challenging cisgenderism in the ageing and aged care sector: Meeting the needs of older people of trans and/or non-binary experience. *Australasian Journal on Ageing, 34*(S2), 14–18.

Asakura, K. (2017). Paving pathways through the pain: A grounded theory of resilience among lesbian, gay, bisexual, trans, and queer youth. *Journal of Research on Adolescence, 27*(3), 521–536.

Asakura, K., Lundy, J., Black, D., & Tierney, C. (2020). Art as a transformative practice: A participatory action research project with trans* youth. *Qualitative Social Work, 19*(5–6), 1061–1077. https://doi.org/10.1177/1473325019881226

Baptista, M. M. R., & de Loureiro Himmel, R. I. P. (2016). 'For fun': (De)Humanizing Gisberta—The violence of binary gender social representation. *Sexuality & Culture, 20*(3), 639–656.

Beemyn, G. (2015). Still waiting for an introduction to gender nonconformity: A review of *Transgender 101: A simple guide to a complex issue. Journal of LGBT Youth, 12*(1), 87–89.

Bith-Melander, P., Sheoran, B., Sheth, L., Bermudez, C., Drone, J., Wood, W., & Schroeder, K. (2010). Understanding sociocultural and psychological factors affecting transgender people of color in San Francisco. *JANAC: Journal of the Association of Nurses in AIDS Care, 21*(3), 207–220. doi:10.1016/j.jana.2010.01.008

Budge, S. L., Rossman, H. K., & Howard, K. A. (2014). Coping and psychological distress among genderqueer individuals: The moderating effect of social support. *Journal of LGBT Issues in Counseling, 8*(1), 95–117.

Crenshaw, K. (1989). Demarginalizing the intersection of race and sex: A black feminist critique of antidiscrimination doctrine, feminist theory and antiracist politics. *University of Chicago Legal Forum, 1989*, 139.

Crenshaw, K.W. (2017). *On intersectionality: Essential writings.* New York: The New Press.

Darwin, H. (2017). Doing gender beyond the binary: A virtual ethnography. *Symbolic Interaction, 40*(3), 317–334.

Factor, R., & Rothblum, E. (2008). Exploring gender identity and community among three groups of transgender individuals in the United States: MTFs, FTMs, and genderqueers. *Health Sociology Review, 17*(3), 235–253.

Hendricks, M. L., & Testa, R. J. (2012). A conceptual framework for clinical work with transgender and gender nonconforming clients: An adaptation of the Minority Stress Model. *Professional Psychology: Research and Practice, 43*(5), 460.

Hinchy, J. (2017). The eunuch archive: Colonial records of non-normative gender and sexuality in India. *Culture, Theory & Critique, 58*(2), 127–146. doi:10.1080/14735784.2017.1279555

James, S. E., & Herman, J. (2017). *The report of the 2015 US transgender survey: Executive summary.* Washington, DC: National Center for Transgender Equality.

Kattari, S. K., Walls, N. E., & Speer, S. R. (2017). Differences in experiences of discrimination in accessing social services among transgender/gender non-conforming individuals by (dis)ability. *Journal of Social Work in Disability & Rehabilitation, 16*(2), 116–140.

Kattari, S. K., Walls, N. E., Whitfield, D. L., & Langenderfer Magruder, L. (2017). Racial and ethnic differences in experiences of discrimination in accessing social services among transgender/gender-nonconforming people. *Journal of Ethnic & Cultural Diversity in Social Work, 26*(3), 217–235.

Keener, E. (2015). The complexity of gender: It is all that and more…. In sum, it is complicated. *Sex Roles, 73*(11–12), 481–489.

Meerwijk, E. L., & Sevelius, J. M. (2017). Transgender population size in the United States: A meta-regression of population-based probability samples. *American Journal of Public Health, 107*(2), e1–e8.

Meyer, I. H. (1995). Minority stress and mental health in gay men. *Journal of Health and Social Behavior, 36*, 38–56.

Moody, C., & Smith, N. G. (2013). Suicide protective factors among trans adults. *Archives of Sexual Behavior, 42*(5), 739–752.

Nadal, K. L., Whitman, C. N., Davis, L. S., Erazo, T., & Davidoff, K. C. (2016). Microaggressions toward lesbian, gay, bisexual, transgender, queer, and gender-queer people: A review of the literature. *The Journal of Sex Research, 53*(4–5), 488–508.

Pemberton, S. (2013). Enforcing gender: The constitution of sex and gender in prison regimes. *Signs: Journal of Women in Culture and Society, 39*(1), 151–175.

Puckett, J. A., Cleary, P., Rossman, K., Mustanski, B., & Newcomb, M. E. (2018). Barriers to gender-affirming care for transgender and gender nonconforming individuals. *Sexuality Research and Social Policy, 15*(1), 48–59.

Richards, C., Bouman, W. P., Seal, L., Barker, M. J., Nieder, T. O., & T'Sjoen, G. (2016). Non-binary or genderqueer genders. *International Review of Psychiatry, 28*, 95–102. doi:10.3109/09540261.2015.1106446

Richmond, K. A., Burnes, T., & Carroll, K. (2012). Lost in trans-lation: Interpreting systems of trauma for transgender clients. *Traumatology, 18*(1), 45–57. doi:10.1177/1534765610396726

Sterzing, P. R., Ratliff, G. A., Gartner, R. E., McGeough, B. L., & Johnson, K. C. (2017). Social ecological correlates of polyvictimization among a national sample of transgender, genderqueer, and cisgender sexual minority adolescents. *Child Abuse & Neglect, 67*, 1–12.

Tebbe, E. A., & Moradi, B. (2016). Suicide risk in trans populations: An application of minority stress theory. *Journal of Counseling Psychology, 63*(5), 520.

Testa, R. J., Habarth, J., Peta, J., Balsam, K., & Bockting, W. (2015). Development of the gender minority stress and resilience measure. *Psychology of Sexual Orientation and Gender Diversity, 2*(1), 65.

Warren, J. C., Smalley, K. B., & Barefoot, K. N. (2016). Psychological well-being among transgender and genderqueer individuals. *International Journal of Transgenderism, 17*(3–4), 114–123.

2 Cutting the Poisonous Roots: Systems Change
A Conversation with Marc Dones

Marc Dones and Jama Shelton

Introduction

Social workers providing direct services may find themselves wanting to contribute to systems change efforts, but may be unable to do so due to their primary responsibility of responding to the individual needs of the person in front of them. Social work practice and education have trended toward the individualization of problems, such that education and practice often focus on relieving an individual's symptoms rather than on identifying and addressing the root causes of social problems (George & Marlowe, 2005). Consequently, social workers are often charged with helping to ensure an individual's access to services and supports, rather than working to eliminate the need for services and supports. This individualization of social problems perpetuates a growing divide between casework/clinical practice and community/macro practice (Mullaly, 1997). This divide can be seen on an organizational level, with agencies providing direct services rarely engaging in macro level change efforts, and agencies engaging in social change efforts rarely also providing direct services (Kivel, 2007; Mullaly, 1997).

Trans and gender expansive (TGE) young people are rarely served well by the social systems meant to support youth, as evidenced by their disproportionate representation in child welfare, homelessness, and carceral systems, pervasive violence and discrimination within educational systems, barriers to accessing physical and mental health care, and reported mental and behavioral health disparities (James et al., 2016; Kosciw, Clark, Truong, & Zongrone, 2020; Shelton et al., 2018). These systems were not set up to meet the unique needs of TGE young people. In fact, TGE young people are frequently invisibilized within social systems, experiencing not only interpersonal violence and discrimination, but also structural violence through exclusionary policies and practices that directly impact their access to care and overall well-being.

It is incumbent upon social workers to understand the importance of systems change efforts, to examine the purpose of the systems within which we work, and to find ways of working alongside TGE young people to envision and create more equitable social structures. The following conversation with

DOI: 10.4324/9780429297687-2

leading systems change expert Marc Dones provides foundational knowledge for engaging in systems change work and poses important questions for social workers and the social work professional to consider if we are to truly engage in socially just practice.

Marc: The logic for systems in almost any context is the same. The world in and of itself by its own nature is actually quite chaotic. We, as relatively high functioning mammals, create systems in order to reproduce outcomes that we think are favorable, right? That's the purpose of a system is to give us a thing on repeat, in some ways, without us having to think about it. And so I what that means is that when you build a system around a certain set of values or ideas or priorities, it continues to deliver on those. Our systems were built on priorities that are cis/heterosexual, patriarchal, racist.

And they continue to deliver on those priorities. **Without substantively taking up the question of systems change, we can't reasonably expect different outcomes**, not beyond the sort of onesy twosy kind of like – I really lucked out and had a great caseworker, or I really lucked out and had a fantastic therapist. **Luck is a really poor mediator of societal outcomes.** In fact, luck mostly mediates bad ones. So, if we're really thinking about how we get to good outcomes en mas for a population with reasonable certainty, the only way to do that is a system.

Jama: Can you talk a little bit about how our current social systems produce and reproduce bad outcomes for trans and gender expansive people, specifically young people?

Marc: I think the first thing is that they really over-index on family, the idea that family holds the keys to solutions, when families are often the substantive site of harm for a lot of these young folks. This, in and of itself, is quite dangerous. And, I want to be really clear that what I'm saying is not that all young people need to be moved out of their families and put somewhere else. That's not what I'm saying. What I'm actually saying is that, because of the nature of systems to vector towards family reunification as rapidly as possible, and frankly, to trust families over young people in terms of who is right about what harm is being caused, the result is that young people who are naming harms that they are experiencing and are saying like – I need help. Like, it's not even that I don't love these people. I need help figuring out how to navigate what safety looks like inside this context that I'm in – are often systemically overridden by belief structures that are embedded. Let's say we believe these parents over this child. I think you can extrapolate that and say you see that same kind of thing happen inside criminal legal systems, where you have a court system that places a preponderance of faith in what an officer says versus what a civilian says when these are both people who can lie and are incentivized to lie in different ways. And frankly, as we've seen, the system of policing incentivizes police to lie more than civilians are incentivized to lie. And so there's a structural bias around the belief of adults and of family leaders, so to speak, that I think is particularly damaging to young folks.

The other thing that is quite lethal, and this is going to sound goofy, but, our systems are fundamentally divorced from our best neuro-psychology. We continue to operate in the past with facts that are 60, 70, 80, 90, a hundred years old and are often no longer facts. So we're continuously having conversations about things like what kinds of decisional capacity or power young people have, or do not have, absent what we understand about literal prefrontal cortex development.

That's a very bridgeable problem, right? But we don't do it. And **we're not building systems that are set up to adapt to changes in our understanding**. Rather, they reassert our old understandings over our new understandings over and over and over again. We see this in particular in thinking about trans folks. I think that we have difficulty talking about it because it requires us to undo messaging that we did to get certain rights. Like the idea of gender as a fixed thing, that if you're a person of transgender experience that you are migrating between two points and that the migration between those points ameliorates gender dysphoric emotions, or experiences, instead of again what is our actual current frontier of understanding, which is that gender is a landscape. It's not a scale. It's a field and you can move around inside that field truly any day in whatever direction you'd like.

And so, again, if I think about a young person who's asserting an identity, and then a set of adultist and unscientific systems that are asserting back something like – you're too young to know that, or you're too young to make these permanent decisions – when what we actually know is you are not too young to know that, and the decision doesn't have to be permanent, and it's not bad if it isn't. Also, when we talk about how a system creates harm and what kind of harm it creates, I think the other thing to be clear about is – what is the actual goal of that system? And I think that, in some ways the goal of many of these social systems is to fix stuff. And fixing implies a very, very, um, well, I don't know … I don't like it. Because I think that it's just a lot of hubris to say that you're going to be fixing people too.

I think that, again, if you look at what we understand currently, it's that most things don't need fixing, That there's, you know, the requirement or the need for support. So there's the need for different kinds of empowerment or there's the need for support. As a middle-class person, I got lots of therapy. If you're getting good therapy, what you know about therapy is it doesn't *fix* things, but good therapy actually makes you aware of some things and then puts you in conversation with them. It doesn't fix them. And so **what does it mean to have systems that are still predicated on the notion of a fix, instead of systems that are predicated on the notion of finding ways to empower you in relationship to the things that you are navigating in such a way that you are not harmed anymore**?

The other thing is just that – and I remember this from the interviews actually that you and I did together – but one of the folks that I interviewed was talking to me about how **we just really don't have a systemic level understanding of the amount of harm that people traverse daily**. And so the deficit that folks are operating out of with regard to just how much harm they have experienced by tonight, compared to their cis/heterosexual counterparts, is significant. And when we don't acknowledge or build as if that harm is real, then we wind up with systems that see cis/heterosexual folks as sort of acting "normally," and then everyone else as overreacting or as a problem. What we need to be doing much more of is actively acknowledging that what we have in place are harmful predatory structures. And so when people show up really put out and very harmed by those structures, that's real.

Jama: I remember something a young person told me once about the homelessness system – they said something like "we show up into these systems and when they can't force us to fit into the system, they kick us out of the system, rather than the system being responsive to us." They said "if I buy a pair of shoes and they don't fit right and I send them back, customer service doesn't say no, make your foot fit in these shoes." No, they say: "they're the wrong size. Let me send you ones that fit." But in social services we don't do that. There's not a customer service lens. There's often a complete absence of recognition of the consumer. Other industries survive by being responsive in a positive way to the people that are engaging with that industry.

Marc: And that's why National Innovation Service (NIS) and our system work uses the word customer instead of other words. Also we work across so many systems, so we use customer rather than having to switch language every time. So in our internal documents or in our reports, we don't refer to, for example, people experiencing homelessness. We say the customers of the homeless services system. The customers of the child welfare system. I mean, it's problematic because it asserts a capitalist paradigm on top of things. And, you know, I have issues with that, but it does do a good job of centering who's supposed to get the good here. Right? Like who are we supposed to be bending over backwards to make sure is satisfied with the work that we've done. And how is it that we have a better idea of how to do that in Best Buy than in child welfare?

Jama: Yeah. Do you have an idea about why that is?

Marc: I mean, it's racism and the patriarchy. I don't think people do this enough, but you can trace the history of any given social system all the way back to its origin points. So for example, child welfare was created by white women and was designed with an idea of taking kids away from families in communities of color. When I say things like that, people are often like, Oh, that can't be true. Or, well, that was the undercurrent racist time, but it's like, no. When you look at the creation of the family shelter system in the 80s, you see this sort of aggressive intertwining of the family shelter system with other carceral systems, because the folks who we're seeing were young black women. Or if you look at the creation of the modern housing market, which finds its foundations in the federal housing administration and red lining and very specific racist policy. **I think that the reasons things are the way that they are is because we explicitly set them up that way**.

If we zoom in and say, so let's talk about trans or nonbinary or gender expansive young people I think that, again, the spaces that discourse grew out of were pathologizing spaces. They were again oriented towards a fix. First it was about documenting something freakish, right? Like the vast majority of psychology and psychiatry arise, not in trying to understand what the zone of normalcy is, but actually sort of seeing fringe behavior and wanting to stare at it. And then after enough staring has been done that then transforms into – can we cure this person? And so when you look back at the early writings – Freud and Lacan and some of the folks who really defined how we do or do not clinically engage – those writings are, I mean, truly bizarre writing that was done around just run-of-the-mill gay stuff. It was first referred to as inversion. It was this idea that the psychodynamics expressed that would bring your romantic impulses out into the world had literally been inverted. And so it was this idea that there was a narcissistic turn in your libidinal impulses. And so much of the treatment was focused on understanding and desolving that narcissistic turn. It doesn't make sense. Like, just to say it out loud in 2020, it's like, Whoa, nah, that's dumb. Right? And ahistorical.

It was actually not that long ago that homosexuality was taken out of the DSM (Diagnostic Statistics and Assessment Manual) as a thing that you could be diagnosed with and like committed for. And now, even in the DSM-5, we still have gender dysphoria as a diagnosis. **We have a medicalized way of interacting with people's gender identities**. I remember talking about this with some students of mine – if you identify as trans and so you have to be diagnosed as having a problem, but the cure for that problem is trans affirming care... I don't know, like, where is the pathology in that? I think that the roots of how we engage with non cisgender identities is so fundamentally rooted in a hundred year old pathologizing discourse, that even inside systems of care that are supposed to be oriented towards helping folks that are experiencing homelessness or housing instability or violence – maybe not even necessarily because of that identity, but certainly not totally disaggregated from it – that those systems have foundations that auto default to pathologizing. There's just no way out of them. **You need a better foundation. You need a foundation that doesn't understand people as problems.** And again, if I'm going back to what I said before, if everything you see is something you're supposed to fix, then you wind up in a real dark space pretty quickly.

Jama: Ok, so who does this? Who changes these systems? I know this is a huge question, but this book is geared towards social workers and there are all kinds of thoughts about the role of the social work profession and the micro and macro divide, which I don't agree with. In my mind, social workers have a key role to play in dismantling systems of oppression like this. I know that there isn't some kind of quick recipe to follow or perhaps we would have already done a lot of this work, but I know that you do a lot of this work every day. So what can social workers do?

Marc: So I consider myself a person who knows a whole bunch of stuff about a bunch of stuff. And knowing things and knowing what to do with things are different. And so at this point I am unfortunately, and literally, unfortunately – because someone should be better at this than I am – but I am literally one of the leading policy experts on the housing sector and its various transformations. But that doesn't actually mean I know how to fix everything. Because I don't necessarily fully understand the dimensions of the problem. And so, if you say to me – Dones, go fix the housing stock problem in rural America. I would be like, I don't know how to do that. And it's in part because I don't know what those folks want their communities to look like. Sitting here in downtown Columbus, in my loft, I can imagine a different tiny Ohio town. I can re-create it from the ground up, like doodling on the back of a piece of paper. Nobody there wants what I wrote down. So, that's not helpful. What I have always said to my students and what I try to say to myself frequently, is that **knowing a whole bunch of stuff does not mean that you know what to do with it. And the best way that you can approach your work is by thinking of yourself as a toolbox for other people to reach into**.

So what I want to be able to do is be in the right relationship with those folks in those small, rural communities who are saying, "Marc, we really want our community to look like that. We want access to these things. These are the things that really concern us." And then I can say back, "Ok, now that I have this understanding, we can work together to create something." Because I have the technical knowledge to know, oh it's these funding streams, it's this kind of zoning problem. These are the things you're going to have to do in order to get to the vision that you have.

Again, it's kind of the same as good therapy, right? A person would show up and say I have a goal for my wellness and it looks and sounds and smells and feels like this. And then a good therapist will have tools that you can pull out and use. That relationship and orientation to the work is really, really critical. And so to understand that, like becoming an expert in social work, in systems design, in public policy is no different than becoming a very skilled craftsmen. You still need the person whose house it is to tell you what kind of addition they want. You don't show up and say what *you* want. That's not the conversation.

Jama: I agree. But it is the conversation sometimes, and that's part the problem, right? One of the things I hear social workers talk about a lot in relation to trans youth, although this is translatable across populations, is that because trans youth are existing in such a contentious and often violent context in their daily lives, that like the focus is on helping. Helping them cope with that and survive. So if that's where social workers are putting all of their energy, then how do they contribute to larger change? I think that's a problem with the way social work has created a macro/micro divide, because you can't actually do one without the other, in my opinion. You can't create macro change without being in right relationship with individual people, and you can't do good micro work without understanding the macro context.

Marc: There are justice oriented frameworks to social work practice, right, although they may be under utilized and perhaps under developed. I have a friend who's a social worker in Maryland. Part of their work is helping people see the political dimensions to what they're experiencing and then helping them figure out how they want to be engaged in those political dimensions. It's more than simply saying – the thing that I can do is work with you to navigate this violence and survive this harm in a way that doesn't kill you. **If we're being honest, these systems are set up to do more harm than good and when the experience of people within them, navigating day-to-day reality, is feeling harmed, to simply say the best I can do for you is give you tools to navigate that harm is insufficient**.

The reality is the best thing I could do would be to migrate towards a conversation that acknowledges **the harm that you experienced is because it is set up this way. It's not because you're doing it wrong**. And because it is set up this way, you are now presented with a choice, which I will help facilitate. Which is, you can choose to say it's not my job to fix this. I just want to figure out how to live in a space that I don't feel harmed in daily. And that is ok, let's see what tools I have that I can help equip you with. Or, and I think this is what frankly often happens when you take this approach, you can say – or do you want to be dismantling this? Do you want to be engaged in some way, shape or form in taking apart all of this nonsense? And if that's the answer, then again, there are tools for that. To me, that is a blending of the sort of macro and micro work. Which is to say that there's no reason other than sort of a precedent and the idea of the billable hour that the therapeutic work can't be door knocking to pass legislation. There's no reason that the therapeutic work can't be running for office. There's no reason, like all of that is in and of itself a form of therapy, a form of clinical action. Because if you're being real, real, real, textbook about it, **it's about the migration of the locus of control out of external structures and into the person, which is the best way we know to deal with any kind of trauma**.

So again, this is applying a systems lens to the work. And if we zoom all the way out and there were enough of us applying that systems lens to the work, then it wouldn't be as hard to have these conversations and say – this is bad. It's just bad. Right? You know, I was giving a panel talk a couple of weeks ago and there was an audience question related to something I said about trauma and navigating time. And the audience question was – isn't life traumatic? And I was like, no, what? No. And I had to do this whole thing then where I basically said – ok, cool, cool, cool. But like, stress is not trauma. Everybody got stress. Not everybody got trauma. And in fact, the collapsing of those things in the common parlance is bad. It's a bad thing. But I was having to say to folks that, you know, if you are inside systems that produce trauma, that is very different from – I lost my car keys or a man I like broke up with me.

Like if you lost your car keys, honey, that's on you. If this system traumatizes you, if you wake up and are like told you're not a person on repeat, by everything you come into contact with, you didn't even do anything. You just existed.

If we're looking at social work as a discipline, that is plugged into multiple different systems, then I would say that the discipline of social work has to have a more rigorous internal look and perspective at where the generative point of the harm is. And is it actually worth it? Is it good? **Is it actually helpful to teach people to navigate harm better or to help people dismantle the harms in their lives? I would say that it is the latter**.

It's actually really important that we start having real conversations about – what is the discourse inside the disciplines conversation? How do we have more reflexivity in that? I did not go to graduate school for anthropology because at the time that I would have gone, there was not a way to do that and work in America. Just the colonialism was so baked into the idea of anthropology, that there was no such thing as being a working anthropologist who didn't speak another language and live in another country half of the year. And every discipline has a part of it – a core component that is rooted in colonialism, rooted in patriarchal structure and that is the part that is scamming us all daily. And so I think that for social work, to take a step back and ask – what is a helping profession, what does that mean? To take a step back and say – what does it mean to always be isolating things in other people or other communities for fixing?

How then do we begin to have field revolutionizing conversations to say – there has to be a real update here where we don't just iterate forward, but we acknowledge some of the poison roots and cut them. And so for, for me, that would really be taking a hard look at the clinical foundations and saying there is a need to fundamentally redo these taxonomies.

References

George, P., & Marlowe, S. (2005). Structural social work in action: Experiences from rural India. *Journal of Progressive Human Services*, *16*(1), 5–24.

James, S., Herman, J., Rankin, S., Keisling, M., Mottet, L., & Anafi, M. A. (2016). *The report of the 2015 US transgender survey*. National Center for Transgender Equality. Retrieved from https://transequality.org/sites/default/files/docs/usts/USTS-Full-Report-Dec17.pdf

Kivel, P. (2007). Social service or social change? In Incite! Women of Color Against Violence (Ed.), *The revolution will not be funded: Beyond the non-profit industrial complex* (pp. 129–149). Cambridge, MA: South End Press.

Kosciw, J. G., Clark, C. M., Truong, N. L., & Zongrone, A. D. (2020). *The 2019 National School Climate Survey: The experiences of lesbian, gay, bisexual, transgender, and queer youth in our nation's schools*. New York: GLSEN.

Mullaly, R. (1997). *Structural social work practice: Ideology, theory, and practice* (2nd ed.). Toronto: Oxford University Press.

Shelton, J., DeChants, J., Bender, K., Hsu, H., Narendorf, S., Ferguson, K., … Santa Maria, D. (2018). Homelessness and housing experiences among LGBTQ youth and young adults: An intersectional examination across seven U.S. cities. *Cityscape*, *20*(3), 9–33.

3 Knowledge for Practice with Trans and Gender Expansive Youth

Gerald P. Mallon

Introduction

More than three decades ago, I met my first young person who was a transgender client. I was at that time the director of a large child welfare facility in New York City that specialized in working with gay teens – in those days we had no knowledge about bisexual or nonbinary young people, actually very limited knowledge about lesbian young people, and no knowledge at all about working with transgender and/or gender expansive (TGE) young people. I had one client, whom I will call Tracey, who told me almost every day "You have it all wrong, Gary, I am not gay, I am transgender." Knowing nothing at the time about TGE young people, I was totally unprepared to work effectively with Tracey and worst of all, I didn't believe that there were differences between being a gay teen and being a trans teen. I realize now, and Tracey and I have since had many conversations about this, how ignorant I was, and how uninformed I was about TGE persons.

Just as those professionals who came before had labeled lesbian, gay, and bisexual persons mentally ill, because they did not understand their circumstances or their nature, TGE youth have similarly been misunderstood. If most social work practitioners are ill prepared to deal with gay bisexual, and lesbian persons, and in most cases, they still are, then certainly they are unprepared to respond to the needs of TGE persons. As a practitioner with almost 45 years of experience, many of them with lesbian, gay, bisexual, transgender, and questioning (LGBTQ) young people, I initially felt very inadequate in my attempts to meet the needs of TGE youth. Apart from its significance as a practice dilemma, this case also illustrates an important truth about TGE youth in contemporary society: That most people, even very experienced practitioners have little or no accurate knowledge about the lives of TGE people.

An Ecological Approach

This chapter will spotlight the importance of knowledge acquisition in working with TGE youth for social work practitioners. The person: environment perspective, has

DOI: 10.4324/9780429297687-3

been a central influence on the social work profession's theoretical base and has usefulness and relevance as an approach to social work practice with TGE persons. Gitterman and Germain (1996, p. 19) underscore the point that disempowerment, which threatens the health, social well-being, and life of those who are oppressed, imposes enormous adaptive tasks on TGE persons. An understanding of the destructive relationships which exists between TGE persons and an environment that is focused on "either/or" male or female binary gender constructions is integral to the process of developing practice knowledge about working with TGE youth. The purpose of this chapter, then, is to define, identify and describe the knowledge base of practice with TGE persons and to review social work's response to the needs of this population.

What the social worker is supposed to do should dictate the boundaries of the profession's knowledge base, noted Meyer (1982). If social workers are supposed to be able to work with TGE young people, then a knowledge-base for practice with them must be within those boundaries. An organized knowledge base is crucial to any profession. Anyone, notes Mattaini (2016, p. 6) "can act." The professional, however is expected to act deliberately, taking the steps that are most likely to be helpful, least intrusive, and consistent with the person's welfare. Further, the social work professional should conduct their work in partnership *with* their clients. In addition to the necessity of an extensive knowledge base from which to draw upon for deliberate, professional practice, social work professionals must also value the dignity and worth of all people (NASW).

Sources of Knowledge

In my earlier chapters (Mallon, 1999b, 2009b), which focused on the acquisition of knowledge for social work practice for TGE young people, I identified several key sources of knowledge, which in a modified version herein, provide a framework for this chapter's discussion on knowledge for practice with TGE youth. These sources include: (1) practice wisdom derived from narrative experiences of the profession and professional colleagues, (2) the personal experiences of the practitioner, (3) a knowledge of the professional literature, (4) a knowledge of history and current events, (5) research issues which inform practice, (6) theoretical and conceptual analyses, and (7) information which is provided by the case itself. All of these, understood within an ecological framework of person:environment, with a consciousness of the reality of oppression in the lives of TGE young people, is called upon to inform social work practice with TGE persons and each contributes to the development of the knowledge base of practice with this population.

Practice Wisdom

Practice wisdom can be viewed as that which is derived from the narrative experiences of the profession, from both professional colleagues and from clients. Although narrative experiences may have drawbacks, in that one person's experience is not generalizable to the experiences of many, listening to the life stories of clients and permitting them to tell their story in their own words is central to the experience of social work practice (Coleman, Means, & Wallace, 2020).

Interest in narrative theory has grown in recent years and the use of life stories in practice has in some organizations replaced elaborate, formalized intake histories (Sharma, 2020; see also https://www.nytimes.com/interactive/2015/opinion/transgender-today). Life stories, which tend to be rich in detail, are usually obtained early in the work with a client and can be a useful means toward not only gathering important data to enhance one's knowledge base, but useful in establishing a rapport and a trusting relationship with a TGE young person. As the client talks and the worker listens empathetically, in the telling and the listening, the story gains personal and profound meanings. This process, particularly with TGE persons who have been oppressed, marginalized, and silenced, can also be a healing process. Finding meaning in life events, or explaining our life experience to ourselves and others, is a way that helps us to move forward.

However, social work practitioners should be cautious about utilizing practice wisdom, especially when most social workers have probably had very limited experience with TGE persons. That being said, listening to life stories can inform practice in meaningful ways. If one really listens to the narratives, with the third ear, and then connects the themes with past practice-based data obtained from previous practice, it can help to make sense of the situation and to guide one's practice.

In addition to listening to the life stories of clients, and the practice experiences of practitioners, social workers practicing with TGE persons can rely on rules which have been handed down by experienced practitioners to others that appear to work. Although practice with TGE persons is a relatively new area of practice for many social workers, heuristic practice (which can be described as principles to guide patterns of professional behavior and that which has shaped and refined practice) may also serve as models for other workers. The acquisition of group-specific language to guide practice, and a knowledge of the myths and stereotypes about TGE persons can be extremely useful forms of heuristic practice. Such fragments of practice wisdom can be valuable as a guide for practitioners interested in enhancing their practice knowledge base in working with TGE young people. **Anytime a young person wants to tell you about their life and to share with you their story, stop whatever you are doing, and listen**.

Personal Experience

The personal experiences of practitioners is the second powerful force which guides knowledge development. Although social workers are guided not only by their own personal experiences, but by a Professional Code of Ethics, most social workers base some of their knowledge about clients by integrating and synthesizing events gathered from their own life experiences. Within the guidelines provided by the Professions' Code of Ethics, basic interpersonal and problem-solving skills that social workers have developed throughout their lives is an important means toward informing one's practice (Moore, 1999).

It is a myth that most people do not know anyone who is TGE, but unquestionably, social workers who have a close friend or a family member who is TGE, may have additional personal experiences that can assist them in guiding their practice with this population. Social workers who themselves are TGE will unquestionably have additional insights into TGE clients. However, being TGE alone does not provide a practitioner with a complete and full knowledge for practice with TGE clients. Individuals who are TGE identified themselves may be at various stages of their own gender identity development and/or assertion and their knowledge may be incomplete and or may not be easily mapped onto the experiences of their clients. Further, there is no one way to be a TGE person. So assuming that a TGE social worker will inherently share processes related to gender identity development with their TGE clients is not only inaccurate, but also overlooks racism, sexism, poverty, and culture, all of which interact with one's experience of gender. Professional practice requires that practitioners conduct themselves in ways that are consistent with professional values and ethics.

Issues of self-disclosure become significant when a social worker has had personal experiences or shares something in common with a client, in this case a TGE identity. A TGE practitioner may find it helpful to disclose their identity with a client who is struggling with whether or not to come out, but in other cases, the worker's disclosure could also inhibit the client from sharing genuine feelings (Dutton, Bullen, & Deane, 2019). Humans have the urge to self-disclose, which is nowadays often satisfied on social media platforms. While contemporary social media applications may have great utility, they also pose a significant challenge. People are usually good at leveraging self-disclosure in a way that gratifications are increased and disadvantages are minimized – for example, by avoiding pitfalls such as revealing too intimate information to a large audience. However, when trying to balance self-disclosure and privacy risks on social media platforms, users are not always able to make rational decisions. Therefore, users of social media need to be supported in order to master self-disclosure decisions (Krämer & Shäwel, 2020). At a minimum, social workers utilizing self-disclosure will need close supervision and consultation to process these issues. Although personal experiences are significant in knowledge development, social workers must always be in touch with their own feelings and must remember that self-disclosure always has to do with the well being of the client, not the practitioner.

History and Current Events

Since practice is embedded in the broader social context of life, a knowledge of the social policies and shifting social forces is important for knowledge development and working with TGE youth. Since historical events are most often documented in the news media, information from multiple media sources can be important sources of information. News stories and talk shows in the mass media are often less than objective and, in many cases, replete with inaccuracies. However, for many, these are the only sources of knowledge about TGE youth and may be an important basis to work from, even in a professional context (Bates, Hobman, & Bell, 2020). However, for a highly illuminating history of transgender people see Susan Stryker's (2017) volume titled *Transgender History: The Roots of Today's Revolution*.

The Internet has provided a very important source of information that individuals can obtain within the confines of their own homes. The Internet has not only grown exponentially during the past several years (and since the first edition of this book, Mallon, 1999a), but the Internet, for many, may be the first place to begin a search about the plethora of issues pertaining to TGE persons. Although there are also inaccuracies on the Internet, one huge benefit for those seeking access to knowledge about TGE persons is that the Web has a reach that exceeds geography. Consequently, persons in remote rural areas, as well as those in more urban centers have equal ability to gather information about and communicate with transgender persons around the world whereas in the past such data was only to be found in urban environs. Although one must have access to a computer or smart phone to make such connections, libraries and schools in many communities can provide individuals with such access and Internet cafes in many communities can provide individuals with such access.

A review of appropriate websites about TGE youth is beyond the scope of this publication, as there are literally tens of thousands and maybe more, that exist on the topic. The reader may find appropriate sites by using one of the numerous search engines (Google, Bing, Baidu, Yahoo, Ask.com, Yandex, DuckDuckGo) and by keying code words and phrases such as transgender, gender expansive, nonbinary, and gender identity.

Social work's history with TGE persons can best be described as contentious relationship. Although the Delegate Assembly of the National Association of Social Workers (National Association of Social Workers, 2000) has proposed to adopt a policy statement on Transgender Issues/ Gender Identity Issues which emphasized its ban on discrimination based on gender identity issues, social work has generally lagged behind other helping professionals in putting resources behind its commitment. The more recent publication, (National Association of Social Workers, 2003) does however do a better job of addressing transgender and gender identity issues.

In a marked improvement over their previous guidance, the Council on Social Work Education in 2016 published its *Guidelines for transgender and gender nonconforming (TGNC) affirmative education: Enhancing the climate for TGNC students, staff and faculty in social work education* (Austin, Craig, Alessi, et al., 2016). The report provides guidelines for the creation of social work educational environments that affirm transgender and gender non-conforming (TGNC) identities. The guidelines for TGNC inclusive social work education emerged from the work of the Council on Sexual Orientation and Gender Identity and Expression (CSOGIE), which is one of the diversity councils of the Council of Social Work Education (CSWE). While the 2015 Educational Policy and Accreditation Standards (EPAS) specifically identified gender identity as one of the dimensions of diversity to be reflected in the learning environments of all CSWE accredited programs of social work, CSOGIE members note a lack of comprehensive guidelines to support social work programs in fostering and promoting environments that are affirmative of diverse gender identities. This concern was expressed in light of evidence revealing that (1) TGNC social work students report a number of unsatisfactory experiences in their social work programs (Austin, Craig, & McInroy, 2016; Craig, Dentato, McInroy, Austin, & Messinger, 2015; McInroy, Craig, & Austin, 2014) and (2) social work students may not be ready to practice competently with TGNC clients after graduation (Craig et al., 2015). Therefore, the document provides a framework to help social work programs assess whether their programs are affirmative of TGNC faculty, students, and staff.

Developing the knowledge and skills of all stakeholders in social work education can contribute to environments that ensure dignity and respect for TGNC students, faculty, and staff and ultimately promote culturally competent social work practice with gender diverse clients. This document can also be used by social work faculty members to incorporate social work content on TGNC issues into the curriculum and to enhance inclusivity of classroom activities.

Austin, Craig, and McInroy (2016) note that social work has professional and academic standards consistent with transgender affirmative education and practice. Nevertheless, a growing body of research suggests that topics related to TGE people and communities are largely absent from social work education, resulting in practitioners who are uninformed or biased about TGE people. Quantitative and qualitative analyses in their study identify barriers to transgender affirmative social work education including (1) transphobic microaggressions within classroom and field settings, (2) the absence of transgender specific education and expertise, and (3) the general lack of visibility of transgender issues.

Despite inclusive policies and accreditation mandates that call for non-discriminatory professional practice, an inherent difficulty in separating personal attitudes from professional prerogatives with respect to TGE issues appears to have made service provision to this population a complex process. Gender-based oppression and the resulting psychosocial difficulties experienced by many TGE individuals demands that social work do more to educate practitioners and students to the needs of this population. Empowering practice calls on social workers to target society's traditional gender dichotomy for change (Burdge, 2007).

The Professional Literature

The scholarship and research with respect to TGE youth has grown exponentially. In 1999, a Socio-Lit, Psych-Lit, and Social Work Abstracts computer search using the words "transgender youth" yielded no articles. Since those early years, in fact, the initial publication of this volume, in the *Journal of Gay and Lesbian Social Services* was the first social work journal to initiate a dialogue about the experiences of transgender youth (Mallon, 1999a) today according to Google Scholar, there are almost 10,000 peer-reviewed articles that focus on TGE youth. Mainstream peer-reviewed social work publications (*Social Work, Social Services Review and Families in Society*) have lagged behind several of the other professional disciplines journals, most notably Psychology and Sociology, in recognizing the legitimacy of TGE youth issues in the professional literature, as evidenced by the special issue of *Clinical Practice in Pediatric Psychology* focusing on advancing the practice of pediatric psychology with transgender youth (Chen, Edwards-Leeper, Stancin, & Tishelman, 2018). Burdge (2007, p. 248) sums up this point best when she notes, "There is also a need for more articles related to transgender issues in mainstream social work journals. Currently, such articles seem relegated to specialty journals, where they risk being read by the 'choir.'"

If one were to look exclusively within the social work professional literature to develop a knowledge-base of practice, one would find a very circumscribed discussion of TGE practice issues in the mainstream social work literature. Although it appears that the major social work journals have been slow to respond to and to publish articles which address the wide and diverse needs of TGE persons, in fairness, it is not possible to know how many articles have been submitted and rejected, or how many in total have been submitted on this population. For a fuller understanding of practice with TGE persons, particularly with TGE youth, practitioners would be wise to look outside of social work for guidance. Practitioners would benefit from not only looking at other disciplines, but also looking to reports from organizations and other community-based resources.

For professionals who work with TGE youth, there are several excellent books which have been published in the past decade Arlene Lev's (2004) book *Transgender Emergence* which focuses on more than TGE youth issues is encyclopedic in its approach, and one of the first to address the topic of TGE persons. Elijah Nealy's (2019) incredible book *Trans kids and teens: Cultivating pride and joy with families in transition* is required reading for any social worker interested in developing their knowledge in practicing with TGE youth. Brill and Pepper's (2008) *The transgender child: A Handbook for Families and Professionals* and Brill and Kenney's *The transgender teen: A handbook for parents and professionals supporting transgender and nonbinary teen* are extraordinary and invaluable resources for social workers, helping professionals, and parents. For a more clinical perspective, Chang, Singh, and Dickey (2018) – *A clinical guide to gender affirming care* is a remarkable resource. It is a comprehensive guide, written by three TGE psychologists, that outlines the latest research and clinical re-commendations to provide professionals with requisite knowledge, skills, and competence in working with TGE persons. Though not focused specifically on youth, the recently released book *Social Work and Health Care Practice with Transgender and Nonbinary Individuals and Communities: Voices for Equity, Inclusion, and* Resilience, edited by Shanna K. Kattari, M. Killian Kinney, Leonardo Kattari, and N. Eugene Walls, is a comprehensive resource for social workers.

Recent publications by Jacob Tobia (2019) and Alok Vaid-Menon (2020) explore nonbinary and gender expansive identities through the author's ex-periences. First-person perspectives can also be found in Jazz Jennings (2016), Kuklin (2014), and Callender's (2020) books that give a powerful and com-pelling voice to TGE teens. Janet Mock shares her experiences as a young trans woman of color in Redefining Realness (2014).

Bornstein's (1994, 1998) books provide practitioners with additional insight into the transworld, from a transgender person's perspective and Feinberg's (1993) deservedly honored classic – *Stone Butch Blues*, and her more scholarly work, *Transgender Warriors: Making History from Joan of Arc to Dennis Rodman* provide social work practitioners with valuable knowledge-building insights.

Transgender activists, Daphne Scholinski (1997), Phyllis Burke (1997) from personal experiences, have documented the brutal adversion therapies to which gender expansive youth have been subjected to coerce them into conformity. Riki Wilchins (1997) raises many provocative questions about the oppressive nature of gender classification, their final chapter documenting hate crimes against transsexuals' underscores the urgency with which Wilchins questions language and gender exclusion.

Randi Ettner's (1996) book *Confessions of a Gender Defender*, provides first-hand insights into a psychologist's reflections on life among transgender persons. Ettner's book helps clinicians examine their own gaps in training and helps to assess their own counter-transference issues surrounding treatment of transgender persons.

Research

The research on TGE youth is growing at a rapid rate. While 10 years ago it was almost non-existent, and if trans youth were at all included it was as part of the LGBT acronym, and then, almost barely mentioned; today Google Scholar identifies that there are almost 10,000 peer-reviewed articles using the term *transgender and gender expansive youth* and using the term *transgender and gender diverse youth*, there are almost 65,000 articles. The current research is both quantitative and qualitative in method. Among the notable published researchers on TGE youth are the following:

Arnie Grossman and Tony D'Augelli (Grossman & D'Augelli, 2006, 2007). Shanna K. Kattari and M. Killian Kinney (Kattari, Kinney, Kattari, & Walls, 2020).

Sari L. Reisner (Reisner et al., 2017).
Jama Shelton (Shelton, 2015, 2016, 2017, 2019)
Anneliese A. Singh (Chang et al., 2018).
Jaimie F. Veale (Veale, Watson, Peter, & Saewyc, 2017)

Questioning gender and sexuality binaries; queer theory, TGE individuals, and researchers can assist social workers in developing their knowledge.

Theoretical and Conceptual Analyses

Theories to guide practice or theoretical constructs, which help one to better understand and practice with a client system also offer explanations to guide practice (American Psychological Association, 2013). Understanding the process of TGE identity formation will undoubtedly enable the practitioner to carry out informed and sensitive intervention with TGE youth (see Bockting & Coleman, 2016). However, practitioners must also be aware of the fact that it is not possible for them to utilize traditional developmental models taught in most human behavior and the social environment sequences (Erikson, 1950; Marcia, 1980; Offer, 1980; Offer, Ostrov, & Howard, 1981) which posit concepts of sex-role identifications which are concerned only with heterosexual development and presume cisgender identity as an eventual outcome. Utilizing these traditional approaches, which view TGE identity from a developmentally pejorative perspective, does not assist or prepare the practitioner to practice competently with TGE persons.

Unlike their counterparts in the cisgender majority, TGE youth experience a social condition which is attributable to their TGE identity: oppression, stigmatization, and marginalization. Oppression, notes Pharr (1988, p. 53) cannot be viewed in isolation because of the interconnected nature of sexism, racism, cis/heterosexualism, classism, anti-Semitism, and ableism, which are linked by a common origin – economic power and control. Backed by institutional power, economic power, and both institutional and individual violence, this trinity of elements acts as the "standard of rightness and often righteousness wherein all others are judged in relation to it."

There are many ways that norms are enforced both by individuals and institutions. One way to view persons who fall outside the "norm" is to label such individuals as *"the other."* It is easy to discriminate against, view as deviant, marginal, or inferior such groups that are not part of the mainstream. Those who are classified as such become part of an invisible minority, a group whose achievements are kept hidden and unknown from those in the dominant culture. Stereotyping, blaming the victim, distortion of reality, can even lead the person to feeling as though they deserve the oppression which they experience. This process, as it relates to TGE identity, is called internalized transphobia (Babits, 2020; Bockting et al., 2020). Other elements of oppression include: isolation, self-hatred, underachievement or over-achievement, substance abuse, problems with relationships, and a variety of other mental health matters.

Violence, as suggested by Domínguez-Martinez and colleagues (2020) as well as Newcomb and colleagues (2020) is also seen as a theoretical construct in the lives of TGE persons. The threat of violence toward TGE persons, particularly TGE youth who must attend community schools, who if they step out of line is made all the more powerful by the fact that they do not have to do anything to receive the violence. It is their lives alone that precipitate such action. Therefore, TGE youth almost always have a sense of safety which is fragile and tenuous and they may never feel completely secure. Social workers who are unfamiliar with TGE youth may view such conditions as a pathology in need of treatment, but for the TGE youth such insecurity is an adaptive strategy for living within in a hostile environment.

Self-Awareness

Many students entering the world of social work think that they are open-minded and while many may have a genuine desire to help others, some have not delved inside of themselves to assess the role that power, privilege, and influence has played in their own lives.

As social work is a values-based profession, we are ethically obligated to address these issues and to work toward increasing the levels of competence and awareness within both students entering the profession and colleagues who continue to make contributions. Although the professional literature has begun to address these areas, as professionals we also must focus on the issue of self-awareness.

The consequence of not considering theoretical analyses and concepts which are transphobic is that many cisgender social workers believe that if they avoid society's fear and loathing of TGE persons then that is all that they will need to do to work effectively with TGE youth. While most social workers have "politically correct" ideas about LGB persons, many professionals have not always had the opportunity to deal with the deeper prejudices and cisgender privileges that they possess. Since most professionals continue to have an inadequate knowledge base about the real lives of TGE persons, this causes them to be, in many cases, more transignorant than transphobic. However, just because one is ignorant and therefore not intentionally or even consciously behaving from a transphobic place, the impact is the same.

Many TGE persons believe that cisgender social workers still harbor the ciscentric assumption that it is less than normal or less preferable to be TGE. Some social workers, particularly those from a more psychoanalytically or-iented perspective, believe that somewhere in the TGE person's system you can find the roots or the cause of TGE identity, and that it secretly has something to do with family dysfunction or childhood sexual abuse.

Research on the intersection between gender identity and mental health is often misunderstood. According to the Diagnostic Statistics and Assessment Manual, DSM-5 (American Psychological Association, 2013), gender dys-phoria (GD), is the distress a person experiences as a result of the sex and gender they were assigned at birth. In this case, the assigned sex and gender do not match the person's gender identity and as such that person would be considered transgender. The broad criterion for a diagnosis of gender dysphoria is "a marked incongruence between one's experiences/expressed gender and assigned gender, of at least six months duration" (American Psychological Association, 2013, p. 452).

Gender identity disorder (GID) which was the previous diagnosis given to people who were TGE, was reclassified to *gender dysphoria* by the DSM-5 (American Psychological Association, 2013). Some TGE people and researchers support declassification of GID because they say that this initial diagnosis pathologized gender identity expression, reinforces the binary model of gender and can result in stigmatization of transgender individuals (Newman, 2002). The official reclassification as gender dysphoria in the DSM-5 may help resolve some of these issues, because the term *gender dysphoria* applies only to the distress experienced by some persons resulting from gender identity issues, not the young person's gender identity itself. The American Psychiatric Association, publisher of the DSM-5, states that gender nonconformity is not in itself a mental disorder. The critical element of gender dysphoria is the presence of clinically significant distress associated with the condition. There is general consensus among medical and psychological experts, consistent with the views of transgender rights advocates globally, that experiencing gender as different from the one assigned at birth is not a disorder or a disease – but rather a natural variation of human experience. Countries such as Argentina, Malta, Nepal, and Norway have made progress in recent years in improving legal recognition of transgender people and not requiring diagnoses. However, many governments continue to deem transgender people "mentally ill," and countries such as Japan, Turkey, and Spain among others, still require a mental health diagnosis to legally change one's name or legal gender marker.

While the change in DSM was intended to reduce the stigmatization of individuals so diagnosed, the continuing presence of a gender-related diagnosis in the DSM is a source of controversy. In May 2019, the World Health Organization removed gender nonconformity from its list of mental disorders in its global manual of diagnoses. The organization's latest version of its International Classification of Diseases, known as ICD-11, no longer calls gender nonconformity a "gender identity disorder" as it was in the last version. It reclassifies it as "gender incongruence" and moves it from mental and behavioral disorders to a section on sexual health (Haynes, 2019). The diagnosis is generally required to access gender-affirming care, but in the process assigns a diagnosis to a person whose distress is largely due to the perceptions and expectations of others rather than intrapersonal dysfunction.

These are complex issues which need to be addressed within the overall context of diversity and yet at the same time, from a specific TGE perspective. Moral, religious, and cultural biases still run deep in many students preparing for practice and in professionals who currently practice. Although there are no simple solutions to helping individuals overcome their biases, beginning an honest dialogue and providing students with accurate and appropriate information about TGE youth is an important place to start.

Knowledge Derived from the Individual Case

Information provided by the case itself is the final means toward the generation of knowledge about TGE youth that will be discussed in this chapter. The client within the individual, couple, or family system and the environmental context within which they live provide a great deal of information that is specific to the case and which can guide practice. Listening to what youth say, and observing what they do from initial engagement, through assessment, intervention, and termination can provide crucial information.

Although some TGE youth present concerns that relate specifically to issues related to their gender, many of which will be discussed in various other chapters in this collection, TGE youth usually seek help for a range of issues that have little to do with their gender per se or are related to it in an indirect way. Like their cisgender counterparts, TGE youth seek help from social work practitioners to deal with a wide array of problems in living. A critical aspect of intervening with a TGE youth is for practitioners to have a firm understanding of the client's identity formation.

The practitioner who is sensitive and affirming in their work with TGE persons need to have a complete understanding of the psychological, behavioral, affectional, attitudinal, and an internal sense of "goodness of fit" as the features of each of the stages of coming out as TGE and direct their interventions accordingly. A lack of familiarity with this process will cause the practitioner to misinterpret the youth's reactions and miss opportunities to assist them in moving forward in the process of developing a comfort with their own identity.

Practitioners need to be aware that certain conditions may be intensified, if not caused by oppression and stigmatization to which TGE youth may have been exposed to in their development and which they may continue to experience as adults. For example, although the coming out process has been conceptualized as a positive developmental step toward healthfulness, the societal or familial response to an individual's disclosure may be less than constructive.

Social work practitioners need to be sensitive to the particular needs and concerns of the TGE youth and must also appreciate that the young person's membership in a stigmatized and oppressed group (Goffman, 1963) has shaped their identity and may play a role in the presenting problem which they may or may not bring to their initial session. Whether or not the presenting problem is related to the client's gender identity, the practitioner who intervenes with the youth must be well-acquainted with the issues and features of TGE life, develop an expertise in working with the population and acquire a knowledge of the community resources which exist to help the young person to thrive and not just survive. It is also important to recognize that there is as much diversity in the TGE community as in all other communities, and therefore, there is no one type of TGE individual or no one correct way to be TGE.

Although Western society has made some positive steps toward altering negative attitudes toward TGE youth, social workers must be aware of the presence of the phenomenon of anti-trans bias, transphobia and possibly the youth's own internalized transphobia. Professionals must help clients refrain from reinforcing it through their own bias and stereotypes. Isolation is another problem that frequently arises as a result of the stigma associated with a TGE identity. Practitioners need to be knowledgeable about existing community resources and if necessary to support the client by going with them to visit these resources. The development of social support networks through involvement in such programs can be an important task for the youth and practitioner to work on together.

Subsequent chapters in this collection will focus on exploring social work practice with TGE persons from the perspectives of multiple systems: individuals, families, communities, and organizations.

Conclusions

The social work profession recognizes TGE identities as valid and TGE people worthy of equitable treatment. TGE persons should be afforded the same respect and rights as cisgender people. Discrimination, oppression, and prejudice directed against any group is damaging to the social, emotional, and economic well-being of the affected group, as well as to society as a whole. All social workers are ethically bound to fight to eliminate such discrimination inside and outside the profession, in both public and private sectors.

Adopting nonjudgmental attitudes toward TGE youth enables social workers to provide maximum support and services to those who are part of TGE communities. Social workers and the profession can support and empower TGE persons through all phases of their coming out process. Utilizing ecological approaches that assist persons in developing adaptation to their environments, social workers should also be aware that they may need to assist in developing supportive practice environments for those addressing issues of gender identity, both clients and colleagues.

Cultivating a knowledge base of practice to prepare students and practitioners to work more competently and effectively with TGE persons, especially with TGE youth, is an essential element of good practice and needs to be integrated into a foundation level curriculum in meaningful and conscientious ways. The Council on Social Work Education should require course content on TGE issues, offer research opportunities for investigating issues of relevance to this population, develop and provide training for instructors and students, and to seek out field opportunities for students interested in working with TGE persons. For specific information on creating trans inclusive and affirming social work classrooms, see Shelton and Dodd (2020) and Shelton, Kroehle, and Andia (2019).

On a societal level we must work to eliminate the psychological and physical harm directed at TGE youth and to work toward portraying them accurately and compassionately. Programs that address the health and mental health needs of clients must work toward developing sensitive and respectful practice with TGE persons and their families that not only affirms TGE youth but also celebrates them.

From a legal and political action perspective, social workers need to join together with other professional associations and progressive organizations to lobby on behalf of the civil rights of TGE persons. An increase in funding for education, treatment services, and research on behalf of TGE persons is essential. Finally, the repeal of laws that limit the ability of TGE people to live authentically and ensuring that individuals will not suffer discrimination against them in inheritance, insurance, healthcare, education, child custody, and property is part of the proud tradition of social work's mission to fight for social justice for all people.

References

American Psychological Association. (2013). *Diagnostic and statistical manual of mental disorders (DSM-V)* (5th ed.). Washington, DC: Author.

American Psychological Association. (2015). Guidelines for psychological practice with transgender and gender nonconforming people. *American Psychologist, 70*, 832–864.

Austin, A., Craig, S. L., Alessi, E. J., Wagaman, M. A., Paceley, M. S., Dziengel, L., & Balestrery, J. E. (2016). *Guidelines for transgender and gender nonconforming (TGNC) affirmative education: Enhancing the climate for TGNC students, staff and faculty in social work education.* Alexandria, VA: Council on Social Work Education.

Austin, A., Craig, S. L., & McInroy, L. B. (2016). Toward transgender affirmative social work education. *Journal of Social Work Education, 52*(3), 297–310.

Babits, C. (2020). Educating against transphobia. *Feminist Collections: A Quarterly of Women's Studies Resources, 41*(1/2), 22–23.

Bates, A., Hobman, T., & Bell, B. T. (2020). "Let me do what i please with it... Don't decide my identity for me": LGBTQ+ youth experiences of social media in narrative identity development. *Journal of Adolescent Research, 35*(1), 51–83.

Bockting, W., & Coleman, E. (2016). Developmental stages of the transgender coming-out process: Toward an integrated identity. In R. Ettner, S. Monstrey, & E. Coleman (Eds.), *Principles of transgender medicine and surgery* (pp. 137–158). New York: Routledge.

Bockting, W. O., Knudsen, G., & Goldberg, J. M. (2006). Counseling and mental health care for transgender adults and loved ones. *International Journal of Transgenderism, 9*(3/4), 35–82.

Bockting, W. O., Miner, M., Swinburne, R. E., Dolezal, C., Robinson, B. E., Simon Rosser, B. R., & Coleman, E. (2020). The transgender identity survey: A measure of internalized transphobia. *LGBT Health, 7*(1), 22–31.

Brill, S., & Kenney, L. (2016). *The transgender teen: A handbook for parents and professionals supporting transgender and nonbinary teens.* Jersey City, NJ: Cleis Press.

Brill, S., & Pepper, R. (2008). *The transgender child: A handbook for families and professionals.* Jersey City, NJ: Cleis Press.

Burdge, B. (2007). Bending gender, ending gender: Theoretical foundations for social work practice with the transgender community. *Social Work, 52*(3), 243–250.

Burke, P. (1997). *Gender shock: Exploding the myths of male and female.* New York: Anchor Books.

Callender, K. (2020). *Felix ever after.* New York: Balzer + Bray.

Chang, S.C., Singh, A. A., & Dickey, L.M. (2018). *A clinicians guide to gender-affirming care: Working with transgender and gender nonconforming clients.* Oakland, CA: Context Press.

Chen, D., Edwards-Leeper, L., Stancin, T., & Tishelman, A. (2018). Advancing the practice of pediatric psychology with transgender youth: State of the science, on-going controversies, and future directions. *Clinical Practice in Pediatric Psychology, 6*(1), 73–83. doi:10.1037/cpp0000229. PMID: 29808159; PMCID: PMC5969520.

Coleman, R., Means, D. R., & Wallace, J. K., (2020). Questioning a single narrative: Multiple identities shaping Black queer and transgender student retention. *Journal of College Student Retention: Research, Theory and Practice, 21*(4), 455–475.

Craig, S. L., Dentato, M. P., McInroy, L. B., Austin, A., & Messinger, L. (2015). *Social work students speak out!: The experiences of lesbian, gay, bisexual, transgender and queer students in social work programs: A study report.* Toronto ON: Authors.

Domínguez-Martínez, T., Robles García, R., Fresán, A., Cruz, J., Vega, H., & Reed, G. M. (2020). Risk factors for violence in transgender people: A retrospective study of experiences during adolescence. *Psychology & Sexuality.* doi:10.1080/19419899.202 0.1802772

Dutton, H., Bullen, P., & Deane, K. L. (2019). "It is OK to let them know you are human too": Mentor self-disclosure in formal youth mentoring relationships. *Journal of Community Psychology, 47*(4), 943–963.

Erikson, E. (1950). *Childhood and society.* New York: W.W. Norton & Co.

Feinberg, L. (1993). *Stone butch blues.* Ithaca, NY: Firebrand Books.

Feinberg, L. (1996). *Transgender warriors: Making history from Joan of Arc to Dennis Rodman.* Boston: Beacon Press.

Gitterman, A. & Germain, C. B. (1996). *The life model of social work practice* (2nd ed.). New York: Columbia University Press.

Goffman, E. (1963). *Stigma: Notes of the management of a spoiled identity.* Englewood Cliffs, NJ: Prentice Hall.

Grossman, A., & D'Augelli, A. (2007). Transgender youth and life-threatening behaviors. *Suicide & Life-Threatening Behavior, 35*(5), 527–537.

Grossman, A., & D'Augelli, A. (2006). Transgender youth: Invisible and vulnerable. *Journal of Homosexuality, 51*(1), 111–128.

Haynes, S. (2019, May 28). The World Health Organization will stop classifying transgender people as having a "mental disorder." *Time,* p. 27.

Jennings, J. (2016). Being Jazz: My life as a (transgender) teen. New York: Ember.

Kattari, S. K., Kinney, M. K., Kattari, L., & Walls, N. E. (Eds.). (2020). *Social work and health care practice with transgender and nonbinary individuals and communities: Voices for equity, inclusion, and resilience.* New York: Taylor and Francis.

Krämer, N., & Schäwel, J. (2020). Mastering the challenge of balancing self-disclosure and privacy in social media. *Current Opinion in Psychology, 31*, 67–71.

Kuklin, S. (2014). *Beyond magenta: Transgender teens speak out.* Somerville, MA: Candlewick Press.

Lev, A. I. (2004). *Transgender emergence: Therapeutic guidelines for working with gender variant people and their families.* New York: Haworth Press.

Mallon, G. P. (Ed). (2008). *Social work practice with lesbian, gay, bisexual, and transgender persons.* New York: Haworth Press.

Mallon, G. P. (1999a). Knowledge for practice with transgendered persons. *Journal of Gay and Lesbian Social Services, 10*(3/4), 1–18.

Mallon, G. P. (Ed.). (1999b). *Social services with transgendered youth.* New York: Haworth Press.

Mallon, G. P. (Ed.). (2009a). *Social work practice with transgender and gender variant youth* (2nd ed.). New York: Routledge.

Mallon, G. P. (2009b). Knowledge for practice with trans youth. In G. P. Mallon (Ed.), *Social work practice with transgender and gender variant youth* (pp. 1–24). New York: Routledge.

Marcia, J. (1980). Identity in adolescence. In J. Adelson (Ed.), *Handbook of adolescent psychology.* New York: Wiley.

Mattaini, M. (2016). Knowledge for practice. In M. Mattaini, C. Holtschneider, & C. T. Lowery (Eds.), *Foundations of social work practice* (5th ed., pp. 59–85). Washington, DC: NASW.

McInroy, L. B., Craig, S. L., & Austin, A. (2014). The perceived scarcity of gender identity specific content in Canadian social work programs. *Canadian Social Work Review, 31*(1), 5–21.

McPhail, B. A. (2004). Questioning gender and sexuality binaries: What queer theory, transgender individuals, and sex researchers can teach social work. *Journal of Gay & Lesbian Social Services, 17*(1), 3–21.

Meyer, C. H. (1982). Social work's conceptual frameworks: Uniqueness and strategies—the time is now. *Social Thought, 8,* 3–13. doi:10.1080/15426432.1982.10383418

Moore, B. (1999). Proposed public and professional policies: Transgender issues/ Gender identity issues. *NASW News,* March: 12–13.

National Association of Social Workers. (2000). *Code of ethics of the National Association of Social Workers.* Washington, DC: Author.

National Association of Social Workers. (2003). Transgender and gender identity issues. In *Social work speaks: National Association of Social Workers, policy statements 2003-2006* (6th ed., pp. 345–349). Washington, DC: Author.

Nealy, E. C. (2019). *Trans kids and teens: Cultivating pride and joy with families in transition.* New York: W.W. Norton & Company.

Newcomb, M. E., Hill, R., Buehler, K., Ryan, D. T., Whitton, S. W., & Mustanski, B. (2020). High burden of mental health problems, substance use, violence, and related psychosocial factors in transgender, nonbinary, and gender diverse youth and young adults. *Archives of Sexual Behavior, 49,* 645–659.

Newman, L. (2002). Sex, gender and culture: Issues in the definition, assessment and treatment of gender identity disorder. *Clinical Child Psychology and Psychiatry, 7*(3), 352–359.

O'Bryan, J., Scribani, M., Leon, K., Tallman, N., Wolf-Gould, C., Wolf-Gould, C., & Gadomski, A. (2020). Health-related quality of life among transgender and gender expansive youth at a rural gender wellness clinic. *Quality of Life Research: An International Journal of Quality of Life Aspects of Treatment, Care & Rehabilitation, 29*(6), 1597–1607.

Offer, D. (1980). Adolescent development: A normative perspective. In S. I. Greenspan & G. H. Pollock (Eds.), *The course of life, vol II: Latency, adolescence, and youth.*

U.S. Department of Health and Human Services Publication No. (ADM) 80-999. Adelphi, MD: Mental Health Study Center, Division of Mental Health Service Programs, National Institute of Mental Health, U.S. Dept. of Health and Human Services, Public Health Service, Alcohol, Drug Abuse, and Mental Health Administration; Washington, DC.

Offer, D., Ostrov, E., & Howard, K. (1981). *The adolescent: A psychological self portrait.* New York: Basic Books.

Pharr, S. (1988). *Homophobia: A weapon of sexism.* Little Rock, AK: Chardon Press.

Reisner, S. L., Jadwin-Cakmak, L., White Hughto, J. M., Martinez, M., Salomon, L., & Harper, G. W. (2017). Characterizing the HIV prevention and care continua in a sample of transgender youth in the U.S. *AIDS Behavior, 21*(12), 3312–3327.

Scholinski, D. (1997). *The last time I wore a dress.* New York: Riverhead.

Sharma, N. (2020). The role of viewers' performance of a narrative on their beliefs about transgender persons. *Atlantic Journal of Communication.* doi:10.1080/15456870.2020.1794866

Shelton, J. (2015). Transgender youth homelessness: Understanding programmatic barriers through the lens of cisgenderism. *Children and Youth Services Review, 59*, 10–18.

Shelton, J. (2016). Reframing risk for transgender and gender expansive young people experiencing homelessness. *Journal of Gay and Lesbian Social Services, 28*(4), 277–291.

Shelton, J., & Bond, L. (2018). "It just never worked out": How transgender and gender expansive youth understand their pathways into homelessness. *Families in Society, 98*(4), 284–291.

Shelton, J., Kroehle, K, & Andia, M. (2019). The trans person is not the problem: Brave spaces and structural competence as educative tools for trans justice in social work. *Journal of Sociology and Social Welfare, 46*(4), 97–123.

Stryker, S. (2017). *Transgender history: The roots of today's revolution* (2nd ed.). New York: Seal Press.

Tobia, J. (2019). *Sissy: A coming-of-gender story.* New York: G.P. Putnam's Sons.

Veale, J. F., Watson, R. J., Peter, T., & Saewyc, E. M. (2017). Mental health disparities among Canadian transgender youth. *Journal of Adolescent Health, 60*(1), 44–49.

Watson, R. J., Wheldon, C., & Puhl, R. M. (2020). Evidence of diverse identities in a large national sample of sexual and gender minority adolescents. *Journal of Research on Adolescence, 30*, 431–442. doi:10.1111/jora.12488

Wilchins, R. (1997). *Read my lips: Sexual subversion and the end of gender.* Ann Arbor, MI: Firebrand Books.

4 Social Work Practice with Nonbinary Youth

Jama Shelton, M. Killian Kinney, and Anthony Ritosa

Introduction

Binaries are ever present in the organization of contemporary society. Binary constructs offer two simple, mutually exclusive, ways of being or identifying. The most prevalent binaries in U.S. society are the sex binary and the gender binary. Both presume that there are only two ways to categorize sex and gender: female/woman and male/man. They also presume that sex and gender are rigidly boundaried, immutable, and interrelated. With these sex and gender categories comes a set of gendered expectations and gender roles. Science has proven that sex is not binary (Fausto-Sterling, 2018). However, the binary construction of sex remains prevalent in contemporary society. Likewise, gender has been explained as a social construct, as existing on a continuum, and as not always correlated with the expectations of assigned sex at birth. However, the binary construction of gender and its correlation with assigned sex at birth remain prevalent in contemporary society, despite the fact that "defining gender as a condition determined strictly by a person's genitals is based on a notion that doctors and scientists abandoned long ago as oversimplified and often medically meaningless" (Grady, 2018, 10A). The prevalence of the gender binary is harmful to everyone, not only those individuals and communities who identify outside of or in between the limited categories allowed within the framework of a binary gender system.

A core value of the social work profession is a commitment to social justice (National Association of Social Workers, 2017). As a core value of the profession, social workers are guided to practice in a socially just manner, as well as to actively engage in addressing barriers to achieving equity for all oppressed groups. This value is articulated in The Code of Ethics: "Social workers pursue social change, particularly with and on behalf of vulnerable and oppressed individuals and groups" (p. 6). The Code of Ethics specifically includes gender identity and expression as distinct categories with regard to discrimination, stating that "social workers should not practice, condone, facilitate, or collaborate with any form of discrimination on the basis of... sexual orientation, gender identity or expression" (p. 21). Similarly, the Council on Social Work Education's (2015) standards for accreditation

DOI: 10.4324/9780429297687-4

require that social workers understand diversity and difference within a context of power, privilege, marginalization and oppression to eliminate biases (Competency 2). Gender identity and expression are aspects of diversity that social work professionals must value and work to understand, thus it is an ethical imperative that social workers engage practice in ways that are inclusive and affirming of all gender identities and expressions (Council on Social Work Education, 2015).

This chapter provides foundational knowledge for social work practice with nonbinary youth. We contextualize the experiences of nonbinary youth within the current social context of the binary gender system, provide current available data about nonbinary individuals, and propose practices for acknowledging and celebrating nonbinary identities in social work practice. This chapter includes a case study and questions for reflection.

The Gender Binary

The *gender binary* can be understood as the pervasive idea that there are two dichotomously existing genders and that a person's gender is biologically determined and will remain the same over time (Hyde, Bigler, Joel, Tate, & van Anders, 2019). Using the gender binary as a way to categorize and classify people is a primary organizing structure of contemporary United States social systems (Shelton, Kroehle, & Andia, 2019). Using a binary classification of gender as a way to organize society makes it challenging for nonbinary individuals to navigate social systems and structures. Nonbinary people are routinely excluded from social systems and structures, or made invisible within them, through cisnormative systems that presume and privilege cisgender identities and that disregard individuals who exist outside of the gender binary (Grossman & D'Augelli, 2006; Shelley, 2009; Shelton & Dodd, in press).

The binary gender system is in relationship with other oppressive ideologies and systems of oppression (Kroehle, Shelton, Clark, & Seelman, 2020). According to postcolonial and Indigenous scholarship, historical conceptualizations of gender throughout the world have not always been limited by binary categories (Mirandé, 2016; Sharyn Graham, 2007; Walters, Evans-Campbell, Simoni, Ronquillo, & Bhuyan, 2006). The creation of systems of categorization as a way to establish hierarchy and control was a key component of colonization. Thus, the colonial roots of the gender binary are connected to other binaries and the enforced hierarchy of European white, male dominance. This bit of history is important because societal norms of appropriate gender presentation and expression are created by the dominant culture to uphold power and privilege. As such, gender based assumptions are raced and classed, with the normative standard (European white, male) having been asserted centuries ago. The result is that individuals are judged against the physicality of those with European skin tones and features who have the ability (including the time and financial means) to dedicate to aligning their appearance with traditional norms of appropriate gender presentation (Kroehle et al., 2020). Therefore, the act of reading one's gender is never race or class neutral (Davis, 2014). These gender-based assumptions are so embedded in U.S. society that they may go unnoticed if not explicitly and intentionally explored. This exploration is required of social workers at the individual level, to eliminate biases, and also at the macro level, to understand and dismantle structural barriers rooted in cisgenderism.

Structural Oppression: Cisgenderism

To understand and effectively address the pervasive discrimination and marginalization faced by nonbinary individuals and communities, social workers must broaden their lens of analysis from the micro level (individual and interpersonal) of discriminatory acts to the structural conditions that allow for (and sometimes encourage) the discriminatory behavior of individuals within public systems and institutions. The attention to structural conditions that produce and maintain marginalization is often referred to as structural discrimination. Structural discrimination is defined as "the policies of dominant race/ethnic/gender institutions and the behavior of the individuals who implement these policies and control these institutions, which are race/ethnic/gender neutral in intent but which have a differential and/or harmful effect on minority race/ethnic/gender groups" (Pincus, 2000, p. 31).

This shift from individual level actions and behaviors (transphobia or anti-trans bias) to structural conditions requires an understanding of cisgenderism. Cisgenderism can be understood as an ideology that "others" people who identify as or who are labeled as transgender or gender expansive (TGE) (Ansara & Hegarty, 2012). Cisgenderism has been defined as "the cultural and systemic ideology that denies, denigrates, or pathologizes self-identified gender identities that do not align with assigned gender at birth as well as resulting behavior, expression, and community" (Lennon & Mistler, 2014, p. 63).

Understanding the challenges nonbinary youth face through the lens of cisgenderism is in alignment with the social work profession's charge to work towards social justice, because it draws the focus to the structural denial and systematic challenging of an individual's self-understanding. In other words, rather than locating the cause of the problem within the individual and focusing interventions solely on the individual level, applying a lens of cisgenderism acknowledges the impact of stressors outside of the individual and encourages social workers to mitigate these societal level stressors as well (Shelton et al., 2019). Reconceptualizing the stressors nonbinary youth face as consequences of the systemic reliance on binary gender categorization also decenters a commonly understood narrative of normative trans identity rooted in constructs of whiteness, ability, and income – ideological structures that limit the possibilities of nonbinary people to become who they are and achieve their full potential.

Who Are Nonbinary Youth?

Nonbinary youth are not a homogenous group. **There is no "right" way to be nonbinary or to express a nonbinary gender**. Some nonbinary individuals may identify as somewhere in between the binary gender constructs of girl/woman and boy/man; some may not identify with any gender at all and some may consider themselves to be a different gender that exists completely outside of the binary gender system (Todd et al., 2019). Nonbinary youth may or may not identify as transgender, and nonbinary youth may claim a range of sexual identity labels. It is important for social workers to understand that nonbinary is a way to describe one's gender, not one's sexual orientation.

Though the social work profession at large has increased its understanding of affirmative practice with transgender individuals and communities, the research literature has often been based on a binary understanding of transgender identity. In other words, much of the research about and the guidance for affirmatively working with transgender individuals has focused on supporting an individual in their transition to the "opposite" gender. This conceptualization reinforces the problematic gender binary while erasing the needs and experiences of nonbinary people. The profession's focus on transition to the "opposite" gender has resulted from reliance upon medical discourses that have shaped understandings of TGE identities and informed the frameworks available to the profession and the population at large (Sanger, 2008). The labeling of TGE people as mentally ill (via the Diagnostic and Statistical Manual of Mental Disorders – the DSM) reinforced the misguided understanding of TGE people as deviants from a gendered norm in need of correction. The corrective action, for decades, was to attempt to force a TGE individual into a gender perceived to be in alignment with their assigned sex at birth. Contemporary medical practice has enabled a different way of "correcting" (for those who could gain access) through hormone treatment and sex confirming surgeries. Though this is the path that feels right for some, it is not right for all TGE people, and it also reinforces the necessity of binary gender conformity (Shelley, 2009; Shelton et al., 2019).

The United States Transgender Survey (USTS) is the largest U.S. survey of TGE people to date with 27,715 respondents. Nearly 35% (9,700) respondents described their gender as nonbinary or genderqueer. The survey was not specifically focused on TGE youth, however 42% of respondents were between the ages of 18 and 24, an age group often included in the definition of youth. Unfortunately, the USTS indicates that nonbinary individuals encounter a range of oppressive experiences in multiple domains of daily life, including within their families and in school settings – places where youth spend a large portion of their time. Nearly one-third of nonbinary USTS survey respondents (N = 9,700) reported experiencing family rejection, and 15% reported leaving school because of the harassment they faced. Over half (53%) sometimes or always avoided using public restrooms in the year prior to the survey. Another 39% reported being mistreated when using public transportation. Nonbinary people also face barriers when seeking gender affirming medical care. Over four-fifths (89%) of USTS survey respondents were denied insurance coverage for surgery and 52% were denied coverage for hormones. Furthermore, there are no options for changing identity documents for nonbinary people. This can place nonbinary people in further danger of harassment, service denial, and marginalization – especially when their gender presentation does not conform to societal expectations associated with the gender marker on their identification documents. Experiencing widespread discrimination and mistreatment can cause psychological distress. Forty-nine percent of nonbinary USTS survey respondents reported experiencing psychological distress, a higher percentage than that reported by respondents identifying as transwomen and transmen (James et al., 2016).

Centering the experiences of nonbinary youth requires particular attention to intersecting identities such as race, class, income, and ability. In what constitutes only a small snapshot of larger themes, USTS respondents of color reported a greater frequency of acts of oppression compared to the U.S. population in general. Black respondents reported experiencing recent serious psychological distress at rates eight times (41%) that of the national average with American Indian and Alaska Native respondents reporting nine times (46%) that of the national average (James et al., 2016).

Perhaps one of the most important roles a social worker can play is not only affirming, but also celebrating a young person's assertion of their identity. The world at large does not affirm or support, much less celebrate, people who are nonbinary. What a difference a social worker can make by serving this role! Actions which affirm a person's unique identiti(es), such as through mentoring, inclusive language, and a focus on social justice, will have positive effects on the psychological and physical well-being of nonbinary youth (Craig et al., 2016). Conversely, reinforcing the gender binary affirms for nonbinary individuals that they must choose between self-affirmation/actualization and self-erasure/silence (Marine, 2017). Social workers who fail to recognize the importance of affirmation of gender diversity work to perpetuate this silence, self-denial, oppression, and erasure (Marine, 2017).

Nearly half (44%) of nonbinary USTS respondents reported that they typically just let others assume that they are women or men; just over half (53%) reported sometimes correcting others and informing them about their nonbinary identity. Nonbinary respondents could choose multiple reasons for not telling others about their identity. The most commonly reported reasons include: people don't understand (86%), it is easier not to say anything (82%), their identity is often dismissed and considered a phase (63%), and fear of violence (43%). Given the experiences of dismissal nonbinary people face in their daily lives, it is crucial for social workers to expand their thinking about gender, avoid making assumptions, and educate themselves so as not to recreate yet another oppressive and dismissive experience for nonbinary youth. Only half (52%) of survey respondents reported ever discussing their gender with a professional (James et al., 2016).

Macro Context – The Importance of Nonbinary-Inclusive Policy

While it is in alignment with social work values to assume that all youth should have access to education, healthcare, and developmentally appropriate socialization, the issue of policy protections for TGE youth has been a contested topic in recent years. Controversies related to school sports, homecoming courts, and bathroom/locker room use have arisen in cities around the country. Notably, many of these topics rely on a binary system of sex and gender categorization. For example, can a trans feminine student play on the girls' soccer team? Can a young transman use the boy's restroom? For schools that require uniforms, what clothing items are allowed to be worn by which students (the boy's uniform or the girl's uniform)?

Title IX is a federal law that bans sex discrimination in schools. Contradicting and confusing messages regarding the inclusion of transgender students under Title IX protections have circulated in the past several years. Despite these contradicting messages, many courts have made it clear that Title IX does protect students who are TGE. Title IX applies to all schools that receive federal funding. Policies like Title IX are an important step in improving the safety of TGE youth and guaranteeing their access to publicly funded systems and services. However, federal, state, local, and even institutional policies often disregard the experiences of nonbinary youth. For instance, a policy that specifies youth may access restrooms and locker rooms in alignment with their gender identity is irrelevant for nonbinary youth if binary restrooms and locker rooms are the only available options. Policies at all levels must focus on an expansion of the sex and gender binary in order to include individuals who identify outside of the female/girl/woman and male/boy/man binary. It is important that policies explicitly define protections as inclusive of nonbinary people, and/or specifically state that nonbinary people are included in protections intended through the implementation of the policy. If not explicitly named, policies are often open to interpretation (as we have seen with Title IX in recent years), and nonbinary people are likely to be erased.

Recommended Practices for Working with Nonbinary Youth

While best practices for working with youth also apply to nonbinary youth, there are several practices that deserve specific attention. It is important to consider the ways our society polices gender, and the ways in which nonbinary youth are marginalized and excluded from most systems, policies, organizations, and practice contexts. Following are some practices for consideration, specifically around building an alliance and navigating language.

Building a Healthy Alliance

Just as with all client populations, when working with nonbinary youth, it is imperative for social workers to build a healthy alliance. As with all people who are marginalized and stigmatized by social systems and dominant ideologies, nonbinary youth may be hesitant to build an alliance with an individual who does not share their identity or someone who is not clearly an ally, for fear of rejection, discrimination, and having to endure the emotional labor of educating those who are meant to support them. This section will provide some suggestions for social workers to build a healthy alliance with nonbinary youth. It is important to note that these suggestions are relevant when working with many groups of youth.

You Don't Need to Be an Expert

In reality, the only person who can completely understand an individual's gender identity is that person. Therefore, it is not expected that social workers will be experts on their clients' gender identity. It is the role of the social worker to make room for a young person to articulate their own unique experience of gender, and to not make judgments about their experiences. Professional codes of practice charge social workers with the task of gaining self-awareness to alleviate biases when working with diverse individuals and communities and to position themselves as learners with their clients serving as informants in their work. Further, the Global Minimum Qualifying Standards Committee of the International Federation of Social Workers and International Association of Schools of Social Work (2004) states that social workers should gain sufficient self-awareness through their education to alleviate personal biases and their impact when working with diverse groups (Craig, Dentato, Messenger, & McInroy, 2014).

Building Trust

Intrinsic to social work practice is building trust and rapport with individuals and communities. Building trust can be a challenge when working with people who are routinely harassed, marginalized, erased, and/or told both explicitly and implicitly that there is something wrong with them. Although mainstream media representations of nonbinary people are on the rise, representation does not immediately result in acceptance or understanding. As such, nonbinary youth may be carrying past negative experiences with them when engaging with a social worker. Social workers can begin to establish trust before a nonbinary youth ever enters the office by being intentional about their physical space. For example, all gender restrooms or single-use restrooms that are not labeled with binary gender labels (men/women) will ensure safe and comfortable access for nonbinary youth. One way that social workers can build rapport is by asking nonbinary youth what their experiences have been like with social workers, school counselors, or other adults in their lives and by listening to their suggestions about how to facilitate a successful working relationship. This should include an exploration of all the "-isms" that impact nonbinary youth, including disability, racism, classism, and adultism (Shelton et al., 2017).

Doing Your Own Internal Work

Social workers are not immune to societal messages about gender. Social workers who identify with the gender binary will have also benefited from the binary gender system at some point in their lives. It is the responsibility of the social worker to do their own internal work to understand the diversity of gender in nonbinary youth, and in themselves. Part of this work is for social workers to recognize their assumptions and biases related to gender, and to examine the ways in which these biases may impact their ability to provide nonjudgmental and supportive care to nonbinary youth. Social workers who have not previously worked with TGE youth should seek supervision from a colleague who has this knowledge and experience (Nealy, 2019).

It is important to use a theoretical framework that does not view nonbinary youth (and their identities) as problems to be fixed, such as the Gender Affirming Model (discussed in chapter 8). It is also important that social workers recognize that many of the challenges nonbinary youth face are, at least in part, the result of living in a cisnormative and binary world that structurally denies their existence. Social workers must develop a proficient structural competence that informs the building of a *brave space* for nonbinary youth (Marine, 2017; Shelton et al., 2019). A brave space is one in which youth of all genders feel they can disclose their gender, even and especially if their understanding of their gender evolves over time. A greater self-awareness in relation to oppressive structures, such as cisgenderism, is necessary for a social worker to increase their self-efficacy in building a healthy alliance with nonbinary youth.

Navigating Language

The way social workers use language – including the terms they use, the questions they ask, and the ways in which they communicate about gender identity – is a critical component of building a healthy alliance with nonbinary youth. Young people may experiment with different labels to describe their gender as they navigate developmental tasks related to identity exploration. Using various terms at various times is not a cause for alarm. Identity labels are also often context dependent, depending on geography, culture, and access to information. The terms people use to describe themselves shift over time, just as language itself evolves over time. Shifting terminology can cause social workers to experience anxiety when discussing gender identity with young people, which can result in stifled and timid conversation and which can come across as discomfort or judgment. Following are several specific considerations when navigating language with nonbinary youth.

Fluency

Using appropriate language that is inclusive of all genders is about more than rote memorization. As previously mentioned, the terms people use to describe themselves may change over time, just as language itself evolves over time. Rather than focusing only on the memorization of terms and definitions, which may shift and change, social workers should practice becoming fluent in gender inclusive language. This includes becoming aware of the ways language perpetuates a binary gender system as well as integrating the use of inclusive language throughout their practice and throughout their lives, not just when in direct contact with nonbinary youth. The following table provides suggestions for shifting from binary-gendered language to gender-inclusive language.

Instead of….	Use this…..
sister/brother	sibling
son/daughter	child
mother/father	parent
wife/husband	spouse
girls/boys	children
ladies and gentlemen	everyone
niece/nephew	nibling
he/she	they
woman/man	person
girlfriend/boyfriend	partner

Fluency also refers to an internalized understanding of the great expanse of the gender spectrum and the diversity of gender fluidity. Through discourse analysis, social workers are empowered to recognize and challenge binary language (Wagaman, Shelton, & Carter, 2018). Fluency allows social workers to identify the infinite ways in which gender is assigned to people, objects, and actions in order to make space for nonbinary and gender expansive expression.

Assumptions

Because we live in a cisnormative society, most people have internalized the belief that they should be able to instantly recognize an individual's gender through a variety of indicators. These indicators may include physical characteristics, such as manner of dress, hair style, facial hair, the size and shape of one's chest, whether or not someone is wearing makeup, or the size and shape of one's body, for example. In the United States, these assumptions are also raced and classed (Davis, 2014; Kroehle, Shelton, Clark, & Seelman, 2020). It is important that social workers become aware of the gendered assumptions they make, both to ensure that these assumptions do not inform their practice with TGE youth and also so they can begin the process of unlearning these internalized manifestations of cisnormativity. As mentioned previously, particular attention must be made through an intersectional lens to recognize and interrupt internalized assumptions based on race, class, income, ability, and gender.

Pronouns

Using the correct pronouns is one way to affirm a person's gender identity. Provide space on paperwork for people to share the pronouns they use, and also make sure to ask a young person what pronouns they use when meeting with them privately. A nonbinary young person may not yet be ready to claim a pronoun on a written form that others may see, so it's important to also ask them in person. When introducing yourself, make sure to share the pronouns you use as well. This practice should be incorporated into your work with everyone, not just when working with someone who you know or think is TGE. This can be done quite simply upon meeting someone by saying something like:

> "Hi, you must be Star. I'm Javier. I use the pronouns he and him. What about you?"

It is also ok to check in periodically to see if the pronoun you are using is still the correct one. You can do this by simply saying something like: I realized that we haven't checked in about pronouns in a while. I am still using the pronouns he and him for you. Are those still the pronouns you use? Social workers can also incorporate pronoun sharing into the agency culture by building a standing pronoun check-in into weekly meetings with service consumers and with colleagues. When in doubt, it is always respectful to use a person's name when referring to them, and when an appropriate opportunity exists, to clarify the pronouns an individual uses.

Sex Assignment

An individual's assigned sex at birth is not necessary information for a social worker to know. Gender is not binary, and neither is sex. If a young person's assigned sex at birth is relevant for them to discuss with you, let them bring it up. Similarly, it's important not to assume that the reason a nonbinary youth is seeking care is related to their gender identity. They may be seeking care and/or support related to their gender identity, or gender may not be related to the reason they are accessing care.

Making Mistakes

Sometimes social workers will make mistakes when working with nonbinary youth, either by using an incorrect pronoun, using someone's dead name, or perpetuating the gender binary through their language choices. The best course of action when this occurs is to apologize, and to move on. One mistake that people often make is to continue to focus on the mistake, which can perpetuate the discomfort for the person who has been misgendered or dead named and also then makes the moment about the person who has made the mistake. Upon realizing a mistake, it is best to acknowledge and move on rather than to continually report feelings of guilt or shame, placing the harmed individual in the position of needing to reassure the person who caused the harm.

Case Study: Misgendering

Angel is a nonbinary 19 year old in couples' therapy with their partner, Keisha. They sought therapy to deal with Keisha's experiences of family violence and the ways in which that was impacting their relationship. In the first several sessions, the social worker referred to Angel as "she" a few times. The first time this happened, neither Angel nor Keisha corrected the social worker because the content in that particular moment was intense and neither felt comfortable interrupting. The next two times, Keisha corrected the social worker in the moment. Once the social worker continued talking and didn't acknowledge it. Angel and Keisha weren't even sure if he had heard the correction. The second time, the social worker corrected himself after Keisha pointed out his mistake. The couple talked about whether or not to continue working with this particular social worker, even though he had been recommended by a local Lesbian, Gay, Bisexual, Transgender and Questioning (LGBTQ) Community Center. They decided to stick it out and after these first several sessions, the issue seemed to be resolved. A month later, the misgendering happened again, repeatedly, two weeks in a row. At this point, the couple felt like they were deep into the work and did not want to start again with someone new. They decided to give it one last try. Angel sent an email to the therapist saying: *"I am having a very difficult time when you refer to me as 'she.' I know you are not doing it on purpose, but it completely takes me out of whatever we are talking about making it difficult for me to remain engaged in the session. It also makes me feel really bad. And so I think it is negatively impacting the work we are trying to do. Keisha and I both think we have been doing some good work and so I really need this to not happen anymore. Thank you."*

Reflection Questions:

1. In the email, Angel says that the misgendering is negatively impacting the therapeutic work. How do you imagine being misgendered made Angel feel?
2. If you received an email like this from someone you were working with, how would you respond? Would you respond to the email? Would you wait until the next session? Why? What would you say in your response?
3. What do you think would be an *inappropriate* way to respond?

Case Study: The Response

Within just a few hours, the therapist responded to Angel's email. Overall, Angel was very pleased with his response. The response is included below, with notes about why different parts of the response were helpful in keeping the couple engaged in therapy.

"Thank you for writing to me and telling me this."

Right away, he communicates gratitude rather than questioning or defensiveness.

"I feel really sorry that my mis-pronouncing mistakes have such a painful and negative impact on you. I will try harder. I believe/hope that you telling me how terribly you experience my mistakes will help me to stay more aware."

He apologizes not only for his mistakes, but also for the ways it has made Angel feel. He also commits to doing better. This validates Angels feelings and communicates to them that he is taking responsibility for his actions and recognizes he needs to do better.

"I thought about the fact that I had used the wrong pronoun after our session and felt badly. I wish now I had written to you about it and apologized. Thank you for reaching out when I did not."

This part of the email demonstrates that he had been thinking about Angel and that he had some self-awareness that he had made a mistake. He takes responsibility again, for the mistake and for not following up with them after the session. He again expresses gratitude to Angel for being willing to communicate their concerns with him.

"Please know that I also understand that what to me are my 'mistakes' and 'stumbles', you experience as blows, which means that unintentional as they may be, when they happen, I truly do hurt you."

Angel was particularly moved by this part of the email, because it became clear to them that the therapist understood the difference between intention and impact, and that regardless of his best intentions, he was causing Angel harm.

"I think that's all I can say right now. I would appreciate hearing back from you, even if it's just that you received my response. I look forward to seeing you and Keisha next week."

In closing out the email in this way, the therapist demonstrated that he would likely be thinking about this interaction further. He also communicated concern for what Angel was feeling, in asking that they acknowledge the email and respond in whatever way they could. He also resolved any fears that Angel had about how he might be when they saw him next, by saying he looks forward to their next session.

Reflection Questions:

1. What are your reactions to the therapist's email response to Angel?
2. Is there anything you were surprised by?
3. What, if anything, would you have done differently?

Summary of Recommendations

This chapter has provided foundational knowledge for social work practice with nonbinary youth. Key take-aways include:

- The gender binary is pervasive and it is oppressive.
- Social workers are ethically obligated to better understand the diverse experiences of gender expression and identity to better serve nonbinary youth and other populations.
- Cisgenderism is structural oppression that reinforces binary gender norms and erases nonbinary people's experiences and identities.
- There is no right or wrong way to express nonbinary gender.
- Social workers can build an alliance with nonbinary youth by positioning themselves as learner, building trust, and doing their own internal work to identify biases and the assumptions they make about gender, so they can better ensure biases and assumptions do not negatively impact their work with nonbinary youth.

- Navigating language around the experiences of nonbinary youth requires working toward fluency of nonbinary language, integrating gender inclusive language in all aspects of their practice, using correct pronouns, and realizing making mistakes is part of the journey.
- Social workers who have not worked directly with nonbinary youth should seek consultation and supervision from colleagues that are experienced in this area.

References

Ansara, Y., & Hegarty, P. (2012). Cisgenderism in psychology: Pathologising and misgendering children from 1999 to 2008. *Psychology & Sexuality*, *3*(2), 137–160.

Council on Social Work Education. (2015). *Educational policy and accreditation standards.* Retrieved from http://www.cswe.org/File.aspx?id=81660

Craig, S. L., Alessi, E. J., Fisher-Borne, M., Dentato, M. P., Austin, A., Paceley, M., … Van Der Horn, R. (2016). *Guidelines for affirmative social work education: Enhancing the climate for LGBQQ students, staff, and faculty in social work education.* Alexandria, VA: Council on Social Work Education.

Craig, S. L., Dentato, M. P., Messenger, L., & McInroy, L. B. (2014). Educational determinants of readiness to practise with LGBTQ clients: Social work students speak out. *British Journal of Social Work*, *1*(20). doi:10.1093/bjsw/bcu107

Davis, H. (2014). Sex-classification policies as transgender discrimination: An intersectional critique. *Perspectives on Politics*, *12*(1), 45–60.

Fausto-Sterling, A. (2018, 15 October). Why sex is not binary. *The New York Times*.

Grady, D. (2018, October 2). Anatomy does not determine gender, experts say. *New York Times*, p. 10A. Retrieved from https://www.nytimes.com/2018/10/22/health/transgender-trump-biology.html

Grossman, A., & D'Augelli, A. (2006). Transgender youth: Invisible and vulnerable. *Journal of Homosexuality*, *51*(1), 111–128.

Hyde, J. S., Bigler, R. S., Joel, D., Tate, C. C., & van Anders, S. M. (2019). The future of sex and gender in psychology: Five challenges to the gender binary. *American Psychologist*, *74*, (2), 171–193. doi:https://doi.org/10.1037/amp0000307

James, S. E., Herman, J. L., Rankin, S., Keisling, M., Mottet, L., & Anafi, M. (2016). *The report of the 2015 U.S. transgender survey.* Washington, DC: National Center for Transgender Equality.

Kroehle, K., Shelton, J., Clark, E., & Seelman, K. (2020). Mainstreaming dissidence: Confronting binary gender in social work's grand challenges. *Social Work*, swaa037.

Lennon, E., & Mistler, B. (2014). Cisgenderism. *TSQ: Transgender Studies Quarterly*, *1*(1–2), 63–64. doi:10.1215/23289252-2399623

Marine, S. B. (2017). *Changing the frame: Queering access to higher education for trans* students.* International Journal of Qualitative Studies in Education. doi:10.1080/09518398.2016.1268279

Mirandé, A. (2016). Hombres mujeres: An indigenous third gender. *Men and Masculinities*, *19*(4), 384–409.

National Association of Social Workers. (2017). *NASW code of ethics*. Retrieved from https://www.socialworkers.org/About/Ethics/Code-of-Ethics/Code-of-Ethics-English

Nealy, E. (2019). *Trans kids and teens: Pride, joy, and families in transition*. New York: W.W. Norton & Company.

Pincus, F. (2000). Discrimination comes in many forms: Individual, institutional, and structural. In M. Adams, W. Blumenfeld, R. Casteneda, H. Hackman, M. Peters, & X. Zuniga (Eds.), *Readings for social justice and social change*. New York, NY: Routledge.

Sanger, T. (2008). Queer(y)ing gender and sexuality: Transgender people's lived experiences and intimate partnerships. In L. Moon (Ed.), *Feeling queer or queer feelings? Radical approaches to counseling sex, sexualities and genders* (pp. 72–88). London and New York: Routledge.

Sharyn Graham, D. (2007). Challenging gender norms: Five genders among the Bugis in Indonesia. *Reference and Research Book News, 22*(1).

Shelley, C. (2009). Transgender people and social justice. *The Journal of Individual Psychology, 65*(4), 386–396.

Shelton, J., & Dodd, S. J. (in press). Binary thinking and the limiting of human potential. *Public Integrity*.

Shelton, J., Kroehle, K., & Andia, M. (2019). The trans person is not the problem: Brave spaces and structural competence as educative tools for trans justice in social work. *The Journal of Sociology and Social Work, 46*(4), 97–123.

Shelton, J., Price, C., & VanCleefe, P. (2017). Authentic youth and young adult partnerships: Broadening the narrative of LGBTQ youth homelessness. *Journal of Family Strengths, 17*(2), 1–10.

Todd, K., Peitzmeier, S. M., Kattari, S. K., Miller-Peruse, M., Sharma, A., & Stephenson, R. (2019). Demographic and behavioral profiles of nonbinary and binary transgender youth. *Transgender Health, 4*(1), 254–261. doi:10.1089/trgh.2018.0068

Wagaman, A., Shelton, J., & Carter, R. (2018). Queering the social work classroom: Strategies for increasing inclusion of LGBTQ people and experiences. *Journal of Teaching in Social Work, 38*(2), 1–17.

Walters, K., Evans-Campbell, T., Simoni, J., Ronquillo, T., & Bhuyan, R. (2006). My spirit in my heart. *Journal of Lesbian Studies, 10*(1–2), 125–149.

5   The Chosen Name Process: Developing Gender Identity & Bolstering Support Networks

M. Killian Kinney and Finneran K. Muzzey

Introduction

Little is known about the process of transitioning to chosen names; however, the existing data has shown that using a chosen name enhances the wellbeing of transgender and gender expansive (TGE) young adults through ameliorating negative health outcomes, namely depression and suicidality (Russell, Pollitt, Li, & Grossman, 2018a, 2018b) and providing support for healthy gender identity development (Muzzey, Kinney, Maas, & McCauley, in preparation). The purpose of this chapter is to review the existing literature on chosen names to raise awareness and inform better practice with TGE young people who are exploring or using a chosen name. The process for changing one's name is discussed, as well as chosen name usage in the context of family, education, workplace, and health care. Practice recommendations are presented for how social workers can support TGE young people in exploring chosen names as part of healthy gender identity development.

Study: Reclaiming Oneself Through a Chosen Name

This chapter will build upon a study by the authors (in collaboration with Drs. Heather McCauley and Megan Maas, see Muzzey et al., in preparation for original study) that explored how TGE young people select and integrate chosen names as part of identity development. In response to community perspective around the importance of chosen names and the lack of literature about this topic, the authors, with Drs. McCauley and Maas, conducted a qualitative study that explored the question "How do trans and nonbinary individuals navigate choosing a new name?" The sample consisted of TGE young people ($N = 12$) who used a chosen name and lived in the Midwest at the time of the study. We conducted in-depth, semi-structured interviews. Interviews were analyzed using content analysis to examine the role of chosen names in TGE identity development and identify the ways TGE young people's support networks inhibit or enhance their wellbeing. Close attention was paid to the ways in which health providers, especially social workers, can support TGE young people in exploring chosen names. While this chapter

DOI: 10.4324/9780429297687-5

does not present the original data (see Muzzey et al., in preparation; Muzzey, Kinney, Maas, & McCauley, under review, for original publications), key findings from the previous research will be integrated throughout this chapter.

Normalizing Name Changes

In modern U.S. culture, some name changes are unquestionably accepted (e.g., Bill or Billy for William) and even socially expected (e.g., marriage). Other common reasons for name changes include nicknames, pseudonyms, adoption, divorce, religious reasons (e.g., christening, confirmation), and witness protection programs. These examples center cisheteronormativity. For instance, in marriage, a woman can easily change her surname to her husband's through the marriage certificate in all 50 states (Brooks, 2013). However, a man must go through the statutory process (fees, paperwork, publication, and court date) to change to his wife's last name (Slade, 2015). This legal process of completing paperwork, publishing the new name, paying fees, and attending a court date applies to any legal name changes outside of a women's surname at the time of a marriage certificate.

For TGE young people, chosen names are often a significant part of gender expression, whether socially and/or legally changed. Name change options include names that are non-gendered (e.g., Seven), names that socially indicate male (e.g., Thomas) or female (e.g., Stephanie), or only initials (Richards et al., 2016). Trans feminine and trans masculine people may be empowered by selecting highly feminine or masculine chosen names, by which TGE individual's identities are communicated and reflected back through binary gender norms. Nonbinary people may intentionally choose ambiguous names to minimize the binary assumptions made by other people. A study using an analytic sample (N = 22,286) from the 2015 U.S. Transgender Survey showed that trans women reported the highest percentage of changed legal documents (some = 35%; all = 45%), followed by trans men (36%; 37%), nonbinary individuals assigned female at birth (AFAB) (23%; 13%), and nonbinary individuals assigned male at birth (AMAB) (6%; 5%) (Scheim, Perez-Brumer, & Bauer, 2020).

TGE Individuals with legal documents that do not match their gender experience discrimination and violence, including verbal harassment, denial of services, and even physical attack (James et al., 2016). Thus, a primary difference between TGE and cisgender individuals related to name changes is the heightened risk of discrimination for TGE individuals and the threat to their emotional and physical safety. The anticipation of these negative experiences can contribute to poor mental health through anxiety, heightened vigilance, and avoidance of social interactions (Byrne, 2014; Glynn et al., 2016). This direct and anticipated discrimination and violence may also increase psychological distress and suicidality (Bockting, Miner, Swinburne Romine, Hamilton, & Coleman, 2013; Perez-Brumer, Hatzenbuehler, Oldenburg, & Bockting, 2015; Reisner et al., 2015). Higher suicidality rates among TGE youth with socially nonconforming gender expressions have been attributed to lack of support, social stigma, and internalized transphobia related to their gender expansiveness (Grossman, Park, & Russell, 2016).

Conversely, TGE people who have legal identification that matches their gender (i.e., name, gender marker) have lower psychological distress and suicidality (Scheim et al., 2020). TGE adults who legally changed their name on both their driver's license and passport were found to have reduced adverse mental health outcomes (anxiety, depression, somatization, and overall distress) and were less upset by gender-based mistreatment compared to those with none or only one document changed (Restar et al., 2020). Notably, legal name changes among low-income trans women of color can be a significant structural intervention, contributing to improved health and well-being outcomes, including economic stability (employment, finances, and housing) and healthcare utilization (general and trans-related care) (Hill et al., 2018). These findings strengthen the hypothesis that name change can act as a protective factor and argue for providing accessible paths for legal name changes for all identification. More work is needed to normalize chosen names for TGE people and to support them in the process, both socially and legally.

Challenges and Advocacy

Coming out with a chosen name and changing identification can be fraught with potential discrimination and systemic challenges, such as:

- Cost: The financial costs (up to several hundred dollars in court fees and other expenses) were identified as the primary barrier to obtaining legal document changes (James et al., 2016).
- Unclear procedures: Some TGE young people described not being aware of the name change process or feeling overwhelmed in anticipation of undertaking the process (Muzzey et al., in preparation).
- Lack of consistent regulations: Statues and regulations for ID changes vary by state and by document, of which birth certificates pose the most difficult. Lambda Legal (n.d.) and the ACLU have filed lawsuits to challenge states that prohibit legal name changes, such as in Ohio, where birth certificates are considered historical documents (Lambda Legal, n.d.). Legal name changes only appear as a footnote to the original Ohio birth certificates (Ohio Department of Health, 2020).
- Discrimination: When filing for a name change, individuals may face discrimination by judges and court staff (James et al., 2016).

In response to the known risks associated with not having legal identification that matches one's gender, advocates have worked to reduce barriers and increase support for chosen name changes. The National Center for Transgender Equality (2020) offers an ID Documents Center on its website that guides one through name and gender marker changes in each state. Local legal advocacy organizations, such as Indiana Legal Services (2020), provide support for ID changes for TGE young people and help work through issues including if one parent is not supportive of a name change. Advocates have fought for an Access to Court Records (ACR) request that can waive the required publication (which publishes the old name, new name, home address, place of birth, and date of birth) and seal the records from the public due to heightened risk for targeting trans and nonbinary individuals (Indiana Legal Services, 2020). New Yorkers have gone further, proposing the Gender Recognition Act that includes several other improvements such as adding an X gender marker, removing required medical documentation, and amending children's birth certificates to identify them as "father," "mother," or "parent" (Empire Justice Center, 2020). Finally, to reduce the financial barrier, several organizations have created mechanisms for funding TGE name changes, including the Trans Lifeline (2020), the Transgender Legal Defense and Education Fund (2020), Tranzmission (2019), and Trans Ohio (n.d.). Social workers can support and advocate for TGE young people exploring chosen names at all levels of practice.

Considerations and Benefits of Chosen Names

Despite the challenges around a chosen name, choosing a name that reflects one's gender can be empowering and a source of coping and resilience. Language is a core part of identity formation as in chosen names for transgender individuals; "it is through names that we are able to project our sense of self into the world and through names that we are empowered to take action and perform our identity" (VanderSchans, 2016, p. 18). This sense of empowerment through the chosen name process was mirrored by TGE young people in the study. Chosen names can make one's gender visible, particularly for binary transgender folx. Some TGE young people choose names that are more ambiguous or not clearly gendered for the goal of minimizing people's assumptions. Gendered experiences are strongly shaped by the names that we share with those around us, through both cultural context (e.g., social norms around gender) (Worthen, 2014) and the subjective experience of navigating one's surroundings as a particular gender (e.g., deciding which bathroom to use) (Moran & Sharpe, 2004). The context and the meaning TGE young people assign to that context were a significant part of the chosen name process.

Several considerations are factored into the chosen name process. Some of the concerns TGE young people may struggle with when choosing a name include:

- Wanting to avoid being misgendered: and using chosen names strategically, based on the environment's perceived physical and emotional safety.
- The impact of a chosen name in professional contexts: One young person said: "I want something that's unique, but something where I'm not gonna be at a disadvantage at a job interview or something if someone

sees my name and thinks like that's a silly name, you know?" (Muzzey et al., under review & Muzzey et al., in preparation)

- Connections between the past and future: Retaining some symbolism behind a given name was a meaningful consideration to some TGE young people. In such cases, TGE young people may opt for a chosen name with the same initials, root name, or name with another familial connection. One TGE young person explained: "I feel like it's a way to pay tribute to my parents' choice of that (ancestral) sound without, of course, keeping the same name" (Muzzey et al., under review & Muzzey et al., in preparation). For some, this connection to the past was particularly harmful.

Chosen names may also act as a protective factor that creates distance from trauma. One TGE young person described their given name as "difficult because unfortunately, my [given name] is almost wrapped up very intrinsically with that trauma" (Muzzey et al., under review & Muzzey et al., in preparation). When asked what their chosen name means to them, they stated, "I would say, definitely stronger, you know? Because sometimes it is weird like it's almost like you are split in half because you have this very real past and this very real present that you are creating ... since you create this name, you almost want to create this person and I can see why my mom thinks it's a person because she's like you act different now and you're this – and I'm like, 'I'm not fucking depressed, mom!'" (Muzzey et al., under review & Muzzey et al., in preparation). For some TGE young people, letting go of given names was freedom from the people who victimized them. Owning one's choice of the name and knowing that it cannot be taken away can be empowering for TGE people (VanderSchans, 2016).

Disclosure of one's chosen name and having that name accepted by others can solidify and strengthen relationships. TGE young people may first explore a chosen name with their TGE peers and other trusted loved ones. During the time of exploring different chosen names, TGE young people may switch and conform to what feels safe and comfortable in different settings and contexts. For instance, sometimes TGE young people might use given names in legal settings if they have not formally changed their names. They may also use given names when it is not safe to be out as TGE. Going through the chosen name process can help TGE young people develop adaptability, self-awareness, and support networks.

> Since I started using like they/them pronouns and my chosen name, I've really tried to dive deeper into the more feminine parts of myself just because those are the things that I wasn't allowed to express when I was younger... It's been a really healthy and really nice process of getting to know myself better...I think nonbinary and queer is about opening myself up to different ways of experiencing the world and of expressing myself. I just feel like I'm more colorful and a more confident person. (Muzzey et al., under review; Muzzey et al., in preparation)

Support Networks for TGE Young People Around Chosen Names

Important supports for TGE young people during the chosen name selection process include:

* Family of origin
* Friends and/or chosen family
* TGE community centers and groups
* TGE-affirming mental health professionals

The functions of these support networks include mixed support, *emotional* support, and *instrumental* support (Muzzey et al., under review).

Family Support Networks

Families of origin, including biological and childhood family members (i.e., parents, siblings, step-parents, caregivers) may be a mixed support – meaning they provide crucial support as well as stress. Many biological parents struggle with accepting their child's choice to discard the name their parents gave them. Within families of origin, chosen names often have to be continually reinforced and defended. Even though families of origin are often described as stressful, it is important not to assume that TGE young people have no support within their families of origin. Sometimes TGE young people will have at least one ally in their family of origin. Friends and/or chosen family, which includes loved ones regardless of biological connections, are often crucial sources of emotional support for TGE young people. TGE young people may first share their chosen name with this support network. Not surprising, friends and/or chosen family are usually a foundational support, while TGE young people disclose their chosen name in other areas of their life (e.g., family of origin, school).

Recommendations for Social Workers

* Affirm and assist TGE young people while navigating the complex considerations of choosing a name that represents their gender identity and processing disclosure.
* Support TGE young people as they share their chosen name with family members, school, healthcare providers, and others.
* Bolster caregivers to work through challenging feelings (confusion, anger, pain, resentment, fear) and disclosure (especially with extended family and faith groups) around chosen names and, ultimately, to proceed with love and respect for their TGE youth.
* Familiarize yourself with community-based resources related to name changes (legal assistance, peer support, community groups) for TGE individuals and families.

Social Support Networks

Lesbian, gay, bisexual, transgender, and questioning (LGBTQ) community groups and TGE peers function as strong *emotional* support networks for TGE young people through finding peers and normalizing shared experiences. Social support networks are crucial for TGE young people for acceptance and resources while transitioning to their chosen name. Being seen and accepted within interpersonal relationships is important and has been found across LGBTQ populations (Riggle et al., 2011; Vaughan & Rodriguez, 2014). Some geographically based social support networks include LGBTQ community centers, support groups, and bars/clubs frequented by LGBTQ community members. These social support networks are particularly important for connecting those who are otherwise geographically and socially isolated, notably for racial and ethnic minority TGE young people. Although community support has consistently been crucial for wellbeing among TGE individuals (Meyer & Frost, 2013; Riggle & Rostosky, 2012; Stanton, Ali, & Chaudhuri, 2017), not all TGE young people experience LGBTQ community groups as safe spaces. Due to feeling isolated and unsupported within LGBTQ communities, some gender expansive and/or nonbinary individuals create their own communities, often composed of other nonbinary individuals with shared experiences (Rankin & Beemyn, 2012).

Recommendations for Social Workers

- Empower TGE young people to find social support with LGBTQ communities or forming their own communities of TGE community.
- Assist TGE young people to create placemaking and programming as they determine for their social support network.
- Facilitate growth within faith-based organizations to welcome and affirm TGE individuals and their families.

Educational Support Networks

Primary and Secondary Schools

Schools are a place where TGE young people spend a significant amount of time. Unfortunately, schools are often sites of harassment and discrimination for TGE students. TGE students experience negative interpersonal interactions as well as unsupportive school policies, resulting in mental and physical distress. The GLSEN 2019 National School Climate Survey confirmed continued interpersonal and structural harassment and violence towards LGBTQ youth, with TGE students reported feeling like they are targets for bullying (Kosciw, Clark, Truong, & Zongrone, 2020). TGE students often feel unsafe at school due to gender identity (84%) and gender expression (70%). Transphobic slurs were heard by 87% of LGBTQ students, of which 44% heard them often or frequently. Discriminatory school policies may include policies that prohibit TGE students from wearing gendered clothes of their choice and preventing them from using the bathroom and locker rooms of choice. As a result, many TGE students experience discrimination related to bathrooms and avoid going to the bathroom altogether.

School Genders and Sexualities Alliances (GSA; previously Gay-Straight Alliance) have been shown to improve the school environment and significantly impact the well-being of LGBTQ youth, as well as lower rates of truancy, tobacco use, alcohol use, attempted suicide, and casual sexual behavior (Poteat et al., 2013). According to the 2019 GLSEN survey, 34% of middle schools and 74% of high schools had a GSA. A GSA's presence was a strong indicator of wellbeing even without active participation by LGBTQ youth (Toomey, Ryan, Diaz, & Russell, 2011). Another service of a GSA is to advocate for school policy (Schindel, 2008). However, GSAs may not always be welcoming places for TGE youth. GSAs have been critiqued for centering LGBQ students while excluding TGE students (Frohard-Dourlent, 2016).

Colleges and Universities

Similar to K–12 schools, colleges and universities may be hostile environments for TGE students, depending on whether or not intentional efforts were made to be TGE-inclusive and affirming. In addition to college's typical demands, TGE students also cope with stressors from marginalization (Nicolazzo, Pitcher, Renn, & Woodford, 2017). This process begins with the application, in which self-identification demographic questions may include biological sex (male or female) without also having a question about gender with inclusive categories, pronouns, or chosen names (Lambda Legal, 2015). Once accepted, TGE students are faced with a new list of possible stressors from student IDs, sex-segregated dorms/housing, restrooms, and locker rooms. In addition to student IDs, the institutional network can be a disconnected and time-consuming process to update. This can prevent TGE students from having correct information and possibly experience misgendering from the first class roster to their diploma and transcripts. The accumulation of these stressors can prevent TGE students from completing their education (Lambda Legal, 2015; Pryor, 2015). Social environments, such as college, play a pivotal role in the overall wellbeing of TGE people; hostility against socially nonconforming gender expressions compromises wellbeing (Rieger & Savin-Williams, 2012).

Two Federal policies help to protect TGE young adults. Under Title IX of the 1964 Civil Rights Act, institutions that receive federal funding are not allowed to discriminate based on sex (inclusive of gender identity), except for religious institutions that can claim religious exemption (Lambda Legal, 2015). The privacy of TGE students' educational records is protected under the Family Educational Rights and Privacy Act (FERPA) (20 U.S.C. § 1232g; 34 C.F.R. §§ 99.00 et seq.). This includes the right to amend records to accurately reflect legal documents (i.e., name change, gender marker). Further, parents are not allowed access to educational documents once a TGE student is 18 years old, unless with their permission. Some state or local laws may provide additional protections, such as anti-bullying policies in New York (the Dignity for All Students Act [DASA]) and California (School Success and Opportunities Act) (Lambda Legal, 2015).

Even within schools of social work, harmful discourse occurs, perpetuated by faculty and students alike, and TGE students are tokenized and othered (Atteberry-Ash et al., 2019). College can be a vulnerable place where the choice to use a chosen name and/or pronouns is weighed against safety and comfort that depends on instructor interaction, size of the classroom, and course content (Pryor, 2015). TGE students are attuned to whether or not professors start their class with pronouns, which can indicate a supportive space (Pryor, 2015). TGE youth report feeling safer in their educational environments when gender diversity and socially nonconforming gender expressions are supported (e.g., asking and using the correct chosen name and pronouns) (Smith, 2016). Educational institutions need to shift away from binary systems of classification to become more inclusive of TGE people, especially nonbinary individuals, and to bolster student success and safety – "college students will expect to have their gender identity honored and protected while they pursue their education" (Nowicki, 2019, p. 4).

At its best, college can be an exciting new and non-judgmental environment where TGE students can explore and openly express their gender. One way that some TGE students navigate the hostile environment of higher education is through trans kinships (Nicolazzo et al., 2017). Trans kinships provide a sense of belonging and are developed and maintained through an emotional investment and connection by each member, which serve as a source for resilience when faced with difficulties and reinforce student success (Nicolazzo et al., 2017). As social workers, we have a professional obligation to constructively address microaggression in our classrooms and model advocacy for future practitioners.

- Integrate TGE-inclusive content throughout the curriculum.
- Advocate for TGE-related reading material in libraries.
- Support the creation and maintenance of a GSA in school and LGBTQ centers at colleges and universities.
- Ensure faculty, staff, and administration are educated on TGE experiences and how to provide support, including the importance of normalizing chosen names and pronouns in the classroom and documents.
- Amend student policies to be TGE-inclusive (e.g., chosen names and pronouns in the classroom, bathroom use, and other transition-related supports).
- Update educational institution's nondiscrimination policy to explicitly include "gender identity" and "gender expression."

- Propose or amend structural policy that can improve the lives of TGE students and mitigate misgendering, dead-naming (using the person's legal or given name rather than chosen name, which often reveals them to be TGE), and outing (e.g., anti-bullying/harassment, housing, sports, streamline updates to name change, pronouns, and gender across systems). Notably, a critical structural improvement has been the conversion of old single-stall bathrooms to all-gender and the creation of all-gender bathrooms in new buildings.

Recommendations for Social Workers

- Disrupt harmful transphobic discourse and end perpetuation of cisnormativity in social work classrooms.
- Educate and affirm TGE students of their rights (e.g., Title IX and FERPA).
- Provide easily accessible TGE resources, for example:

  - The Trevor Project 1-866-488-7386 (available 24/7). Crisis intervention and suicide prevention services to LGBTQ youth ages 13–24. https://www.thetrevorproject.org/
  - The Trans Lifeline US: (877) 565-8860 or Canada: (877) 330-6366 (available 24/7). Peer support, crisis hotline, and microgrants **by and for** transgender people. https://translifeline.org/
  - Fenway Health Binding Resources Guide https://fenwayhealth.org/wp-content/uploads/Binding_Resource_Guide.pdf

Healthcare Support Networks

Health providers would benefit their clients by educating themselves about their TGE clients' needs, including ways to integrate chosen names and pronouns into their practice. A study of TGE youth and caregivers found barriers to gender-affirming health care included a lack of TGE training among healthcare providers, irregular use of chosen name and pronoun, and inconsistent protocol for trans-related care (e.g., lack of awareness and adherence to professional guidelines), among several other barriers (Gridley et al., 2016, p. 257). The prevailing approaches to TGE health care, the Gender Affirmative Model (GAM) and the Wait and See approach, were compared and found GAM to be a better practice for medically supporting TGE youth (Kinney, Meininger, & Wiener, 2020). In the GAM, youth are acknowledged as experts on their gender and should be free to express their gender unrestricted. Further, the GAM tasks providers with examining their biases and assumptions about gender to understand how these beliefs may harm TGE youth and disrupt such patterns (Kinney et al., 2020).

A primary structural mechanism for including chosen names and pronouns in health care are electronic medical records (EMR). It is recommended that EMRs contain chosen names, pronouns, and gender in addition to other demographics (e.g., sex, race) (Deutsch et al., 2013). Virtually streamlining intake forms and documents allows for all personnel interacting with the TGE client to see this crucial information – if the EMR is formatted to include such information.

The *nickname* field can record the chosen name and gender/pronouns, and alerts can notify personnel of this information (Deutsch et al., 2013). Logically, TGE individuals prefer returning to providers who use structural mechanisms to record chosen names and pronouns, which can be shared in the future to help individuals be seen and avoid misgendering. Politely asking for chosen names and pronouns, especially if unsure, are foundational to communicating sensitivity to gender (Kosenko, Rintamaki, & Maness, 2015). Even when forms are inclusive, it can be reassuring to check with a quick follow up question, such as "Are the name and pronouns on your form the ones you would like me to use today?" Professionals can mirror these behaviors by wearing pronouns on lanyards, nametags, and other visible markers. When chosen name and pronouns are used in healthcare settings, the relief and joy felt by TGE youth is significant – "It's really cool to be able to go somewhere that I wasn't immediately uncomfortable as soon as I got there" (Gridley et al., 2016, p. 258).

Mental health professionals function as strong *instrumental* support, providing guidance on name transition and connecting TGE young people to resources (e.g., support groups, legal aid) (Muzzey et al., under review). Within the GAM, a mental health provider's role is a supportive partner with the TGE youth through a client-centered transition – social, medical, and surgical if desired (Kinney et al., 2020). Mental health professionals working with TGE young people would be well informed to anticipate occupying a gatekeeper role and educate themselves on how to navigate this bureaucratic necessity while collaborating with their clients to access their desired gender-affirming interventions (Abrams, Golden, & Cohen, 2020).

For some TGE individuals, social workers are the first person gender expansiveness is shared with and, if supported, is the first line of acceptance (Kinney, 2018). Notably, thwarted belonging and perceived burdensome contribute to suicidality among TGE people (Grossman et al., 2016). As a coping mechanism to avoid stress and discrimination, some TGE individuals choose to selectively and strategically share their chosen name and pronouns (Dietert & Dentice, 2009; Muzzey et al., under review), which speaks to the importance of a strong therapeutic alliance. Building this trust is not only asking for chosen names and pronouns once, but instead creating a space for trying on different gender expressions without holding them to the first chosen name or pronouns (Kinney, 2018).

Recommendations for Social Workers

- Practice ways in which providers can respectfully ask chosen names and pronouns ("Are the name and pronouns on your intake the ones you would like me to use today? If this changes, I am happy to adjust.")

- Model chosen names and pronouns by sharing them during introductions and professional identification (e.g., work badge, lanyard, email signature).
- Create a supportive therapeutic space where TGE young people can try on chosen names and other forms of gender expression without holding someone to the first interaction.
- Modify all paper and virtual documents to include chosen names, pronouns, and expansive options for gender.
- Promote hiring and training client advocates to be well-informed of TGE experiences in healthcare, including discrimination and gender-specific needs.
- Develop protocols for caring for TGE youth and their families (e.g., How can you best proceed when a young trans woman is referred to your sex-segregated in-patient ward). Be proactive – waiting is irresponsibly negligent, posing probable harmful to TGE youth.
- Establish a TGE community advisory board (CAB) to center the perspectives of TGE people and their families/caregivers. Create a regular working relationship between the TGE community and social workers that provide incentives for their valuable time and expertise. The strength of this relationship is contingent on a meaningful feedback loop between discussions (improvements to documents, policy, program evaluation, and new directions) and action to meet the TGE community's needs.
- Mandate continuing education in the Gender Affirmative Model, cultural humility with gender expansiveness, and other trans-health care guidelines (WPATH Standards of Care – https://www.wpath.org/publications/soc)
- Advocate for reduced gatekeeping in TGE standards of care guidelines, medical institutes, and insurance policies.

Conclusion

As social workers, we have the opportunity and responsibility to improve the lives of TGE youth and their families through direct practice, education, research, and policy. This chapter discussed the benefits of chosen names as a healthy part of identity development, helping TGE young people explore and affirm their gender and build resilience. Overall, the chosen name process involves complex considerations concerning the past, present, and future, during which social workers can play a pivotal role in providing individual and systemic support for a healthy, smooth process. Understanding the significant role of chosen names helps social workers prioritize using chosen names over legal names. Otherwise, not recognizing chosen names can lead to distance and distrust between clients and providers. Similarly, misnaming through a wrong name and misgendering by inappropriate pronouns are extremely corrosive microaggressions frequently experienced by TGE young people and should be addressed through training, structure, policy, and accountability.

For many TGE young people, gender-specific resources and services are largely inaccessible due to geography, financial costs, and lack of insurance coverage. In addition to strengthening TGE support networks, social workers can increase TGE-inclusive and affirmative settings, policies, and programming at existing social service agencies to bridge this gap. Recommendations have been provided that focus on increasing awareness of the importance of chosen names, continual learning as the language and understanding of gender changes and expands rapidly, and reducing both interpersonal and structural barriers to care. In addition to recommended actions for social workers, the TGE community would benefit from the recruitment and retention of TGE educators, social service providers, and healthcare providers in all fields of care – to see oneself reflected in these roles is invaluable. Though this chapter focused on chosen names, these recommendations can be applied broadly to help TGE young people feel seen and supported and contribute to greater social equity.

References

Abrams, M., Golden, R. L., & Cohen, J. R. (2020). Affirming and inclusive mental health care for transgender and nonbinary young people. In S. K. Kattari, M. K. Kinney, L. Kattari, & N. E. Walls (Eds.), *Social work and health care practice with transgender and nonbinary individuals and communities: Voices for equity, inclusion, and resilience* (pp. 76–88). London: Routledge.

Atteberry-Ash, B., Speer, S. R., Kattari, S. K., & Kinney, M. K. (2019). Does it get better? LGBTQ social work students and experiences with harmful discourse. *Journal of Gay & Lesbian Social Services, 31*(2), 223–241. doi:10.1080/10538720.2019.1568337

Bockting, W. O., Miner, M. H., Swinburne Romine, R. E., Hamilton, A., & Coleman, E. (2013). Stigma, mental health, and resilience in an online sample of the US transgender population. *American Journal of Public Health, 103*(5), 943–951. doi:10.2105/AJPH.2013.301241

Brooks, M. (2013). For nontraditional names' sake: A call to reform the name-change process for marrying couples. *University of Michigan Journal of Law Reform, 47*(1), 247–282.

Byrne, J. (2014). *License to be yourself: Law and advocacy for legal gender recognition of trans people.* Open Society Foundations. Retrieved from https://www.opensocietyfoundations.org/publications/license-be-yourself

Deutsch, M. B., Green, J., Keatley, J., Mayer, G., Hastings, J., & Hall, A. M. (2013). Electronic medical records and the transgender patient: Recommendations from the World Professional Association for Transgender Health EMR Working Group. *Journal of the American Medical Informatics Association, 20*(4), 700–703. doi:10.1136/amiajnl-2012-001472

Dietert, M., & Dentice, D. (2009). Gender identity issues and workplace discrimination: The transgender experience. *Journal of Workplace Rights, 14*(1), 121–140. doi:10.2190/WR.14.1.g

Empire Justice Center. (2020, February). *Joint Memo of Support Gender Recognition Act A.3457-B (Ortiz)/S.0056-B (Hoylman).* Retrieved from https://empirejustice.org/wp-content/uploads/2020/03/Joint-Memo-of-Support-Gender-Recognition-Act-February-2020.pdf

Frohard-Dourlent, H. (2016). Muddling through together: Educators navigating cisnormativity while working with trans and gender-nonconforming students. Doctoral dissertation, University of British Columbia.

Glynn, T. R., Gamarel, K. E., Kahler, C. W., Iwamoto, M., Operario, D., & Nemoto, T. (2016). The role of gender affirmation in psychological well-being among transgender women. *Psychology of Sexual Orientation and Gender Diversity, 3*(3), 336–344.

Gridley, S. J., Crouch, J. M., Evans, Y., Eng, W., Antoon, E., Lyapustina, M., ... Breland, D. J. (2016). Youth and caregiver perspectives on barriers to gender-affirming health care for transgender youth. *Journal of Adolescent Health, 59*(3), 254–261. doi:10.1016/j.jadohealth.2016.03.017

Grossman, A. H., Park, J. Y., & Russell, S. T. (2016). Transgender youth and suicidal behaviors: Applying the interpersonal psychological theory of suicide. *Journal of Gay & Lesbian Mental Health, 20*(4), 329–349. doi:10.1080/19359705.2016.1207581

Hill, B. J., Crosby, R., Bouris, A., Brown, R., Bak, T., Rosentel, K., ... Salazar, L. (2018). Exploring transgender legal name change as a potential structural intervention for mitigating social determinants of health among transgender women of color. *Sexuality Research and Social Policy, 15*(1), 25–33. doi:10.1007/s13178-017-0289-6

Indiana Legal Services. (2020, September 21). *Indiana name & gender marker change FAQ.* Retrieved from https://www.indianalegalservices.org/namegendermarkerfaq

James, S., Herman, J., Rankin, S., Keisling, M., Mottet, L., & Anafi, M. A. (2016). *The report of the 2015 US transgender survey.* Washington, DC: National Center for Transgender Equality. Retrieved from https://transequality.org/sites/default/files/docs/usts/USTS-Full-Report-Dec17.pdf

Kinney, M. K. (2018, March). "The first line of acceptance": Bolstering resilience among non-binary clients through affirming health care practice. Poster presentation at the 2018 Annual Meeting of the Society for Adolescent Health and Medicine, Seattle, WA. *Journal of Adolescent Health, 62*, S48–S49. doi:10.1016/j.jadohealth.2017.11.098

Kinney, M. K., Meininger, E., & Wiener, S. (2020). Transgender and nonbinary youth and access to medical care. In S. K. Kattari, M. K. Kinney, L. Kattari, & N. E. Walls (Eds.), *Social work and health care practice with transgender and nonbinary individuals and communities: Voices for equity, inclusion, and resilience* (pp. 29–41). London: Routledge.

Kosciw, J. G., Clark, C. M., Truong, N. L., & Zongrone, A. D. (2020). *The 2019 National School Climate Survey: The experiences of lesbian, gay, bisexual, transgender, and queer youth in our nation's schools.* New York: GLSEN.

Kosenko, K., Rintamaki, L., & Maness, K. (2015). Patient-centered communication: The experiences of transgender adults. In L. G. Spencer & J. C. Capuzza (Eds.), *Transgender communication studies: Histories, trends, and trajectories* (pp. 93–110). Washington, DC: Lexington Books.

Lambda Legal. (2015, July 22). Transgender college students. In *Transgender rights toolkit: A legal guide for trans people and their advocates* (pp. 39–44). Retrieved from https://www.lambdalegal.org/publications/trt_transgender-college-students

Lambda Legal. (n.d.). *FAQ about identity documents.* Retrieved from https://www.lambdalegal.org/know-your-rights/article/trans-identity-document-faq

Meyer, I. H., & Frost, D. M. (2013). Minority stress and the health of sexual minorities. In C. J. Patterson & A. R. D'Augelli (Eds.), *Handbook of psychology and sexual orientation* (pp. 252–266). New York: Oxford University Press.

Moran, L. J., & Sharpe, A. N. (2004). Violence, identity and policing: The case of violence against transgender people. *Criminal Justice, 4*(4), 395–417. doi:10.1177/14 66802504048656

Muzzey, F. K., Kinney, M. K., Maas, M. K., & McCauley, H. L. (in preparation). Making a name for your self: Reconciling, rejecting, or reflecting external environments through chosen names among transgender and nonbinary young adults.

Muzzey, F. K., Kinney, M. K., McCauley, H. L., & Maas, M. K. (under review). Support networks of transmasculine and nonbinary young adults during chosen name transition.

National Center for Transgender Equality. (2020, May). *Id documents center.* Retrieved from https://transequality.org/documents

Nicolazzo, Z., Pitcher, E. N., Renn, K. A., & Woodford, M. (2017). An exploration of trans* kinship as a strategy for student success. *International Journal of Qualitative Studies in Education, 30*(3), 305–319. doi:10.1080/09518398.2016.1254300

Nowicki, E. (2019). Supporting trans and nonbinary community success in higher education: A new paradigm. *College and University, 94*(1), 2–9.

Ohio Department of Health. (2020, October 15). *Changing or correcting a birth record.* Retrieved from https://odh.ohio.gov/wps/portal/gov/odh/know-our-programs/vital-statistics/changing-correcting-birth-record

Perez-Brumer, A., Hatzenbuehler, M. L., Oldenburg, C. E., & Bockting, W. (2015). Individual- and structural-level risk factors for suicide attempts among transgender adults. *Behavioral Medicine, 41*(3), 164–171.

Poteat, V. P., Sinclair, K. O., DiGiovanni, C. D., Koenig, B. W., & Russell, S. T. (2013). Gay-straight alliances are associated with student health: A multischool comparison of LGBTQ and heterosexual youth. *Journal of Research on Adolescence, 23*(2), 319–330. doi:10.1111/j.1532-7795.2012.00832.x

Pryor, J. T. (2015). Out in the classroom: Transgender student experiences at a large public university. *Journal of College Student Development, 56*(5), 440–455.

Rankin, S. & Beemyn, G. (2012). Beyond a binary: The lives of gender-nonconforming youth. *About Campus, 17*(4), 2–10. doi:10.1002/abc.21086

Reisner, S. L., Hughto, J. M. W., Dunham, E. E., Heflin, K. J., Begenyi, J. B. G., Coffey-Esquivel, J., & Cahill, S. (2015). Legal protections in public accommodations settings: A critical public health issue for transgender and gender-nonconforming people. *The Milbank Quarterly, 93*(3), 484–515.

Restar, A., Jin, H., Breslow, A., Reisner, S. L., Mimiaga, M., Cahill, S., & Hughto, J. M. (2020). Legal gender marker and name change is associated with lower negative emotional response to gender-based mistreatment and improve mental health outcomes among trans populations. *SSM-Population Health, 11,* 100595. doi:10.1016/j.ssmph.2020.1 00595

Richards, C., Bouman, W. P., Seal, L., Barker, M. J., Nieder, T. O., & T'Sjoen, G. (2016). Non-binary or genderqueer genders. *International Review of Psychiatry, 28*(1), 95–102. doi:10.3109/09540261.2015.1106446

Rieger, G., & Savin-Williams, R. C. (2012). Gender nonconformity, sexual orientation, and psychological well-being. *Archives of Sexual Behavior, 41*(3), 611–621. doi:10.1 007/s10508-011-9738-0

Riggle, E. D., & Rostosky, S. S. (2012). *A positive view of LGBTQ: Embracing identity and cultivating well-being.* Maryland: Rowman & Littlefield Publishers.

Riggle, E. D., Rostosky, S. S., McCants, L. E., & Pascale-Hague, D. (2011). The positive aspects of a transgender self-identification. *Psychology & Sexuality*, *2*(2), 147–158.

Russell, S. T., Pollitt, A. M., Li, G., & Grossman, A. H. (2018a). Chosen name use is linked to reduced depressive symptoms, suicidal ideation, and suicidal behavior among transgender youth. *Journal of Adolescent Health*, *63*(4), 503–505. doi:10.1016/j.jadohealth.2018.02.003

Russell, S. T., Pollitt, A. M., Li, G., & Grossman, A. H. (2018b). Transgender youth allowed to use their chosen name have fewer mental health problems. *PRC Research Brief Series*. Retrieved from http://hdl.handle.net/2152/65222

Scheim, A. I., Perez-Brumer, A. G., & Bauer, G. R. (2020). Gender-concordant identity documents and mental health among transgender adults in the USA: A cross-sectional study. *The Lancet Public Health*, *5*(4), e196–e203.

Schindel, J. E. (2008). Gender 101— beyond the binary: Gay-straight alliances and gender activism. *Sexuality Research and Social Policy*, *5*, 56–70. doi:https://doi.org/10.1525/srsp.2008.5.2.56

Slade, M. (2015). Who wears the pants? The difficulties men face when trying to take their spouse's surname after marriage. *Family Court Review*, *53*(2), 336–351.

Smith, J. (2016). *Gender nonconformity in youth and safety: Utilizing photo-elicitation and thematic analysis*. Doctoral dissertation, Georgia State University. Retrieved from OpenDissertations (590E4C9B170794D8).

Stanton, M. C., Ali, S., & Chaudhuri, S. (2017). Individual, social and community-level predictors of wellbeing in a US sample of transgender and gender non-conforming individuals. *Culture, Health & Sexuality*, *19*(1), 32–49. doi:10.1080/13691058.2016.1189596

Toomey, R. B., Ryan, C., Diaz, R. M., & Russell, S. T. (2011). High school gay–straight alliances (GSAs) and young adult well-being: An examination of GSA presence, participation, and perceived effectiveness. *Applied Developmental Science*, *15*(4), 175–185. doi:10.1080/10888691.2011.607378

Transgender Legal Defense & Education Fund. (2020, November 10). *Name change project*. Retrieved from https://transgenderlegal.org/our-work/name-change-project/

Trans Lifeline. (2020). *Microgrants*. Retrieved from https://translifeline.org/microgrants

Trans Ohio. (n.d.). *Name change financial assistance program*. Retrieved from http://www.transohio.org/?page_id=3740

Tranzmission. (2019). *Name change project*. Retrieved from https://tranzmission.org/programs/name-change-project/

VanderSchans, A. (2016). The role of name choice in the construction of transgender identities. *Western Papers in Linguistics*, *1*(2), 1–21.

Vaughan, M. D., & Rodriguez, E. M. (2014). LGBT strengths: Incorporating positive psychology into theory, research, training, and practice. *Psychology of Sexual Orientation and Gender Diversity*, *1*(4), 325–334. doi:10.1037/sgd0000053

Worthen, M. G. (2014). The cultural significance of homophobia on heterosexual women's gendered experiences in the United States: A commentary. *Sex Roles*, *71*(3–4), 141–151. doi:10.1007/s11199-014-0389-1

6 Social Work Practice with Trans and Gender Expansive Youth and Their Families

Kristian Gambardella

Introduction

The parent–child relationship is positioned to be one of the most influential factors that promote the well-being of transgender and gender expansive (TGE) youth (Turban & Ehrensaft, 2018; Wallace & Russell, 2013). The parent–child relationship can also be a source of distress, denial, rejection, and shame, even in the case of well-intentioned parents (Malpas, 2011). At the crux of this phenomenon is how a family system makes meaning of their TGE child's gender identity. This chapter will review stressors, strengths, and supports for TGE youth and their families, with an emphasis on primary caregivers. The discussion will draw from attachment theory, minority stress theory, and systems theory. This chapter will also highlight social work practice guidelines as to how to support TGE youth and their families.

Understanding TGE Youth and Their Families

Affirming Attachment Relationship

An affirming attachment relationship is defined by the presence of an attachment figure or primary caregiver who affirms the young person's authentic gender identity. Caregiver support can take many forms including using the child's affirming name and pronouns, creating space for the child to explore their gender via play and presentation, and instilling a sense of agency and self-determination within the child. The gender-affirmative approach is in line with an attachment-based framework (Wallace & Russell, 2013). Wallace and Russell (2013) suggest that the affirmative approach can strengthen the attachment relationship and decrease the shame a child experiences, thus promoting healthy development of the child's sense of self.

The Diagnostic Statistics and Assessment Manual (DSM-V) defines gender dysphoria as distress regarding the incongruence between ones's externally perceived gender and their authentic gender identity; this distress can also manifest itself as a desire to have different genitals and/or secondary sex characteristics. Gender dysphoria is defined as intrapsychic; however, it is

DOI: 10.4324/9780429297687-6

primarily influenced by the responses of the youth's primary attachment figures (Ehrensaft, Giammattei, Storck, Tishelman, & Keo-Meier, 2018; Spivey, Huebner, & Diamond, 2018; Turban & Ehrensaft, 2018; Wallace & Russell, 2013). The literature indicates that gender-expansive youth whose family supports their transition and affirms their identity experience better mental and physical health outcomes compared to youth with unsupportive families (Ehrensaft et al., 2018; Hill, Menvielle, Sica, & Johnson, 2010; Turban & Ehrensaft, 2018; Wallace & Russell, 2013). Parental support should be rooted in what feels authentic to the child and cautions against parents trying to protect by correcting or policing their child's gender (Ehrensaft et al., 2018; Turban & Ehrensaft, 2018; Wallace & Russell, 2013).

Role of Primary Caregivers

The presence of a gender-affirmative parent is a crucial protective factor for gender-expansive youth as parents can help promote safety and advocate for their child across the different systems they interact with such as education, health care, legal, and community. For example, a caregiver may advocate for their TGE child at school by meeting with their child's teacher(s) and administrator(s) in advance of their child expressing their authentic gender identity at school to develop a plan as to how the school is going to support their child's gender diversity. Caregivers are often tasked with educating other adults their child interacts with regarding affirming language, practices, and policies, ensuring their child has access to gender-affirming facilities (bathrooms and locker rooms) and is afforded the same opportunity to participate in extracurricular activities, as well as championing the correct use of name and pronouns. It is not uncommon for a TGE youth to be the only gender-diverse student in their class, grade, or even school. As such, caregivers are sometimes paving the way for not only their child, but for other gender diverse youth to come.

TGE children and youth often experience chronic social stressors as they navigate their daily lives. These chronic social stressors include being misgendered by others, being referred to as a prior or no longer affirming name, bullying, harassment, erasure as a result of less than inclusive practices or language, being discriminated against via transphobic policies, and fear of violence. A caregiver's acceptance and affirmation of their TGE child's gender identity has the potential to mitigate these chronic social stressors that TGE youth endure in the settings outside of their family of origin. When a TGE child knows their caregiver is affirming of their gender identity, they are much more likely to communicate relevant needs and stressors, which informs the caregiver as to how they can best support their child in different settings.

Many TGE children experience anxiety regarding the physical development of their body as they approach an unwanted puberty that corresponds to their sex assigned at birth. It can be distressing for TGE youth to feel as though their body is moving in a direction that doesn't align with their identity. For example, a transgender boy may find the onset of menstruation and/or development of breast tissue triggering. A caregiver who is supportive of their child's access to gender-affirming medical care, such as puberty blockers, can help ameliorate these traumatic physical reminders. Without caregiver consent, it is nearly impossible for TGE minors to access gender-affirming medical care.

TGE youth are also dependent on their primary caregivers until they are of consenting age to make legal decisions and predominantly reliant on their primary caregivers for financial support. As such, a caregiver can have a tremendous impact on a TGE youth's ability to socially transition. Let's take Lucy for example, a 10-year-old trans girl whose parents are supportive of her gender identity. Lucy expressed wanting to wear dresses and skirts to school, styling her hair in a more feminine way, and participating on the local girls' soccer team. From a resources perspective, Lucy's parents can support her social transition by allowing her access to clothing and grooming styles that are representative of her gender identity. From an interpersonal/community perspective, her parents can advocate for her inclusion on the girls' soccer team by meeting with coaches and league organizers. In terms of legal support, Lucy's parents can file legal paperwork to update Lucy's legal documents with her affirming name and gender marker to prevent Lucy from being misgendered or being outed as transgender if Lucy wishes to live stealthy (not sharing her transgender gender identity with others beyond immediate family or close friends).

Primary caregivers have the potential to protect their child from harm by supporting their social and/or medical transition, advocating for their child across systems, and simply being an affirming adult in their child's life. As social workers in the lives of TGE youth and their caregivers, it is our duty to harness the strength of caregiver support to better serve an incredibly vulnerable population. In order to harness this strength, we must first understand how families make meaning of their TGE child's gender identity.

Aren't They Too Young?

Though there has been an increased awareness among mental health providers in regard to gender diversity in adolescents and adults, there is often oversight of gender diversity in prepubescent children. A child is able to express their core gender identity between 18 and 24 months; this development in sense of self is no different for gender-expansive youth (Ehrensaft et al., 2018). Early findings of an ongoing longitudinal study conducted by the TransYouth Project (TYP) at the University of Washington indicate that transgender children who have socially transitioned know and understand their gender ("I am a boy," "I am a girl," "I am both," "I am neither," etc.) just as a cisgender children know and understand their gender (Olson, Key, & Eaton, 2015). These findings debunk the common misconception that gender-expansive children are confused or being oppositional in their assertion of a gender expansive identity (Olson, Key, & Eaton, 2015). Gender specialists concur TYP findings are consistent with their clinical observations of a "persistent, consistent, and insistent" gender-expansive identity in TGE youth (Ehrensaft, 2016).

A TGE child may express their core gender identity in a range of ways. Depending on a child's environment and developmental stage, they may not have the language to verbalize feeling "transgender" or "gender expansive" explicitly. Instead they may send gender messages to those around them via their behaviors and gender presentation, including but not limited to preferences in clothing, hairstyle, peers, and play. Some examples of gender messages may be more subtle and not necessarily indicative of gender diversity such as gravitating towards certain clothing, haircuts, or activities; others are more overt like expressing aversion or distress towards one's natal sex or body parts.

Some children communicate feeling like a boy, girl, neither, both, or something else. A child is considered to have a binary transgender identity if they identify within the binary, meaning a child is assigned female at birth and identifies as a boy, or a child is assigned male at birth and identifies as a girl. A nonbinary child identifies outside the gender binary as neither, both, or something else and often refutes sociocultural expectations of gender.

A child's assertion of their gender identity is largely influenced by the child's experiences with their surroundings. For example, a child assigned female at birth may communicate feeling "like a boy" via their style of behavior and play and express a preference towards shorter hairstyles and clothing typically associated with masculinity. However, if these gender messages are received negatively by those around them, especially primary attachment figures, the child may begin to internalize shame and try to conceal their core gender identity in fear of abandonment or rejection.

It is imperative for those who support TGE youth (caregivers, teachers, social workers, providers, etc.) to understand that there is no one way to be transgender or gender expansive. Some children may consistently assert a binary transgender identity throughout their life beginning at the age of two years old, while others may explore and play with their gender expression and presentation over time and have a more dynamic gender identity journey. This ambiguity does not invalidate one's gender identity, it should rather be viewed as a component of one's gender identity, presentation or expression. Let's take Jay for example, a 16-year-old nonbinary Black youth assigned female at birth. Jay expressed feeling like a boy starting when they were 4 years old and experienced distress regarding their chest when they began puberty. Jay began their social transition when they were 11 years old. Initially, Jay requested to be referred to using he/him pronouns. As Jay connected with more gender expansive youth, they realized they felt most affirmed when referred to using gender neutral language (they/them/theirs). When Jay was younger they had no exposure to gender identities beyond the binary. It wasn't until Jay saw themselves represented in others that they were able to understand how they felt about their own gender.

Static or dynamic, all gender identities are valid. A child needs room to play and explore, and caregivers can create space for a child to do so. This can be achieved by allowing the child to lead the way. For example, a caregiver can practice this on a regular basis by asking their child what they would like to wear to school, checking in on how the child feels regarding their name and pronouns, modeling openness towards gender diversity, and using affirming communication like "I love you as you are" or "I love you no matter what."

Sociocultural Influence

Over the past several years there has been a marked increase in prevalence of gender diversity along with societal progress towards acceptance of gender diversity. There has been a greater awareness of the existence of gender diversity, an increase of visible transgender and gender expansive people in mainstream media, a heightened focus on gender diversity within public policy, and a surge of ways to be in virtual community with other gender expansive folks. This has led to an increase in the number of TGE youth and their families seeking services.

However this progress has not been made without setbacks – the current political environment includes a myriad of anti-trans legislations such as bathroom bills, banning access to gender-affirmative care, and limiting TGE youth's participation in extracurricular activities, as well as the removal of legal protections demonstrated by the omittance of gender identity from Title IX. In recent years, states have attempted to ban TGE individuals from using restrooms that correspond with their gender identity, and require individuals to use facilities that correspond to their sex assigned at birth. Similar attempts to categorize one's gender based on biological sex at birth have also impacted TGE youth's participation in gendered extracurricular activities. In April 2020, Idaho became the first state to pass a law that bars transgender girls from participating in girls' and womens' sports and requires athletes to un-dergo DNA testing to confirm anatomical sex. Until a federal precedent is established, TGE children and youth are at the mercy of their state and local legislation and governing bodies.

TGE youth and their primary caregivers exist within a larger society which is cisnormative and predominantly transphobic. These sociocultural influ-ences largely impact how both the child and caregiver make meaning. For example, a caregiver may refuse to accept their child's gender identity as a result hearing anti-trans rhetoric and messaging throughout their life. In an attempt to protect their child from a "harder" or "complicated" existence the caregiver may instinctively want to correct their child's gender identity.

A family's cultural values also impact meaning making when it comes to accepting and embracing their TGE child's authentic gender identity. When working with TGE youth and their families, a social worker must explore how a family's culture has shaped their view of gender diversity. Far too often, is it assumed that families of color are less accepting of gender diversity among youth in comparison to white families. This is reinforced by lack of re-presentation of TGE children of color in mainstream media, research, and academic literature (Brown & Mar, 2018). Brown and Mar (2018) highlight that as providers and support figures in the lives of TGE children of color we must take into account how "Christianity and colonization have impacted communities of color by reinforcing the gender binary and devaluing gender diversity" (p. 66).

There is a rich history of gender diversity in indigenous culture as well as communities of color, and in spite of oppressive colonization and Christianity there is resilient representation of gender diversity within these cultures and communities today (Brown & Mar, 2018). By stereotyping families of color or expecting that families of color conform to dominant white and western practices, we lose sight of the TGE youth and family in need of support, as well as perpetuate these oppressive forces.

Every family is unique, each influenced by their culture, community, larger society, and historical context. Similarly to how there is no one way to be transgender and gender expansive, there is no one way to be a supportive and affirming caregiver. However there are some basic tenets to follow – cor-recting a child's expression of authentic gender and enforcing gender norms is detrimental to the child's development of sense of self. These corrective at-tempts made by primary caregivers causes a child to internalize shame. Furthermore these responses from caregivers represent a breakdown in parent-child attunement and can erode the attachment relationship.

Secondary Minority Stress

The social worker must consider the minority stress associated with parenting a gender-expansive child. These stressors extend beyond wit-nessing discrimination and victimization of their gender-expansive child (Hidalgo & Chen, 2019). Primary caregivers of TGE youth face a number of distal stressors including experienced and perceived peer, societal, and travel-based discrimination related to their child's gender identity or expression (Hidalgo & Chen, 2019). Caregivers may experience distress when they are unsure of how their family will be treated based on their child's gender diversity. For example, when traveling caregivers are often concerned with availability of gender neutral bathrooms, whether their child's name and pronouns will be respected by those in the immediate environment, and if they will encounter any gender-based harassment or possibly violence. To complicate matters, legal protections can vary state to state, which can heighten the level of fear and distress experienced by the TGE youth and their family. Caregivers also experience distal stress pertaining to experienced and perceived rejection from other family members and friends (Hidalgo & Chen, 2019). Caregivers are also often grappling with their own internalized stigma towards gender diversity (Ehrensaft et al., 2018).

A caregiver's concern for the safety of their TGE child can manifest itself as rejection or policing of their child's gender identity or expression. Additionally, if a child has experienced discrimination or victimization outside of their family of origin (i.e., school or community), a caregiver may respond by blaming the child as opposed to responding in an affirming way due to their own distress. For example, a TGE child tells their caregiver they have been bullied at school on a day they expressed their authentic gender identity thru affirming clothing. The child's caregiver may respond by saying the child "was asking to be picked on" and prohibit the child from wearing clothing that aligns with their authentic gender identity in fear that the bullying may continue and escalate to physical violence. Caregivers often feel that these policing or corrective measures are a way of protecting their TGE child. This also speaks to a caregiver's lack of understanding of the experiences of their TGE child, as most primary caregivers don't share this aspect of identity.

Supporting Families

Caregiver Supports

Caregivers undergo their own emotional process of transition as their child transitions. It is recommended that caregivers have space to share their feelings and thoughts regarding their child's gender identity. The literature highlights the importance of caregiver supports which may include clinical and/or peer supports (Ehrensaft et al., 2018; Johnson & Benson, 2014; Riley, Clemson, Sitharthan, & Diamond, 2013; Turban & Ehrensaft, 2018; Wallace & Russell, 2013).

Peer support groups for parents can help reduce feelings of shame and isolation while increasing understanding and connection with other parents and their own child (Johnson & Benson, 2014; Riley et al., 2013). Peer support groups can also be a space for caregivers to share resources and information with each other. Depending on where a family is geographically located will determine the availability of in-person support groups. However within the last several years more and more support groups have moved to online platforms to increase access for families everywhere. Gender spectrum facilitates online support groups for caregivers that are topic based and specific to the TGE child's age.

Additionally, social supports for children can often create opportunities for caregivers to connect with one another. Similar to in-person caregiver support groups, these may or may not be available depending on the family's geographic location. Local LGBTQ youth organizations, pediatric gender clinics, or other mental health providers who work with TGE youth may be helpful when looking for more regional resources and programming.

Clinical supports are recommended if social stressors become barriers to the parent's acceptance of the child's authentic self (Hidalgo & Chen, 2019).

Malpas's (2011) Multidimensional Family Approach (MDFA) is one of the primary therapeutic frameworks specifically designed to provide clinical support to parents of TGE youth. The MDFA incorporates psychoeducation, parent coaching, and family therapy (Malpas, 2011). The therapeutic work focuses on the parent's realization that their support and acceptance is a form of protection for their gender-expansive child (Malpas, 2011).

The Family Acceptance Project (FAP) supports model addresses specific issues related to sexual orientation and gender identity diversity. FAP is a family-related approach which is geared to help ethnically, racially and religiously diverse families support their LGBTQ children's well-being by accepting their child's sexual orientation and/or gender identity (Cohen, Mannarino, Wilson, & Zinny, 2018). Findings from FAP's research indicate that among LGBTQ youth family acceptance and support leads to better mental and physical health as well as social outcomes, while family rejection increases a youth's risk for depression, suicidality, illegal drug use, and STI contraction (Cohen et al., 2018).

Role of the Social Worker

Social work practice will vary depending on the type of setting in which a worker is engaging with a TGE child and their family. There are four roles a social worker will commonly take on when working with this population regardless of setting. These include witness, psychoeducator, advocate, and resource referral.

Witness

A primary function of a social worker is to bear witness to the gender journey of the TGE child and their family. The presence of an affirmative figure who is seeing the child for who they authentically are and holding space for their caregivers to process their own emotional transition is paramount to the wellbeing of the family unit. This isn't to say that every child and caregiver dyad will be attuned with one another. Even supportive and loving caregivers experience distress regarding their TGE child's gender identity. As previously mentioned, there are significant secondary minority stressors that caregivers endure when parenting a TGE child. A social worker should create a separate space for caregivers to express their own feelings and thoughts regarding their child's gender identity. This is recommended to reduce harm to the TGE child and provide caregivers a safe space to explore their feelings of uncertainty, loss, fear, denial, and shame.

When working with a parent-child dyad it is fundamental that the social worker is using the child's appropriate name and pronouns. Upon introduction a worker should introduce themselves and volunteer their own pronouns. By doing so, this not only creates an opportunity for the child to share their pronouns instead of placing the work on the child to carve out that space, but it also models usage of affirming language to the caregivers. Throughout a child's journey, the name and pronouns that feel most affirming to them may change. A worker should acknowledge this possibility and create space for the child's most authentic self to shine through.

Here is an example of a possible introductory exchange between a social worker and a parent-child dyad:

Worker: Hi, my name is Steve. I use he/him pronouns. What name and pronouns do you go by?

Child: Hi Steve. My name is Alex. I use they/them pronouns.

Worker: Nice to meet you, Alex. Thanks for sharing your pronouns with me. I'm also glad your grown-up could join us today. What name and pronouns do you go by?

Parent: Hi. I'm Alex's father. My name is Frank and I use he/him pronouns.

Worker: Wonderful to meet you Frank. I know sometimes the name and pronouns we would like others to use when referring to us can change. If at any point you would like me to use a different name or pronouns for you, please let me know. Alex, I might check in with you every now and then to see how you feel about your name and pronouns. Would this be alright?

Child: Okay.

Worker: I know sometimes it can be hard or even scary to ask someone to call you something different, so if at any point it feels scary or you don't know how to tell me I have these name tags here that you are welcome to use.

Child: Cool.

Psychoeducator

A large component of the work is often supporting parents and families to help them become more comfortable in affirming their child's authentic gender identity; this is predominantly done via psychoeducation. When engaging with a TGE child and their family a social worker should assess their need for psychoeducation, more specifically assess where there may be gaps in information that is interrupting parent-child attunement.

For example, if a parent is consistently questioning the validity of their child's nonbinary identity because they are 6 years old, it could be helpful to provide the parent with information on gender identity formation as well as gender diversity beyond the binary. As mentioned earlier, a child begins to express their gender identity during early childhood. The social worker could also approach the topic by exploring with the parent when they first knew or understood their own gender identity. This creates an opportunity for reflection and empathy. The social worker could explain how gender expansive youth have the same capacity to know their gender identity as their cisgender peers.

Psychoeducation can also be focused on the usage of affirmative language and responses. This includes coaching caregivers to promote their usage of appropriate name and pronouns for their TGE child, or even role playing with caregivers to improve their responses to gender messages their child is sending them. A social worker is often coupling coaching with information to support a caregiver's progression towards attunement with their child.

Another possible avenue for the social worker to take in regards to psychoeducation is providing the parent with information on their child's developing sense of self associated with their gender identity, and the negative impact of not being affirmed by attachment figures, as well as increased risk for potential victimization and discrimination by those outside of the family unit. It should be highlighted that it is not always the most appropriate approach to begin with psychoeducation on negative consequences and risk factors as this could potentially create more distress for the caregivers.

Advocate

The majority of systems a TGE child will encounter are riddled with cis-normative and transphobic policies and practices. These policies and practices are sometimes in direct contradiction with existing anti-discrimination laws. It is important that a social worker stays current on anti-discriminatory protections to best support TGE children and their families to know when their legal rights are being violated.

I met Kate (she/her), a white 15-year-old transgender girl at a pediatric gender clinic in California. Kate informed me she had recently been suspended for using the girls' locker room during participation in extra-curricular activities. Kate proceeded to tell me the principal had threatened her with suspension after seeing her use the facilities that corresponded to her gender identity. Kate had socially transitioned at school earlier that year and her parents had previously disclosed her gender identity to school administration. Despite their frustrations Kate nor her parents protested the suspension. The school insisted that because Kate had not legally transitioned (typically done by updating legal name and/or gender marker on legal documents) the suspension was valid. This however was in contradiction to California state law which stated that a child was free to use the facilities at school that corresponded with their affirmed gender identity and that no legal documentation denoting a gender marker or name change was required in order to do so. Kate and her parents were unaware of this legal protection. By informing Kate and her family that the school was in violation of state law the family was able to get the suspension expunged from her records.

Resource Referral

It is common that a social worker will refer families to resources to support them in meeting needs outside their scope of practice. Resource referrals typically fall within the following categories: medical, legal, and social supports.

Below are some examples of possible referrals for each of the listed categories:

Medical
* Pediatrician who is well-versed on gender diversity to provide affirming general primary care
* Pediatric gender care provider, endocrinologist, or clinic that offers puberty blockers or HRT

Legal
* Tutorial information on name and gender marker change
* Attorney or law center which specializes in anti-discriminatory gender and racial justice – there are some law centers that have name and gender-marker change clinics and do pro bono work

Social
* Caregiver peer support group
* Summer camp or local playgroup geared towards TGE youth or is known for having inclusive practices and culture

Conclusion

Primary caregivers of TGE youth have the potential to mitigate chronic social stressors associated with gender diversity and foster a healthy development of sense of self by affirming their child's authentic gender identity. As social workers engaging with TGE youth and their families, we can promote this protective relationship by taking on several roles – witness, psychoeducator, advocate, and resource referral. It is essential to explore how the youth and their family make meaning of the youth's gender identity as it relates to their culture and lived experiences. The social worker must prioritize gender affirmative language and practices in order to create a safe space for TGE youth and their families to share their thoughts, feelings, and needs related to their unique gender journey. By doing so, the social worker and the family can work together to identify stressors and plan supports to promote the child's well-being.

Helpful Resources

Family Acceptance Project

http://familyproject.sfsu.edu

Gender Spectrum

www.genderspectrum.org

National Center for Transgender Equality

http://www.transequality.org

PFLAG (Parents, Families, and Friends of Lesbians and Gays)

www.pflag.com

Transgender Law Center

www.transgenderlawcenter.org

Transgender Legal Defense and Education Fund

https://transgenderlegal.org/

Trans Youth Family Allies

www.imatyfa.org

World Professional Association for Transgender Health

www.wpath.org

References

Brown, E. E., & Mar, K. (2018). Culturally responsive practice with children of color. In C. Keo-Meier & D. Ehrensaft (Eds.), *Perspectives on sexual orientation and diversity. The gender affirmative model: An interdisciplinary approach to supporting transgender and gender expansive children* (pp. 55–69). Washington, DC: American Psychological Association.

Cohen, J. A., Mannarino, A. P., Wilson, K., & Zinny, A. (2018). *Trauma-focused cognitive behavioral therapy LGBTQ implementation manual*. Pittsburgh, PA: Allegheny Health Network.

Ehrensaft, D. (2016). *The gender creative child: Pathways for nurturing and supporting children who live outside gender boxes*. New York: Experiment.

———. (2012). From gender identity disorder to gender identity creativity: True gender self child therapy. *Journal of Homosexuality, 59*(3), 337–356.

Ehrensaft, D., Giammattei, S., Storck, K., Tishelman, A., & Keo-Meier, C. (2018). Prepubertal social gender transitions: What we know; what we can learn – A view from a gender affirmative lens. *International Journal of Transgenderism, 19*(2), 251–268.

Hendricks, M. L., & Testa, R. J. (2012). A conceptual framework for clinical work with transgender and gender nonconforming clients: An adaptation of the minority stress model. *Professional Psychology: Research and Practice, 43*, 460–467. doi:10.1037/a0029597

Hidalgo, M., & Chen, D. (2019). Experiences of gender minority stress in cisgender parents of transgender/gender-expansive prepubertal children: A qualitative study. *Journal of Family Issues, 40*(7), 865–886.

Hill, D., Menvielle, E., Sica, K., & Johnson, A. (2010). An affirmative intervention for families with gender variant children: Parental ratings of child mental health and gender. *Journal of Sex & Marital Therapy, 36*(1), 6–23.

Johnson, S., & Benson, K. (2014). "It's always the mother's fault": Secondary stigma of mothering a transgender child. *Journal of GLBT Family Studies, 10*(1–2), 124–144.

Malpas, J. (2011). Between pink and blue: A multi-dimensional family approach to gender nonconforming children and their families. *Family Process, 50*, 453–470.

Olson, K., Key, A., & Eaton, N. (2015). Gender cognition in transgender children. *Psychological Science, 26*(4), 467–474.

Riley, E., Clemson, L., Sitharthan, G., & Diamond, M. (2013). Surviving a gender-variant childhood: The views of transgender adults on the needs of gender-variant children and their parents. *Journal of Sex & Marital Therapy, 39*(3), 241–263.

Spivey, L., Huebner, D., & Diamond, L. (2018). Parent responses to childhood gender nonconformity: Effects of parent and child characteristics. *Psychology of Sexual Orientation and Gender Diversity, 5*(3), 360–370.

Turban, J., & Ehrensaft, D. (2018). Research review: Gender identity in youth: Treatment paradigms and controversies. *Journal of Child Psychology and Psychiatry, 59*(12), 1228–1243.

Wallace, R., & Russell, H. (2013). Attachment and shame in gender-nonconforming children and their families: Toward a theoretical framework for evaluating clinical interventions. *International Journal of Transgenderism, 14*(3), 113–126.

7 The Affirmative Potential of Sex-Positive Sex Education with Trans and Gender Expansive Youth

Maggie Dunleavy and S. J. Dodd

Introduction

Considerable progress has been made in societal understanding and acceptance of gay, lesbian, bisexual, and pansexual people (Riggs & Bartholomaeus, 2018). While there are gains to be celebrated due to advocacy efforts and shifts in policy, there are also gaps and blind spots that still need to be addressed in the path towards equity. This is particularly true in relation to gender identity, and in the protection of those who are transgender and gender expansive (people whose gender is not in alignment with the expectations associated with their assigned sex at birth). The transgender community is a vibrant and diverse one, including those who are binary trans men and women, as well as those who find their gender to be undefinable by the traditional male/female binary and claim an ever-evolving array of language and labels. Some of these gender identities include gender nonbinary, genderqueer, gender fluid, agender (without gender), third gender, and two spirit, although this is by no means a comprehensive list. Now more than ever, there are innumerable ways to explore one's gender identity and find the word and the community that feels right. That process can be a confusing one, especially when one does not have the language, educational tools, or community support to do so safely. For many young people in particular, who find themselves coming to terms with their gender identity in adolescence, there can be few places to find informative, affirming, celebratory spaces to grapple with the challenges and pleasures of discovering their authentic gender and sexuality. Transgender and gender expansive (TGE) youth all need spaces where they can be themselves and find support in figuring out exactly what that means for them. When working with TGE youth, sex-positive and trans-inclusive sex education offers a unique opportunity through which conversations about sexual agency, desire, and pleasure can empower youth with the invitation to listen to their bodies, explore their curiosities and boundaries and evolve their gender identities and sexual orientations concurrently.

Adolescence is a crucial stage of development, one in which people come into their personhood in an entirely new way. The developmental tasks of

DOI: 10.4324/9780429297687-7

adolescence center around identity development and role testing (Erikson, 1959; Hutchison, 2015). Much of adolescence is spent trying on a range of personal, social and political roles, with friends, family, and community to see which ones feel right and seem to fit, and which ones don't. When working in practice with youth, it is important to keep in mind their unique developmental stage in order to support their growth in a way that is affirmative and nurturing. However, when it comes to education and social work practice around the emerging sexuality of youth, students are often failed by educators who employ shame, fear, and condescension in curriculum that is cis-heteronormative, centering abstinence and heterosexual, monogamous relationships as the only form of safe sexual expression (Dodd, 2020; Haley, Tordoff, Kantor, Crouch, & Ahrens, 2019; McNeill, 2013; Muzzey, Shelton, & Dunleavy, in press; Ullman, 2018). Similarly, complex discussions around the relationship of sexuality and gender identity and student exploration of what feels right are shut down or avoided, and students are once again failed and forced to seek other avenues for their sex education (Dodd, 2020; Haley et al., 2019; McNeill, 2013; Robinson, Bansel, Denson, Ovenden, & Davies, 2014). This narrow approach to sexuality and complete erasure of gender identity can have dire consequences for trans and gender expansive youth who largely feel unsafe in their schooling environments, disproportionately face bullying and violence, and are at greater risk for suicidality (Kosciw, Clark, Truong, & Zongrone, 2020; Goodrich & Barnard, 2018; James et al., 2016; Johns et al., 2019; McNeill, 2013; Robinson et al., 2014; Shelton & Lester, 2018).

With the advent of extensive online resources and communities, including social media and user-generated information sharing platforms like YouTube, youth are likely to augment their formal education on sex and gender, finding online and informal spaces to discuss and discover the information they are missing (Dodd, 2020). In one study young people described learning about diversity and possibility through hashtags (Bragg et al., 2018). Access to the internet and social media can offer the potential for gaining concrete information about sexual health when conversations around sexuality are not happening at home or in school (Stevens et al., 2017). However, when left on their own, online exploration can lead to an avalanche of information that may or may not be developmentally appropriate for young people to comprehend and can even lead to false expectations, exposure to transphobia, negative gender bias, and even dangerous personal attacks (Cipolletta, Votadoro, & Faccio, 2017; Springate & Omar, 2013). Therefore, an important opportunity remains within educational settings and clinical social work with TGE expansive youth not only to harness the positive potential of social media while protecting against negative experiences, but also to facilitate sex education that is sex-positive, inclusive, and affirming of the emerging (and often multiple) identities and desires the young people are beginning to explore and claim (Dodd, 2020). In order to do this, it is critical to consider what could be included in the facilitation of such conversations.

In approaching social work with trans, nonbinary and gender expansive youth, we recommend a paradigm shift which replaces the worker as expert with the student as expert. This shift centers the lived experience of youth as well as their demonstrated facility with rapidly evolving language around gender and sexuality and curiosity about their own desires. Listening to youth's interests, experiences, and priorities while bringing in essential concepts like consent makes for education and clinical work that is inclusive and affirming of all identities. Additionally, we offer a series of pillars of trans-inclusive, sex-positive education to lean on in the planning and facilitation of sex-positive conversations with TGE youth about sexuality and gender. Working from this place of collaborative, knowledgeable respect is useful for sex education with students of all genders, but is especially important when working with trans, nonbinary, and gender expansive youth, who may not have other spaces in their lives that provide the opportunity for them to work through the feelings, fears, and desires that are part of the complicated and creative process of exploring their gender identity alongside their emerging sexuality.

Burden on Trans Students: Establishing the Problem

Adolescence and young adulthood are spent growing into identities that will shape the rest of adult life. Using Erik Erikson's (1959) eight stage developmental model, the primary developmental conflict to be resolved during adolescence can be seen as identity versus role confusion. Adolescents try on a range of different roles within their social systems to discover which ones feel right and which ones don't, working over time to solidify their own identities and making sense of significant changes they experience physically, emotionally, and socially. Not only are young people asking themselves who they are, they are bombarded with the pressures of who they are expected to be, both in their immediate social groups and communities, and in the context of a larger culture that stigmatizes forms of expression outside of traditional gendered roles and compulsory heterosexuality. When engaging youth who have already begun to see themselves as outliers in these cultural scripts, it is crucial that they are able to get the support they need to develop into their authentic selves.

Trans and gender expansive youth in particular need the support and affirmation of the important adults in their lives. Transgender students report significantly higher rates of experiencing physical violence, engaging in substance use, and experiencing suicidal ideation (Johns et al., 2019). Likely contributing to these risk factors is a widespread school culture of harassment and bullying targeting those who openly identify as LGBTQ as well as students whose gender presentation does not conform to binary expectations of masculinity or femininity. In GLSEN's 2019 national survey of LGBTQ students, an overwhelming number of students (98.8%) reported experiencing or witnessing derogatory language and insults about sexuality and gender presentation from other students, and also reported that it was largely tolerated or even endorsed by school faculty and staff (Kosciw, Clark, Truong, & Zongrone, 2020). In fact, two-thirds (66.7%) of the students reported actually hearing negative comments about gender expression from their teachers or other staff (Kosciw, Clark, Truong, & Zongrone, 2020). For students of color, this verbal harassment is disproportionally accompanied by a sense of real physical danger. Black and Hispanic LGBTQ students not only face a greater risk of physical violence for their queer and trans identities but also of interpersonal violence in their relationships, with one study reporting physical victimization from an intimate partner being 1–4 times higher among nonwhite youths than among white youths (Johns et al., 2019, p. 22). Students without white privilege experience the compounding effects of everyday experiences of racism and white supremacy in addition to the ways they are harassed for their gender identity and/or sexual orientation.

Similar rates of exposure to harassment and violence were reported in Australian schools with 65% of participants from one study reporting verbal abuse at school because of gender difference and 21% reporting physical abuse (Jones et al., 2016). Studies from the United States, UK, and Australia have also identified that schools are very gendered environments, from school buildings to school uniforms and dress codes, to permitted sports involvement and activities (James et al., 2016; Jones & Hiller, 2013; British LGBT Awards, 2020). Clearly, trans youth are not being served effectively by their school environments, the place where they spend most of their time and learn how to navigate their identities publicly.

Meyer's (2003) Minority Stress Model identifies four relevant processes including:

1. external, objective events that are stressful to experience;
2. the impact of expecting such events, which are stressful to experience (here amplified by the hostile school environment and the consistent expectation of verbal and even physical harassment related to sexual and gender identity);
3. the internalization of negative social attitudes; and
4. the impact of concealment (in this case of one's gender identity).

Utilizing Meyer's (2003) Minority Stress Model, the burden carried by trans and gender expansive youth can be conceptualized as the compounding stress of directly experienced violence and bullying, anticipation of future harm, and the vigilance required to be on guard against such threats of violence, as well as the internalized transphobia and homophobia that is reinforced by a heteronormative and cissexist school environment (Hendricks & Testa, 2012; Robinson et al., 2014). Trans students learn that they are unsafe and largely on their own, with even the adults in their learning environments either ignoring attacks on them or contributing to them by using derogatory or insulting language themselves (Kosciw, Clark, Truong, & Zongrone, 2020).

Students overwhelmed by this matrix of stressors may turn the resulting frustration and pain inward, leading to suicidal ideation and self-harm (James et al., 2016; McNeil, Bailey, Ellis, Morton, & Regan, 2012). For students like Erica, a 13-year-old white trans feminine seventh grader, the stress of being visibly different to her fellow classmates at school is met by teachers who tell her that her long hair and decorative barrettes and clips are not up to uniform code for boys, sending her to the administrative office for disciplinary action multiple times. By the time she has ended up in the school social worker's office, she is visibly withdrawn and defeated, and shares that she knows her chosen name and pronouns won't matter to anyone at school, they'd just be another reason for everyone to make her feel worse about herself. Over and over again, from the moment she walks into school, she receives the message that her gender identity is wrong. For many TGE youth trying to live authentically as themselves at school, this is a familiar experience.

Across the globe, transgender, nonbinary, and gender expansive young people report devastatingly high rates of self-harm behaviors, suicidal ideation, and suicide attempts. The US Transgender Survey (USTS), reporting data based on a sample of 27,715 TGE people, found a staggering 82% had experienced suicidal ideation and 40% reported an actual suicide attempt, far exceeding the 4.6% attempt numbers reported by the general population (James et al., 2016). McNeil et al. (2012) found comparable rates in their UK-based sample of 889 transgender participants, with 84% expressing thoughts of suicide and 35% reporting an attempt. Similarly, Jones and Hiller (2013) found significantly higher rates of suicide attempts and self-harm behaviors in a smaller sample of transgender and gender diverse young people in Australia. TGE mental health is a crisis, and youth are being failed by those who might give them the tools to work through their feelings and fears, and create space to celebrate themselves and what does feel good or exciting to them as they come into their gender and sexuality. Providing inclusive and affirming sex education for everyone can begin to expand notions of gender and can create a protective buffer, which affords greater safety for everyone. In fact, students in states that have a higher proportion of LGBTQ-inclusive sex education had reduced risk of school-based violence and negative mental health outcomes (Proulx et al., 2019). Unfortunately, in most places sex education is narrowly conceived, reinforcing of cishetero narratives, and poorly delivered (Riggs & Bartholomaues 2018; The Terrence Higgins Trust, 2017).

Sex Ed: Abstinence and Risk vs. Sex-Positive

From an early age, children are curious about their bodies, the bodies of others, and the rules of the world. Sexual exploration and experimentation are born out of the uninhibited pleasure of physical exploration and masturbation as self-soothing (Dodd, 2020). As children grow into adolescence, that relationship of pleasurable exploration may change, shaped by the gendered expectations placed on them by their family and culture. In North

American culture, there are familiar stereotypes to be negotiated. Girls must be feminine, small, and withholding, while boys are expected to be strong, unemotional, and dogged pursuers sexually (Crooks & Baur, 2017). This familiar paradigm is built out of limiting, heterosexist ideas of gender that limit all people's freedom to claim and express themselves fully. For TGE youth, there is likely to be a present and even painful dissonance between the gendered messaging they are receiving according to the sex they were assigned at birth and the way they feel internally about themselves and their gender. This may have implications for their relationships, their comfort levels in dating, or how they express themselves to their peers. However, in educational settings, there is little space available to youth to support an exploration of their gender or their emerging adult sexuality as positive or encouraged.

Additionally, in sex education, one of the few concrete places where youth engage in conversation about their bodies, desires, and curiosity, there is a dominant assumption that youth cannot handle complex discussions of sexuality and cultivating a sexual identity. Mainstream sex education is instead focused on abstinence and controlling sexuality into a handful of acceptable forms of expression, namely heterosexual marriage (Hall, McDermott Sales, Komro, & Santelli, 2016). The goal of this education is warning youth of the impending likelihood of unplanned pregnancy, sexually transmitted illnesses, and sexual assault if one chooses to have sexual intercourse out of the context of marriage. However, while many government-funded programs exclusively promote abstinence from sexual activity until marriage, research has shown that this strategy is not effective at delaying initiation of sexual intercourse, reducing the number of sexual partners, or shifting sexual behaviors (Santelli et al., 2017). Sex education that solely promotes abstinence is harmful in the lack of information it offers students, and the stigmatizing way it portrays students who are already sexually active as inferior to those who have yet to have sexual intercourse. For students who are survivors of sexual violence, are parents, or simply have already begun having sex when they enter into this educational setting, their lived realities are shamed and disparaged. The moralistic shame and fear employed in these programs and the often rigid gender roles they unquestioningly reinforce also leaves sexual and gender minority youth feeling invisible, isolated, and othered (Robinson et al., 2014). For all students, the gaps in information provided to them often leave them uninformed on the use of other effective contraceptives, relevant reproductive health information, or a strong understanding of ongoing enthusiastic consent as a requirement for all sexual activity.

While not all sexual education programs in the United States are based solely in abstinence only education, the majority are framed around the assessment and control of sexual risk (Chin et al., 2012). This approach seeks to educate those engaging in sexual activity about the potential negative outcomes of their choices, namely unplanned pregnancy, and sexually transmitted illnesses such as HIV.

Though more helpful than an abstinence-based curriculum, because of its slightly more educational aims, a sexual risk framework is also limited in many ways. First, discussions centered on minimizing sexual risk often focus solely on individual choice and fail to acknowledge systemic factors which may shape the choices available to individuals, such as racism, poverty, and discrimination (Muzzey, Shelton, & Dunleavy, in press). A sexual risk framework for sex education also makes assumptions of what is an inherently negative outcome of sexual activity, such as teenage pregnancy, without evaluating with the youth themselves what they value or aspire to. A sexual risk framework often locates risk within specific communities in a stigmatizing and alienating way. LGBTQ students, for example are often posited as a more "at-risk group" than their cisgender, heterosexual peers because they are cited as being likely to engage in sexual risk-taking behaviors, "including earlier age at first sexual intercourse, more lifetime and recent sex partners, and drinking alcohol or using other drugs prior to last sexual intercourse; and are less likely to use a condom during intercourse" (American Psychological Association, 2014). However, this picture of LGBTQ youth fails to include the systemic factors contributing to the decisions they make in their sexual lives, or how they feel about the choices available to them. It can be challenging, then, to find a place to feel encouraged or seen in conversations framed around outcomes that may not even apply to them (i.e., pregnancy) without space to openly discuss areas of their sexual life that are specific to their experience.

Consider the experience of Alex, a 17-year-old Asian, nonbinary student who goes through a final year of sex education in their high school focused primarily on sexually transmitted infections and pregnancy prevention. They know that when they go to college, they want to start testosterone, and one day maybe even get top surgery. But they also know how important it is to their parents that they, an only child, have grandchildren, and they've always imagined themselves having kids on their own. Too nervous to bring it up in front of the rest of the class, Alex wonders if the hormones would render that impossible, or maybe even act as a kind of birth control? They sit in the back of the class overwhelmed by questions and feeling frustrated and alone, thinking that maybe they can do some internet searching on their own, but feeling very intimidated by the thought. For all students, framing adolescent sexuality exclusively as risky or dangerous and failing to provide comprehensive and inclusive education around concerns unique to TGE populations prevents youth from expressing themselves authentically and owning their sexual autonomy, desires and sexual experiences, both positive and negative, as valid and educational (Muzzey, Shelton, & Dunleavy, in press).

In stark contrast, inclusive and sex-positive sex education centers personal sexual agency, desire, and pleasure (Dodd, 2020). It honors consent as an ongoing, collaborative process that is woven into every moment of a sexual encounter between those participating. Sex-positive education also gives permission to not want to have sex, affirming asexuality and aromatic identities, while also making space for sex to be wanted and enjoyed by everyone (Dodd, 2020). In order to achieve inclusive and affirming sexuality education, work with students must be based on a respectful encouragement of each person to explore what they want or do not want, what feels good in their body, and how to express their desires, preferences, and boundaries. It is a shift from control and risk-management to building a thoughtful dialogue with oneself and feeling empowered to make decisions from that place. The focus is on the development of an authentic sexual autonomy. Sex-positive conversations come from an affirmative place, asking students what feels good and what they enjoy more. Sex-positive conversations also invite them to understand what things they don't like, so they can practice clear communication around boundaries and engage in fully informed consent conversations. This practice opens space for all students to be curious about their bodies and desires in a non-judgmental way, and for them to learn how to build positive intimate relationships with themselves and others.

Youth are now finding themselves growing up in a time where countless online communities offer space for LGBTQ+ people to explore identities and language around gender and sexuality. When working with adolescents, who have had access to social media for most of their lives and are incredibly digitally literate, it's reasonable to expect the students to become the teachers in some ways. Working collaboratively with youth themselves to center not only their questions but also their own knowledge of their identities and the communities through which they find safety and affirmation, social workers and educators can facilitate conversations that are nuanced and inclusive, encouraging respectful curiosity on both sides of the dialogue. Combined with a larger institutional commitment to supporting gender diversity, including educational opportunities for faculty and staff around how to best support trans, nonbinary, and gender expansive youth, sex-positive sex education offers a positive and affirming framework through which youth can build their own understanding of healthy sexuality.

Sex-Positive / Trans Inclusive – Useful for All Students

Regardless of the identities of students, those existing outside of binary gender expectations are likely to incur harassment and bullying. One does not need to be gay or trans to be called homophobic and transphobic slurs. Gender nonconformity in particular is targeted and weaponized as a way to belittle and demean students who are different. Students almost unanimously report hearing negative remarks about gender expression in their school settings, including specifically derogatory language about transgender people (Kosciw, Clark, Truong, & Zongrone, 2020, p. xix). And although the impact of homophobic and transphobic violence and harassment is most often measured in its impact on LGBTQ students, it is witnessed by all students, and reinforces a schoolwide culture that accepts the policing of others' gender expression, and limits what is acceptable to largely traditional gender roles. For boys this can mean a narrow view of masculinity that is organized around homophobia, the intense fear of being seen as gay and therefore weak (Kimmel & Mahler, 2003). For girls, it may show up as a compulsory femininity, pressure to be thin or pretty by Eurocentric standards of beauty. For TGE youth, the limited choices of acceptable expression available to them can leave them feeling backed into a corner with few options offering them the chance to feel like their authentic selves at school.

One entry point into creating safer learning environments or inclusive education for youth is understanding the impact of shame on all adolescents. If the goal of administration is to reduce bullying or to combat violence in schools, a strategy for achieving that goal may be to provide outlets for shame to be processed and worked through by students. All adolescents have in common the developmental moment they are navigating, and the ways in which those changes show up in their bodies, emotions, and desires. These changes are disorienting, and without the tools to process through them, can result in feelings of shame and self-consciousness (Dodd, 2020; Hutchison, 2015). TGE youth may have, in some ways an added layer of shame, as they mitigate the confusion of an internal pull towards discovering and finding the words for a gender more authentic than the one they were assigned at birth. For TGE youth, the developmental changes happening in their bodies may be the catalyst for intense waves of gender dysphoria, and learning to find safety and even pleasure in their bodies can be extremely challenging on their own.

However, growing into the gender one was assigned at birth, for cisgender youth, also comes with often rigid expectations of how to perform one's masculinity or femininity in a socially acceptable way, and may be the source of body dysmorphia, disordered eating, or other painful and confusing conditions (Douglas, Kwan, Minnich, & Gordon, 2019; Fisher, 2018). Shame, particularly in heterosexual boys and men, has been linked to acts of violence as extreme as school shootings and homophobic hate crimes (Kimmel & Mahler, 2003). When boys are backed up to the wall of rigid masculinity, needing to "prove" themselves, there is no room for them to hear the subtler echoes of their desires, fears, and curiosities.

In conversations with youth of all genders, inclusive and affirming sex education holds the potential for safe and empowering self-exploration. All young people can benefit from sex education centered on building a positive relationship with emerging desires and noticing how pleasure and discomfort feel in one's body, normalizing an ongoing process of checking in for consent, and finding their own way of communicating their boundaries and needs with others. Youth of all genders need space to get information that will shape their choices around sex, to ask questions and feel seen and affirmed in the identities they are growing into.

Institutional Component: What Is Expected/Recommended?

It can be tempting to position gender and sexuality education for youth as exclusively meeting the needs of youth who identify as queer, trans, or gender expansive. Often, these initiatives are framed as a way to address bullying and teach other kids not to pick on those who are different from them (Ullman, 2018). This, in a way, addresses the violence that queer and trans kids face as they navigate their identities and gender expression. However, it limits the scope of what is possible, and locates the problem in their difference. Teaching the straight, cis kids how to tolerate the non-straight, non-cis ones does not address the currents of shame, desire, and fear that run through all adolescents, or give them constructive spaces in which to process these feelings and learn how to make healthy choices. Additionally, educators and social workers speaking to youth about inclusivity around sexuality and gender as an anti-bullying measure may fail to see ways in which they themselves contribute to the social marginalization of LGBTQ+ students, locating the problem outside of the school environment they themselves have the power to shape (Ullman, 2018). Additionally, while bullying is definitely a large concern for those working with an adolescent population, there is much more to be gained for all students in sex-positive education alongside minimizing harm to vulnerable populations.

TGE students are navigating a school environment that is likely to be inherently gendered, from the way they are addressed by educators and fellow students to the sex segregated bathrooms they are likely to face and be forced to choose between. Additionally, in the process of choosing how and when to come out formally to their family and community as trans, TGE students are confronted with the often daunting process of asking their schools to respect and formally recognize their gender identities through their social transition. "This process may include using a different name and/or third-person pronouns, using different toilets and changing rooms, changing the gender marker on class lists and adopting an appearance in accordance with societal expectations for their gender" (Frohard-Dourlent, 2018, p. 329). In their social transition and beyond, students need the backing of a school culture that respects and values gender diversity, making it an institutional priority to support TGE youth and center their needs.

For social workers and educators seeking guidance on how best to approach facilitating sex-positive conversations with TGE youth, the task can seem daunting. And while it is understandable to want some kind of script or template for getting these conversations started, or navigating their more murky or unpredictable areas, it's important to acknowledge that any such script written today would likely be out of date almost immediately. As language and identities themselves evolve so will the unique needs of any population. Instead of trying to find the perfect way to have these conversations, it is useful to return to a series of pillars, described below, which will help inform educational conversations around sex, sexuality, and gender with youth of all identities.

Pillars of Transgender Inclusive Sex Education

No Judgment, No Assumptions

The first step in developing inclusive and affirming sex education is to come to the table with an open mind, free from expectations about the youth you will be in conversation with. This includes suspending expectations regarding the partners students may have or aspire to have, the number of people they've partnered with or are currently with, the gender of those partners, and what sexual roles they take on with their partners regardless of their genders or anatomy. In the same vein, avoid assuming what kind of behaviors, desires, or feelings students may have about themselves, their bodies, or their relationships. Without assumptions to overcome, youth may feel more encouraged to speak from their own perspective.

Trust the Youth

While young people may be in the process of discovering what their identities mean to them, or how to articulate them, it's important to trust them as the experts of their own bodies and experiences. Supporting them by listening deeply when they articulate their experiences and validating the complicated and even conflicting feelings that arise in that process is an integral part of making them feel seen and safe in moments of vulnerability.

Promote Sexual Autonomy

Sexual autonomy is an essential concept to explore and encourage in conversations around sexuality. Creating space where youth can connect with their desire, notice what feels good in their bodies and articulate their boundaries to themselves and others, all offer the chance for deep self-reflection and the opportunity to forge a more connected and intuitive relationship with themselves. For trans, nonbinary, and gender expansive youth, this can come with additional layers of navigating the ways they feel in their body, how they want to be touched and what they want their body parts to be called. The young people may have feelings of dysphoria about their genitals or their bodies, which lead them to avoid intimacy or to have specific boundaries around the activities they engage in. Providing a safe non-judgmental space for young people to explore what sexual autonomy means for them can help navigate dysphoric feelings and facilitate confidence around decision-making related to sex and intimacy. For example, some young people rename or regender their body parts in a way that feels congruent for them.

Communication and Consent

Without a thorough understanding of consent and the communication required to maintain ongoing consent, a potential curriculum leaves youth unprepared to navigate crucial aspects of romantic and sexual relationships with others. Conversations about consent should also address the tension between sexual desire and emotional readiness. Riggs (2017) recommend allowing space for young people to explore what is motivating them to consent to sex and intimacy. In this context, it is also important to discuss the ways that cisnormativity and anti-trans bias have influenced young people's beliefs about who is sexy and desirable, and whether motivation is around their need to feel desired and wanted. Additionally, it can be useful to include an exploration of asking for consent and communicating feelings around the use of gendered words with partners, as well as what names or words feel best when referring to a partner's or one's own body parts inside and outside of sex.

Avoid Gendered and Binarizing Language

Avoiding gendered and binarizing language is always important but is especially important when engaging in conversations about sexuality. Discuss body parts and their functioning without assigning them a particular gender.

Embrace Fluidity

It's important to keep in mind that sexuality and gender are often flexible and evolving, meaning that conversations about them need to be as well. Language is constantly changing, and it is crucial as facilitators to stay as current as possible and be willing to let go of previously held ideas about what may be "typical" categories of identity or expression. Honoring the fluidity of gender and sexuality can open up space for students to feel comfortable trying new pronouns or chosen names in class, or to open up about the uncertainty or pressure to "choose" that they may be feeling.

Conclusion

Sexuality education is one of the few subjects where educators often follow the premise that with less information, youth will make better decisions or experience fewer negative outcomes (Dodd, 2020). Abstinence-only sex education and sexual risk frameworks position sexuality first and foremost as a dangerous thing to be controlled, rather than providing a space for youth to constructively explore the pleasurable and exciting aspects of their developing sexuality. Now more than ever, students need that space to claim themselves fully, ask questions, and get crucial information that will set them up for success in their future sexual and romantic relationships. TGE youth face intense cultural waves of doubt, scrutiny, and violence as they navigate their evolving identity alongside their sexuality (James et al., 2016; Kosciw, Clark, Truong, & Zongrone, 2020). By creating trans affirmative and inclusive sex education grounded in sex-positive practices encouraging curiosity, consent, and sexual autonomy, all students stand to gain from the conversation. Encouraging youth to bring their full selves into conversations that may be uncomfortable, awkward, or funny provides a valuable opportunity for exploration and community across identity and an invitation to find safety, joy, and self-acceptance by being curious about ourselves, our bodies, and our desires.

References

Bragg, R., Renold, E., Ringrose, J., & Jackson, C. (2018). "More than boy, girl, male, female": Exploring young people's views on gender diversity within and beyond school contexts. *Sex Education, 18*(4), 420–434. doi:10.1080/14681811.2018.1439373

American Psychological Association. (2014). Youth at Disproportionate Risk. Retrieved from https://www.apa.org/pi/lgbt/programs/safe-supportive/disproportionate-risk

British LGBT Awards. (2020). *LGBT<25 Survey, conducted by the British LGBT Awards.* Retrieved from https://www.britishlgbtawards.com/wp-content/uploads/2020/01/LGBT25-Report-Headlines-Final.pdf

Chin, H. B., Sipe, T. A., Elder, R., Mercer, S. L., Chattopadhyay, S. K., Jacob, V. J., ... Santelli, J. (2012). The effectiveness of group-based comprehensive risk-reduction and abstinence education interventions to prevent or reduce the risk of adolescent pregnancy, human immunodeficiency virus, and sexually transmitted infections: Two systematic reviews for the guide to community preventive services. *American Journal of Preventive Medicine, 42*(3), 272–294. doi:10.1016/j.amepre.2011.11.006

Cipolletta, S., Votadoro, R., & Faccio, E. (2017). Online support for transgender people: An analysis of forums and social networks. *Health and Social Care in the Community, 25*(5), 1542–1551. doi:10.1111/hsc.12448

Crooks, R., & Baur, K. (2017). *Our sexuality* (13th ed.). Belmont, CA: Thomson Wadsworth.

Dodd, S. (2020). *Sex-positive social work.* New York: Columbia University Press.

Douglas, V. J., Kwan, M. Y., Minnich, A. M., & Gordon, K. H. (2019). The interaction of sociocultural attitudes and gender on disordered eating. *Journal of Clinical Psychology, 75*, 2140–2146. doi:10.1002/jclp.22835

Erikson, E. H. (1959). *Identity and the life cycle.* New York: W. W. Norton.

Fisher, A. (2018). Gender differences in the presentation of body dysmorphic disorder: A systematic review. *Research Gate.* Retrieved from https://www.researchgate.net/publication/327437889_Gender_Differences_In_The_Presentation_Of_Body_Dysmorphic_Disorder_A_Systematic_Review

Fisher, C. (2009). Queer youth experiences with abstinence-only-until-marriage sexuality education: "I can't get married so where does that leave me?" *Journal of LGBT Youth, 6*(1), 61–79. doi:10.1080/19361650802396775

Frohard-Dourlent, H. (2018). "The student drives the car, right?": Trans students and narratives of decision-making in schools. *Sex Education, 18*(4), 328–344. doi:10.1080/14681811.2017.1393745

Goodrich, K., & Barnard, J. (2018). Transgender and gender non-conforming students in schools: one school district's approach for creating safety and respect. *Sex Education*, 1–14. doi:10.1080/14681811.2018.1490258

Haley, S., Tordoff, D., Kantor, A., Crouch, J., & Ahrens, K. (2019). Sex education for transgender and nonbinary youth: Previous experiences and recommended content. *Journal of Sexual Medicine, 16*(11), 1834–1848. doi:10.1016/j.jsxm.2019.08.009

Hall, K. S., McDermott Sales, J., Komro, K. A., & Santelli, J. (2016). The state of sex education in the United States. *The Journal of Adolescent Health: Official Publication of the Society for Adolescent Medicine, 58*(6), 595–597. Retrieved from https://16/ j.jadohealth.2016.03.032

Hendricks, M. L., & Testa, R. J. (2012). A conceptual framework for clinical work with transgender and gender nonconforming clients: An adaptation of the Minority Stress Model. *Professional Psychology: Research and Practice, 43*(5), 460–467. doi:10.103 7/a0029597

Hutchison, E. (2015). *Dimensions of human behavior: The changing life course* (5th ed.). Los Angeles: Sage.

James, S. E., Herman, J. L., Rankin, S., Keisling, M., Mottet, L., & Anafi, M. (2016). *The report of the 2015 U.S. transgender survey*. Washington, DC: National Center for Transgender Equality.

Johns, M. M., Lowry, R., Andrzejewski, J., Barrios, L. C., Demissie, Z., McManus, T., ... Underwood, J. M. (2019, January 25). Transgender identity and experiences of violence victimization, substance use, suicide risk, and sexual risk behaviors among high school students – 19 states and large urban school districts, 2017. *Morbidity and Mortality Weekly Report, 68*(3), 67+. Retrieved from https://link.gale.com/apps/doc/ A579537523/AONE?u=cuny_hunter&sid=AONE&xid=06cac299

Jones, T., Smith, E., Ward, R., Dixon, J., Hillier, L., & Mitchell, A. (2016). School experiences of transgender and gender diverse students in Australia. *Sex Education, 16*, 156–171. doi:10.1080/14681811.2015.1080678

Jones, T., & Hillier, L. (2013). Comparing trans-spectrum and same-sex-attracted youth in Australia: Increased risks. *Increased Activisms, Journal of LGBT Youth, 10*(4), 287–307. doi:10.1080/19361653.2013.825197

Kimmel, M. S., & Mahler, M. (2003). Adolescent masculinity, homophobia, and violence: Random school shootings, 1982–2001. *American Behavioral Scientist, 46*(10), 1439–1458. doi:10.1177/0002764203046010010

Kosciw, J. G., Clark, C. M., Truong, N. L., & Zongrone, A. D. (2020). *The 2019 National School Climate Survey: The experiences of lesbian, gay, bisexual, transgender, and queer youth in our nation's schools*. New York: GLSEN.

McNeill, T. (2013). Sex education and the promotion of heteronormativity. *Sexualities, 16*(7), 826–846.

McNeil, J., Bailey, L., Ellis, S., Morton, J., & Regan, M. (2012). Trans Mental Health Study 2012. Scottish Transgender Alliance. Retrieved from http://worldaa1 .miniserver.com/~gires/assets/Medpro-Assets/trans_mh_study.pdf

Meyer, I. H. (2003). Prejudice, social stress, and mental health in lesbian, gay, and bisexual populations: conceptual issues and research evidence. *Psychological Bulletin, 129*(5), 674–697. doi:10.1037/0033-2909.129.5.674

Proulx, C. N., Coulter, R., Egan, J. E., Matthews, D. D., & Mair, C. (2019). Associations of Lesbian, Gay, Bisexual, Transgender, and Questioning-Inclusive Sex Education with Mental Health Outcomes and School-Based Victimization in

U.S. High School Students. *The Journal of Adolescent Health: Official Publication of the Society for Adolescent Medicine, 64*(5), 608–614. https://doi.org/10.1016/j.jadohealth.2018.11.012

Riggs, D., & Bartholomaeus, C. (2018). Transgender young people's narratives of intimacy and sexual health: Implications for sexuality education. *Sex Education, 18*(4), 376–390. doi:10.1080/14681811.2017.1355299

Robinson, K. H., Bansel, P., Denson, N., Ovenden, G., & Davies, C. (2014). *Growing up queer: Issues facing young Australians who are gender variant and sexuality diverse.* Melbourne: Young and Well Cooperative Research Centre.

Santelli, J. S., Kantor, L. M., Grilo, S. A., Speizer, I. S., Lindberg, L. D., Heitel, J., ... Ott, M. A. (2017, September). Abstinence-only-until-marriage: An updated review of U.S. policies and programs and their impact. *Journal of Adolescent Health, 61*(3), 273–280. doi:10.1016/j.jadohealth.2017.05.031

Shelton, S. A., & Lester, A. O. S. (2018). Finding possibilities in the impossible: A celebratory narrative of trans youth experiences in the Southeastern USA. *Sex Education, 18*(4), 391–405. doi:10.1080/14681811.2017.1421920

Springate, J., & Omar, H. A. (2013). The impact of the internet on the sexual health of adolescents: A brief review. *Pediatrics Faculty Publications, 135*. Retrieved from https://uknowledge.uky.edu/pediatrics_facpub/135

Stevens, R., Gilliard-Matthews, S., Dunaev, J., Todhunter-Reid, A., Brawner, B., & Stewart, J. (2017). Social media use and sexual risk reduction behavior among minority youth: Seeking safe sex information. *Nursing Research, 66*(5), 368–377. doi:1 0.1097/NNR.0000000000000237

Terrence Higgins Trust. (2017). *Shh no talking: LGBT inclusive SRE in the UK.* Retrieved from https://www.tht.org.uk/sites/default/files/2018-07/Shh%20No%20talking %20LGBT%20inclusive%20SRE%20in%20the%20UK.pdf

Ullman, J. (2018). Breaking out of the (anti)bullying 'box': NYC educators discuss trans/gender diversity-inclusive policies and curriculum. *Sex Education, 18*(5), 495–510. doi:10.1080/14681811.2018.1431881

8   Trans and Gender Expansive Youth: Emerging Models of Identity Development

Ryan Karnoski, Ryan Papciak, and Liam Waller

Introduction

Although there are as many understandings of gender identity development as there are individuals who develop a gender identity, conceptual models of gender identity development can provide a schematic way to share commonly held ideas about when, where, and how gender identity emerges. In social work, **bio-psycho-social models** are often used as a **conceptual framework** to contextualize human behavior in and across social environments. Contemporary perspectives on gender identity development largely reflect this model, which delineates a construct of gender based on three primary areas: an individual's "biological sex," psychologically situated gender identity, and outward gender expression. Models such as these play a role in many aspects of how social workers learn about gender identity development.

Social workers may encounter research studies online or in academic journals which incorporate contemporary models of gender identity development into their investigations. Such studies have resulted in attention grabbing findings about "cross-gender" behaviors, which may occur as early as age 2 for some transgender children. Furthermore, these so-called "cross-gender" behaviors may precede or be accompanied by the child's "consistent, persistent, and insistent" rejection of their sex assigned at birth and declaration of an "opposite gender identity." Using a **life course perspective**, social workers may be tasked with evaluating "early-onset" gender dysphoria (occurring in early childhood) or "late-onset" gender dysphoria (occurring in adolescence). Although this conventionally used model of identity development may be well suited to some transgender youth, emphases on binary gender identity, early occurrence (pre-adolescence) of cross-gender behavior, and presence of dysphoria can further marginalize and exclude many transgender and gender expansive youth. Social workers play a pivotal role in understanding, improving, adapting and developing models of identity development to be more inclusive of youth whose experiences have not been captured by these constructs. To prepare for this, social workers must familiarize themselves with the origin and implications of emerging models of gender identity development.

DOI: 10.4324/9780429297687-8

Introduction: What Is Gender? What Is Gender Identity? How Does It Develop?

Regardless of whether a person considers themselves to be cisgender or transgender, most people would agree that gender identity (or the absence of thereof) can play an enormously influential role in personal and social life. In order to best understand emerging models of gender identity development, social workers should first consider three key questions that play a focal role in such models: (1) What is gender? (2) What is gender identity? (3) How does gender identity develop?

Responses to these questions are likely to differ across cultures and professional fields. As an interdisciplinary profession, social workers are tasked with establishing common understandings of various models and the terms and concepts embedded within them. Social workers should also be able to assess and determine whether a particular model is appropriate for a given clinical practice setting, helpful for an individual client, or compatible with social work ethics and values.

The information in this chapter will equip social work practitioners with a foundational understanding of emerging models of identity development to use in social work practice with transgender and gender expansive youth. Within this chapter, past, present, and emerging models of gender identity development within and outside the field of social work are presented, explored, and evaluated for their utility in social work practice with transgender and gender expansive youth. As advocates for their clients with a commitment to social justice, social workers must be equipped with the skills to evaluate how particular models of gender identity development may affirm or disaffirm the diverse array of gender identities and expressions of T/GE youth. The overview section of this chapter encourages social workers to exercise critical discernment to assess how a particular model of gender identity development may be applied in a manner that is as gender-affirming as possible, and how to improve cultural literacy and humility when exploring gender development with transgender youth.

Following an overview of emerging models of identity development, best practices and helpful suggestions are offered for social workers who aim to integrate emerging models of gender identity development into their practice. Within this chapter, social workers will have the opportunity to analyze two case studies that demonstrate where and how models of gender identity development may arise in clinical settings. Following these case studies, reflective questions explore how social workers' integration of particular models of gender identity development can impact a youth's experience while receiving services. Finally, a selection of resources are presented to aid social workers in the process of deepening their understanding of the emerging models of gender identity used in service provision for transgender and gender expansive youth.

Addressing Key Questions:

1. What is gender?

    In social work, the idea of "gender" has been influenced by social theorists, activists, social service administrators, and the lived experiences of individuals from many walks of life. Although many people believe that gender identity is an innate, inherent, and immutable characteristic of a person's... personhood, it can sometimes be helpful to consider other conceptualizations of how gender is **manifested** and **embodied**. Philosophers such as Judith Butler have described gender as a social construct which individuals "**perform**" through social customs, behaviors, and mannerisms. For example, a person may perceive themselves to be "acting ladylike" in how they perform their gender, but how exactly does one decide whether this characteristic will become an intrinsic aspect of their self-concept? How do we, as individuals and societies, define what these characteristics look like for ourselves and others? Butler and other social theorists toiled over these and similar questions, making major contributions to the **discourse** on how **gender identity** is discussed today.

2. What is gender identity?

    In simple terms, gender identity is an aspect of an individual's self-concept that can play a role in how a person might express themselves physically, emotionality, aesthetically, or spiritually. Gender is typically associated with culturally influenced traits which are associated with physical sex. Gender identity presents a paradoxical challenge between the relationship between physical bodies, personal beliefs and experiences, and social customs. Identities are subjective, yet generalizable enough to be shared with others, to the point where gender roles are often described as though they are universal. The question of gender identity evokes many others: What does it *truly* mean to "identify as male," "female," "two-spirit," or "genderqueer"? With whom do we disclose these identities? How do we actualize them? If gender is socially constructed and subjective, are some people "actually" transgender while others are not? Is it possible to quantifiably or qualitatively measure how "male" or "female" somebody is? What about those who are agender or demi-gender? Can somebody "become transgender" through identity alone?

    While these types of questions are very interesting (and make excellent conversation starters) this chapter does not seek to definitively address any of them with universality or finality. Here, such questions are presented to help social workers consider their own perspectives and beliefs about gender and its origins. This is an important first step in thinking critically, thoughtfully, carefully, and empathetically about how social workers can engage with youth about their conceptualizations of gender.

3. How is gender identity developed?

    Although nearly all individuals develop a gender identity (with the exception of those who are **agender**), the exact mechanism by which gender development occurs is something of a mystery. Researchers who investigate this type of "**etiological**" question examine how gender identity develops at different **levels of analysis**. Researchers do this by studying the experiences of particular individuals, groups, or even entire cultures in order to draw conclusions that are **generalizable**. While some **empirical research** has resulted in findings that show some common themes of gender identity development across certain groups of research subjects, other approaches to understanding gender identity development purport findings that are highly personal, subjective, and context dependent. **Dialectically**, gender identity can be thought of as both rigid and flexible, present and absent, personal and interpersonal, static and dynamic, immutable and situational, subjective and objective, boring and interesting, ad infinitum. Social workers may benefit from integrating this dialectic understanding of gender identity into their own emerging concepts of gender identity development, thinking of gender identity as both "developed" and "developing" through the **life course**.

Gender as a Construct: Identity vs. Status

Many current models of gender identity development feature a **taxonomical** concept of gender. A taxonomy is a system of classification that is based on sorting individuals into particular groups based on characteristics they either have or do not have. Thus, many current models of gender identity development actually exist with the purpose of determining gender "status," not identity. Gender "status" is typically relevant in contexts where medical, legal, educational, or administrative information is being collected about an individual. This inquiry is usually presented as a simple checkbox inquiring as to whether an individual is transgender or not, for example, on a medical form in a doctor's office or as a question in a "back to school" survey to students in a classroom. Gender status is used to denote whether an individual is cisgender or transgender. Although **transgender** is an umbrella term which encompasses many different gender identities, "transgender" is not typically considered to be its own discrete gender identity. Examples of **gender identities** may include male, female, genderqueer, nonbinary, two-spirit, and many others.

All Models Are Wrong, but Some Are Helpful

Understanding Models of Identity Development in Social Work Practice

The aphorism "all models are wrong, but some are helpful" can be a helpful way for social workers to frame models of gender identity development which seem to contradict or supersede each other. In social work research, models are frequently used to "map" dynamic concepts, including "**bio-psycho-social**" models, a "**person in environment**" perspective, or a "**socio-ecological**" framework. These types of **multidimensional models** are very helpful for considering how factors such as social relationships and environments impact how an individual constructs and conveys their gender identity. Many models of gender identity incorporate some of these same types of methodologies that social workers are likely already familiar with.

One particular area of importance in emerging models of gender identity development is the etiological role of **social learning**. Judith Butler described the "learned" aspects of gender identity and performance as a process of "**citationality**," which refers to the process of informing our own gender identity by mentally "citing" the actions of others as we develop our own schematic understanding of gender. It is important to note that researchers who study transgender children and youth currently seeking to explain gender identity development have different motivations for doing so, which will be discussed later on in this chapter.

Many models of transgender identity and the development thereof have focused on capturing the differences between processes of gender identity development between cisgender and transgender people. In a manner reminiscent of Cartesian Dualism's "mind-body problem," early models of gender identity highlighted the **incongruence** between the "**physical sex**" (or "**assigned sex at birth**") and **gender identity** of transgender people. The term for the distress a transgender individual may experience as a result of this so-called incongruence is typically referred to as **gender dysphoria**.

Gender identity development is a phrase used to describe any individual's process of developing their gender identity through the construction of ideas and beliefs about one's own relationship to the construct of gender. **Gender transition** (sometimes written as simply **"transition" i.e., "my transition"**) typically refers to a transgender individual's experience of changes to gender expression or how they embody the particular characteristics of a **gender role**. **Transitioning** may include a name change, using different pronouns, dressing or emoting differently, or medical treatment such as hormone replacement therapy, surgeries, etc. It is important to remember that while **all people develop a gender identity**, only some people consider themselves to have "**transitioned**" with respect to their gender role, identity, or expression. In fact, many transgender people who desire to "transition" are unable to do so due to inadequate access to resources or supportive environments in which to do so, nor do all transgender people desire to undergo some form of gender "transition."

Both cisgender and transgender people undergo "transitions" to new gender roles throughout the lifespan, especially during late childhood, adolescence, and early adulthood. Consider the case of a teenage parent who was assigned female at birth "transitioning" to a new gender-associated role as a "mother." Because the role of mother is "**congruent**" with a typical female gender role, this would not be considered a "gender transition." To take this example a step further, let's imagine this teenage parent to be a transgender male who uses he/him pronouns. This youth may identify with a gendered parental role as a "father" or "mother," or simply as a "parent," regardless of his gender identity, assigned sex at birth, or physical anatomy he has. If this youth previously wore typically "masculine" clothing in the style of other males in his community and began wearing "feminine" or "maternity" clothing during his pregnancy, he may or may not consider this change in appearance to be a form of **"gender transition,"** even if it results in an appearance that others may consider to be "congruent" with his assigned sex at birth for the duration of his pregnancy. This example of a "gender transition" demonstrates how "gender transition" is not always intended to be an aspect of **self-actualization**, to be **permanent**, or to establish "congruence" between **societal expectations** of gender identity and gender expression.

If a transgender youth expresses themselves as a gender or sex other than that which was assigned at birth, a parent or caregiver may consider themselves to be assisting the child to "transition." In the case of transgender youth whose transitions are formally supported by parents or other care providers, special care should be taken to prioritize autonomy, authentic self-expression, and self-actualization. This is especially relevant for social workers who may need to advocate on behalf of a youth's individual needs and desires in settings where the other **stakeholders** in the youth's life are imposing *their own* concepts of "congruence" between the youth's identity and outward expression.

Present Models of Gender Identity Development

Theoretical Perspectives: How Do We Imagine Gender?

How social workers "imagine" gender plays a large role in the types of models we are drawn to. Present models of gender identity development tend to focus on three primary perspectives of gender identity. Some perspectives on gender identity are based on a **binary** model of gender identity, the most common of which features a model where an individual is either male or female. Another application of a binary model of gender identity is one in which an individual is either transgender or not transgender. Additionally, a binary model of gender may be one that categorizes individuals between those who identify as experiencing gender, and those who do not, who tend to refer to themselves as "agender," and sometimes identify with the transgender/gender minority community. Those who reject the idea of binary gender may refer to themselves as **non-binary** or **enby** (pronounced like "nb" as in, non-binary).

Another conceptual model of gender is that of gender as a spectrum. A **gender spectrum** typically features an array of traits such as "masculine," "feminine," "both," or "neither." These models are sometimes used to capture **demi-gender** identities. Those with demi-gender identities tend to describe their gender in terms of the degree or magnitude to which they identify with a certain gender identity or gendered trait, as if to measure it using a spectrum.

Other models of gender aim to take a more inclusive and affirming approach to gender, which is particularly important for youth who may be questioning or exploring their gender identity. Models such as these tend to consider the unique and dynamic aspects of gender (Turban & Keuroghlian, 2018) and gender identity development. These models are sometimes referred to as **gender inclusive, gender expansive, gender creative,** or **gender diverse**.

Visual Models: Mapping Constructs of Gender

The Genderbread Person V 4.0 is a commonly referenced visual model developed by Sam Killerman, a graphic artist who has described himself as "straight" and "cisgender." Killerman has spoken about the importance of ally ship and education on issues related to gender and sexuality, particularly related to his own experiences with bullying based on his perceived identities. Note the use of the term "anatomic sex" and the binary spectrum of "male-ness" vs. "female-ness" next to the transgender symbol, as well as the category "sex assigned at birth," with a "male," "female," and "intersex" category (see Figure 8.1).

The Gender Unicorn is a widely used infographic type figure that demonstrates similar aspects of gender identity, expression, sex assigned at birth, and attraction. This graphic was produced by the transgender youth-led organization, Trans Student Educational Resources (TSER). Note the inclusion of an "other" category for gender, and the integration of age-related identity categories in the gender identity graphic for "Male/man/boy." The "sex assigned at birth" category uses the symbol of a chromosome rather than the transgender symbol, and specifies an "other/intersex" category, as intersex babies are typically assigned either a male or female sex at birth, unless parents specifically request a designation of "X" or "other" in a state where the designation is legally permitted (see Figure 8.2).

Gender Affirming vs. Disaffirming Models

Broadly speaking, models of gender identity development can be seen as originating from two primary bases: Models which are gender-affirming, and models which are disaffirming. **Gender-affirming** models of identity development prioritize the validation of a client's lived experiences. Gender-affirming models of gender identity development may be integrated into varying approaches to clinical practice that are intended to support and

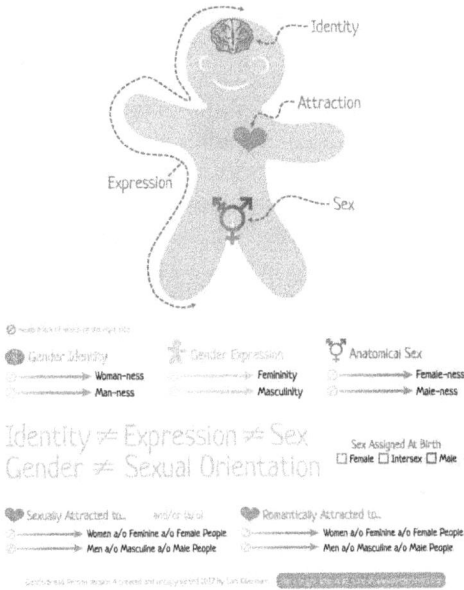

Figure 8.1 The Genderbread Person.

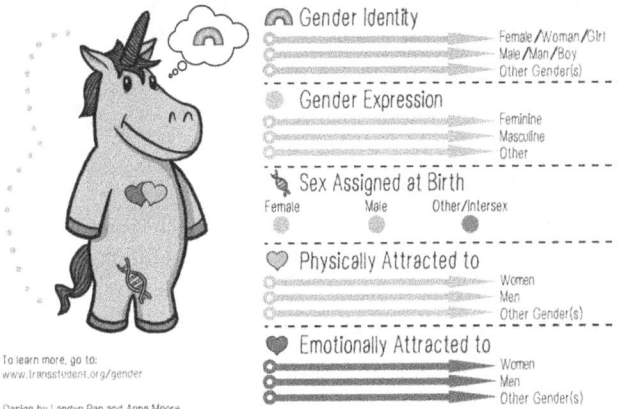

Figure 8.2 The Gender Unicorn.

nurture the gender identity development of both cisgender and transgender individuals. While "affirming" models of gender identity development tend to purport themselves as such in order to attract clients seeking this type of service, it is less likely to encounter a practice setting which readily identifies itself as "disaffirming" of transgender or gender expansive identity development. Some clinical practice settings following "disaffirming" models may be doing so in ways that are intended to go "under the radar," such as clinics which offer "conversion therapy." However, some clinics who intend to support and affirm transgender clients may be unintentionally using disaffirming models of gender identity development. This is often true in cases of **gatekeeping**, a term which refers to barriers created by healthcare providers which inhibit access to gender-affirming healthcare (Ashley, 2019a). Gatekeeping can be observed in models such as **"the live in your own skin"** (Zucker & Bradley, 1995) and **"watchful waiting"** (Cohen-Kettenis & Pfäfflin, 2003) approaches to gender-related care for transgender youth. The live in your own skin model is a disaffirming model of gender identity development which aims to coerce children into identifying with the assigned gender role that typically corresponds with their assigned sex at birth. The watchful waiting model is a disaffirming model which takes its name from the field of oncology, in which a precancerous pathology is monitored and assessed to determine whether it warrants interventive care. Under the "watchful waiting" model, transgender status and gender expansiveness are addressed as pathological conditions for which gender related healthcare are a "last resort" treatment option.

Disaffirming models of gender identity have inspired the **"gender-critical" movement**, which has argued for increased gatekeeping to gender affirming care, particularly for transgender youth. This movement was spurred by a dubiously designed research study which manipulated ecological systems theory to offer an etiological explanation for adolescent transgender identity development, dubbed **"rapid onset gender dysphoria."**

Models of Gender Identity Development Across Practice Settings

It is difficult to separate present and historical models of transgender identity development from the systems where they are most typically encountered. Because social work occurs across social service systems, including medical settings (in-patient and out-patient), in community-based organizations, and across **micro-**, **mezzo-**, and **macro-**level practice settings, it is important to consider the purpose that a particular model serves in a given setting. Key questions to consider when assessing a particular model in a practice setting include:

• Who is the intended audience of this model? Will it be used as a teaching tool for clients, or for other practitioners?

- Does this model look like it was designed with youth in mind? If not, are there ways that it could be adapted to be more helpful for a youth audience? Weigh strengths and challenges of adapting a model, or asking for clients' and stakeholder impressions of the model's validity or applicability in a particular setting or circumstance.

Profession-Based Perspectives

Social work is an interdisciplinary field, and social workers may expect to encounter differing models and perspectives of gender identity development. Features of these different models may serve distinct purposes unique to the fields in which they are used, but these differences are not always obvious or explicitly stated. Social workers can increase their awareness of how particular models of identity development are being used in their practices by examining keywords in training materials, presentations, internal documents, or policies that define "Standards of Care," "Best Practices," or "Community Agreements" used in a particular practice setting.

Social workers working in clinical settings will likely be most familiar with **psychological models** of gender identity. Psychological models of gender identity tend to revolve around the assessment, diagnosis, and treatment of gender dysphoria. Until 2013, the Diagnostic and Statistical Manual of Mental Disorders (DSM) classified transgender status with a diagnosis of "Gender Identity Disorder." This diagnosis was replaced by the diagnostic label of "gender dysphoria" in the DSM-V, which is used to indicate a "clinically significant distress" due to the incongruence between one's sex and one's gender. However, this diagnostic label is frequently used as a method for indicating transgender status in Electronic Health Record (EHR) systems, and does not necessarily accurately reflect a transgender person's subjective experience of their gender identity (which may not involve gender dysphoria at all).

Psychological models of gender identity also tend to discuss **processes** or **pathways** of Gender Identity Development, as well as concepts of **latency** and **deferral**. Latency is a term which can be used in reference to an identity that is presently unknown or has not yet developed, whereas deferral may be described as a period where gender identity is known, but not yet disclosed, and may not be considered final or permanent. Psychological models of gender identity development may also feature concepts such as **bracketing** or **self-actualization**. **Bracketing** is a term used to describe the psychological segmentation of events within an individual's **life course**. In regards to gender identity development, this may look like a period of self-exploration and gender identity development which would result in an experience of self-actualization and self-discovery of one's gender identity.

Other models of gender identity development that social workers may encounter are **sociological models** and **medical models**. **Sociological models** such as those described earlier in this chapter explore gender identity development and gender performativity as social phenomena, and are particularly helpful for describing distinctions between facets of gender as a social construct. **Medical models** of gender identity development tend to focus on **biological** aspects of the relationship between gender and sex. These models may include information about chromosomes, hormone exposure in utero, "Disorders of Sexual Development" (DSDs) and certain intersex conditions, such as Partial Androgen Insensitivity Syndrome (PAIS).

Emerging Models of Gender Identity

Timelines and Transactional Pathways: How and When Does Gender Identity Develop?

Historical perspective on gender identity has broken gender identity development into two groups: those who are cisgender, and those who are transgender. Historically, cisgender individuals' gender identity development has tended to be seen as a "natural" part of early childhood development, occurring between ages 2 and 3 (Kohlberg, 1966). A difference between models of cisgender and transgender identity development is that the **onset** of transgender identity has typically been associated with adolescence, the developmental period when most youth begin puberty, as well as many other aspects of social, emotional, and cognitive development (Kar, Choudhury, & Singh, 2015).

Dysphoria, De-Pathologization, and "Trans-Medicalists"

Within the transgender community, individuals may have varying opinions about the **medicalization** or **pathologization** of transgender identity or gender dysphoria. **Trans-medicalists** (sometimes referred to as "truscum") tend to believe that gender dysphoria is a requisite aspect of transgender identity development. Those who call for **de-pathologization** of transgender identity tend to believe that medical models that focus on the presence and treatment of dysphoria further marginalize nonbinary and gender expansive individuals who may or may not experience gender dysphoria (Vincent, 2018).

Moving the Conversation Forward

As a profession, social work's ethical values of social justice and anti-oppressive practices set it apart from other fields. For this reason (and many others) social workers can (and should) demonstrate their commitment to advancing the ways we consider, discuss, and incorporate models of gender identity development into our practices.

Suggested Best Practices for Affirming Approaches to Gender Identity Development

A social worker's efforts toward understanding, evaluating, and applying emerging models of gender identity development to their own practices neatly integrates many ethical principles of the social work profession. Of these values, two are of particular significance as they pertain to emerging models of gender identity development, **respecting a clients' right to self-determination**, and **continuing education** in the area of emerging (and affirming) models of identity development.

Self Determination

Create Opportunities for ALL Youth to Explore and Develop Their Gender Identity

Consider whether gender identity is related to a client's primary treatment goal.

- Ask permission to use a client's own self-expressive language regarding their gender

  - Example: "I heard you say that your experience of 'figuring out your gender' felt like a 'gender tornado.' Is it okay with you if I refer to that process as a 'gender tornado'?"
  - This type of reflective statement can help a client set their own boundaries about what self-expressive language is okay for other people to use when referencing their experiences.

Use a Youth's Chosen Language and Conceptualization of Their Own Gender Identity Development

- If a client is struggling to put words to their experience, consider encouraging alternate forms of communication, such as drawing, dance, singing/vocalizing, or other non-verbal forms of communication.

There Is No "One Size Fits All"

Consider whether your existing model of gender identity development is helpful for your client. If your personal conceptualization of gender identity is not a good fit for your client, or if you recognize current limitations in your level of understanding of a particular model of gender identity, be open and honest with your client. While some models of gender are intended to be affirming (or even disaffirming), the most critical aspect in goodness of fit of a particular model of gender identity is whether it is helpful for a particular client.

For example, experiences of self-actualization may look and feel very differently from one youth the next. Sometimes experiences of self-actualization are described in terms of living or expressing one's "true gender" or living as one's "authentic self." Terms such as these can reflect **binarist attitudes** toward gender identity development, and can imply that an individual did not feel authentic or truly "themselves" prior to developing their present gender identity.

Gender Identity Development as an Ongoing Process (or Not!)

Rather than assuming that a client will develop or express a transgender identity at a particular point in time, remember that for many individuals, gender identity development is a lifelong process. This can be just as true for clients who do not necessarily identify themselves as transgender or gender expansive. Alternatively, some transgender youth who "transition" in early childhood and are raised as their chosen gender may not identify with dominant narratives about "coming out" or be interested in thinking critically about their gender identity. In each case, it is important for social workers to develop a clear understanding of the perspective of the individual they are serving in order to provide equitable and responsive opportunities for self-discovery with respect to gender identity development.

Continuing Education

Consider the Source: Who Made This? Why?

When examining a model of gender identity development, consider the source. If a model is presented without information about the authors or researchers who constructed it, consider doing further research to gather more information to determine the appropriateness of this model for your own purposes as a social worker.

Consistently Reconsider Your Conceptualizations

Continuing education to deepen your knowledge and broaden your exposure to emerging models and conceptual frameworks of gender identity is an ongoing process. Remember to mindfully integrate new information and critically assess the relative helpfulness of a particular model or theoretical approach for each individual client based on their own unique beliefs and circumstances.

Case Studies

Case Study 1   Chloe, Alex, and Their Dads

Imagine that you are a social worker working in a private practice setting. Recently, you were contacted by Christopher and Gerard, a married couple whom you worked with several years ago. Previously, you worked with Christopher and Gerard as they navigated the process of adopting their two children. Since then, Christopher and Gerard have reached out over the years for therapeutic support regarding various life stressors, including occasional bouts of extreme marital conflict. You have noticed that Gerard, a stay-at-home parent, tends to reach out for support more readily than Christopher, who has appeared somewhat disinterested in your attempts to build clinical rapport. Their children, Chloe and Alex, both attend a middle school close to the family's home. Chloe, who is in 9th grade, is a 14-year-old transgender girl. Supported by both parents, Chloe "transitioned" at age 4 after expressing that she "just knows she's a girl." Although Chloe began taking Lupron (a hormone blocker) at age 11, she recently began taking estrogen to, in her words: "live as her true self." Alex, who is 12 years old and in 7th grade, recently transferred from a K–8 school across the district after being bullied for having gay parents. Shortly after changing schools, Alex began seeing a school-based mental health counselor. One day after school, Alex told their parents that they would like to be referred to with "they/them" pronouns.

Christopher and Gerard have reached out to you for support mediating some of their recent conflicts at home. They give you several examples of recent disputes within the family, including a fight between Chloe and Alex which erupted after Alex borrowed Chloe's track team jacket without asking. Christopher reports that during this argument, Chloe began yelling "at the top of her lungs," called Alex a "transtrender," then collapsed to the ground, sobbing. Over the phone, Christopher described Chloe as "emotional and PMS-y since she started taking those pills." Gerard insists that he "tries to stay out of it," but that "Alex needs to stop picking fights." A few days ago, Christopher and Gerard received a call from the vice-principal of the middle school saying that a parent needed to pick Chloe up from the office because she was unwilling to attend class. On the drive home from the school, Chloe begins to cry, saying "I can't go back there! Now that Alex thinks it's cool to be trans, people will think I'm like that too. I'll never get to just live my life." Today, in a one-on-one appointment with Christopher and Gerard, both parents mention that Chloe and Alex used to attend a support group for transgender/gender expansive kids and their siblings, but they had recently stopped attending after Chloe "finished her transition." Christopher and Gerard tell you they aren't sure how to approach the conflict between the siblings because they "understand why Chloe is upset" and although they want their children to be able to "express themselves freely," they don't want to "have to schedule a whole new set of doctor's appointments for Alex."

Reflection Questions:

1. What are your initial thoughts about this scenario? What are your initial feelings about this scenario? Why would this type of self-reflection be important when preparing to work with this family?
2. Which types of natural supports/resources might be helpful for this family with respect to the issues they have identified? Which strengths and vulnerabilities do you think are most relevant to your work with this family?
3. Assuming the entire family system is your client, what are the key issues related to gender identity development you would want to discuss? Are there any key areas where you think more information would be helpful? How might this approach look different for each family member?
4. How do you think social positionality and/or systems of privilege and oppression could be affecting the attitudes, behaviors, or beliefs of different family members? How do these relate to conceptualizations of gender identity development?
5. To assess how various models of gender identity development appear in the case of Chloe, Alex, and their dads, assume that Christopher and Gerard consider themselves to be "supportive of transgender people," but are not very familiar with emerging models of gender identity development. How might you encourage Christopher and Gerard to broaden their understanding of gender identity development using a gender-affirming and de-pathologizing approach?

Case Study 2   Hunter and Their Father

As the social worker for a juvenile court system in a rural county, your role involves coordinating case management and clinical services for juvenile justice system-involved youths and their families. Earlier in the month, you received case information for Hunter, a 12-year-old child who was recently released from the regional juvenile correctional facility. Hunter entered the juvenile justice system after being charged with assaulting another child in a fight at school. Hunter is an only child and is currently living with their father Bill. As a condition of Hunter's probation, Hunter and Bill are required to regularly check in with a juvenile probation counselor. All members of Hunter's case management team have releases of information and regularly communicate with each other. Hunter has told Bill that it is "an invasion of privacy" to talk about them "behind their back," and "doesn't want to get labeled by anyone."

A few days ago, you received a call from an advocate on Hunter's educational support team who is concerned about Hunter being mistreated for being "a girl in a boy's body" tells you about a recent meeting in which Bill met with Hunter's juvenile probation counselor and school principal to discuss Hunter's return to school. During the meeting, Bill stated that he and Hunter argue frequently at home, saying, "I don't know what's wrong with the kid." During the meeting, Bill mentioned that he wasn't sure why "Hunter hasn't grown out of the costume stuff... even after living with tough guys." The principal shared that Hunter had disclosed experiences of being harassed at school for wearing dresses and wigs. In addition to this, the principal reported that Hunter had gotten in trouble for "disrupting class" after few students became upset with Hunter for "lying" after Hunter described themselves as "sometimes a boy, sometimes a girl." The advocate tells you that at the end of the meeting, Hunter's probation counselor stated that if family therapy was not enough to adequately address "Hunter's behavioral problems at home and at school," Hunter may need "residential mental health treatment."

The educational advocate tells you that they have always known Hunter to be a very sweet child, but experiences bursts of anger that are triggered when "people don't know how to respond to him, if they try to put him in one box or the other, he gets too upset." You call the juvenile probation counselor to review the referral for in-home therapy, assess risks and protective factors in the case, and discuss safety concerns prior to meeting with Hunter and Bill. During your call, the juvenile probation counselor states, "I can't figure out why this kid gets so angry at others when he's the one dressing like an outcast."

Reflection Questions:

1. If you were referring Hunter and Bill to a family therapist, how might you use models and perspectives on gender identity development to assess whether a particular therapist might be a good fit for Hunter? What types of questions would you ask? What other information might be helpful to you?
2. Imagine that you have called Bill to schedule an intake appointment. During the call, Bill tells you he believes family therapy is unnecessary because "Hunter's issues are his sh*t to work on."

How might Bill's comment inform your approach toward promoting a gender-affirming environment for Hunter?

3. How would you explain the relationship between gender expression and gender identity to other members of Hunter's case management team?

4. What questions would you ask Hunter to better support them? What are some natural supports in the community that you would recommend to this family?

5. What information or resources might you share with Bill to help him understand and support Hunter's experience? Reflect on how you might share information about models of gender identity development.

References

American Psychiatric Association. (2013). *Diagnostic and statistical manual of mental disorders* (5th ed.). Washington, DC: Publisher.

Ashley, F. (2019a). Gatekeeping hormone replacement therapy for transgender patients is dehumanizing. *Journal of Medical Ethics, 45*(7), 480–482.

Ashley, F. (2019b). Thinking an ethics of gender exploration: Against delaying transition for transgender and gender creative youth. *Clinical Child Psychology and Psychiatry, 24*(2), 223–236. doi:10.1177/1359104519836462

Cohen-Kettenis P. T., & Pfäfflin F. (2003). *Transgenderism and intersexuality in childhood and adolescence.* Thousand Oaks, CA: Sage Publications.

Ho, F., & Mussap, A. J. (2019). The gender identity scale: Adapting the gender unicorn to measure gender identity. *Psychology of Sexual Orientation and Gender Diversity, 6*(2), 217–231. doi:10.1037/sgd0000322

Kar, S. K., Choudhury, A., & Singh, A. P. (2015). Understanding normal development of adolescent sexuality: A bumpy ride. *Journal of Human Reproductive Sciences, 8*(2), 70–74. doi:10.4103/0974-1208.158594

Katz-Wise, S. L., Budge, S. L., Fugate, E., Flanagan, K., Touloumtzis, C., Rood, B., ... Leibowitz, S. (2017). Transactional pathways of transgender identity development in transgender and gender nonconforming youth and caregivers from the trans youth family study. *The International Journal of Transgenderism, 18*(3), 243–263. doi:10.1080/15532739.2017.1304312

Kennedy, N. (2020). Deferral: The sociology of young trans people's epiphanies and coming out. *Journal of LGBT Youth.* doi:10.1080/19361653.2020.1816244

Keo-Meier, C., & Ehrensaft, D. (2018). Introduction to the gender affirmative model. In C. Keo-Meier & D. Ehrensaft (Eds.), *Perspectives on sexual orientation and diversity. The gender affirmative model: An interdisciplinary approach to supporting transgender and gender expansive children* (pp. 3–19). Washington, D.C.: American Psychological Association. doi:10.1037/0000095-001

Kohlberg L. (1966). A cognitive-developmental analysis of children's sex-role concepts and attitudes. In E. E. Maccoby (Ed.), *The development of sex differences* (pp. 82–173). Stanford, CA: Stanford University Press.

National Center on Parent Family and Community Engagement. (n.d.). Healthy gender development and young children a guide for early childhood programs and professionals. Retrieved from https://eclkc.ohs.acf.hhs.gov/publication/healthy-gender-development-young-children

Pan, L., & Erlick, E. (2017). *The gender unicorn – Trans student educational resources.* Retrieved from http://www.transstudent.org/gender

Schimmel-Bristow, A., Haley, S. G., Crouch, J. M., Evans, Y. N., Ahrens, K. R., McCarty, C. A., & Inwards-Breland, D. J. (2018). Youth and caregiver experiences of gender identity transition: A qualitative study. *Psychology of Sexual Orientation and Gender Diversity, 5*(2), 273–281. doi:https://doi.org/10.1037/sgd0000269

Turban, J. L., & Keuroghlian, A. S. (2018). Dynamic gender presentations: Understanding transition and 'de-transition' among transgender youth. *Journal of the American Academy of Child & Adolescent Psychiatry, 57,* 451–453. doi:10.1016/j.jaac.2018.03.016

Vincent, B. (2018). *Transgender health: A practitioner's guide to binary and non-binary trans patient care* (pp. 126–127). London: Jessica Kingsley Publishers. ISBN 978-1785922015

West, C., & Zimmerman, D. (1987). Doing gender. *Gender & Society, 1*(2), 125–151. doi:10.1177/0891243287001002002

Zucker K., & Bradley S. (1995). *Gender identity disorder and psychosexual problems in children and adolescents.* New York, NY: The Guilford Press.

9 When There Was No Space for Us, We Made a Space: The House and Ballroom Community

A Conversation with Twiggy Pucci Garçon

Twiggy Pucci Garçon and Jama Shelton

Introduction

Mother, organizer, twin, leader, sibling, healer, sister, designer, father, activist, parent, artist, peer … these are just some of the roles an individual may fulfill as a member of the house and ballroom community. For many trans and gender expansive (TGE) youth, particularly Black and Latinx TGE youth, the house and ballroom community provides support, affirmation, and celebration in a world that too often enacts violence upon TGE people of color. While formal systems of care struggle to figure out how to best support TGE young people, the house and ballroom community has nurtured TGE young people of color for decades. Any consideration of resilience and resistance, of protective factors and leadership development, among TGE youth of color should look to the house and ballroom community. In the following conversation, Twiggy shares the history and structure of the community, as well as her own personal journey within the community.

The House and Ballroom Community

Twiggy: The house and ballroom community is an autonomously created and organized community that was created in Harlem in the 1920s and 1930s during the Harlem Renaissance. It was originally known as the Harlem Drag Ball scene and it was created in resistance to homophobia and transphobia from the Black church. Many of the queers of the time would create these spaces called drag balls to, first and foremost, create a safe space where they could exist as their true selves and to express themselves completely and wholly. And so for some folks that might be more feminine than they could be in the day-to-day lives. For some folks, it would be at the time called drag and for other folks because they didn't have language such as trans and non-binary but particularly trans folks that, you know, would have liked to have actualized living their lives as their true selves all

DOI: 10.4324/9780429297687-9

the time and not having to go back out of drags. So do you get in and out of drag, but like, it provided a place where they could live out their true selves completely all the time. And so the drag balls were organized by groups of people that consider themselves families. And they considered themselves families because most of them had been rejected or kicked out by their own families. And so, there were mothers or fathers who were the leaders of these families, and the members of the families were the kids just like in any other family. Now we have the language of chosen family.

Eventually we find ourselves in the late 60s, needless to say it was in the middle of a huge moment in the civil rights movement, but it was also a huge moment in the queer liberation movement. We know about Stonewall, but just around the same time as Stonewall there was a queen named Crystal LaBeija who thought that she lost this particular drag pageant or drag ball because of racism and colorism. And over the course of the time from the '20s to '30s, like many other things, the ballroom scene became colonized by white people. So many of the judges were these huge, sort of rich celebrities and artists from high culture and from downtown who would come up and judge the balls in Harlem. Andy Warhol for example, is one of the people who would come and judge the balls. Anyway Crystal storms off, goes off, reads them to filth. You can see all of this on a documentary called "The Queen." Eventually her family became the first house. And so Crystal sort of birthed the transition from drag ball to house ball.

Crystal LeBeija Bay pretty much birthed the first of these families, which was the House of LaBeija. They were named houses because they took on a family structure. So again, the parents were the mothers and the fathers. But also, at the time, many of the members sort of stay together in an actual physical house. The third reason for houses is that many of them, not all, but many of them were named after fashion houses. I think all of the original houses were like family names. I don't think any of them were named after fashion lines until later, like mid to late '70s.

Through the '60s and '70s, the first five houses, which are all created by trans women – we call them the terrible five, but it's just because they were so stern and they read and were shady. **I think it's important to note that transwomen created the scene in this format and were the leaders of it until patriarchy had its way** and what we call butch queens started to take over in the '80s and '90s.

These houses were, and still are, chosen families that LGBTQ young people form – actually LGBTQ people of all ages, because you've come into this scene and then to come into this community at whatever point in your life – it is a sense of family assistance and support. It is not "in a sense" it *is* family and it *is* support. And years down the line we find ourselves, at least in the housing space where you have these things called host homes, and that we've been doing in the ballroom scene for years. And through our own ways, but without the means of support of any sort of stipend or grant or federal funding that comes from the state. **It's just really Black and Brown LGBTQ people making a way out of no way and learning to survive and learning to create our own support mechanisms, um, and learning how to, um, really just be**.

The Balls

Twiggy: About the balls – while they are competitions, they are also a place where anyone who is participating in them is exploring their gender expression, exploring their sexual identity in some categories. They're exploring their, um, you know, what is comfortable on the spectrum of gender performance, if you will. I'll use one specific category as an example. Realness, which is this category, this umbrella of term or word or category. That means how much you pass, how well you pass. And so if you're a Butch queen and you walk a type of realness, it means how much you pass as heterosexual. If you're a trans woman it's how much you pass as a cis woman. If you're a drag queen it's how much you pass as a cis woman. And the realness categories are broken into sub categories, which are sort of themes if you will. And I think, you know, on one hand I considered this category a bit problematic in many ways, then and now, but on one hand, this was a way for people to practice their passibility, such that they could be safe in the streets on a day-to-day basis. Balls were always held pretty much overnight. So that folks wouldn't get bashed or beat or killed, getting to and from the balls. And so, the realness provided a way for folks to practice their passibility in many ways. So it was a bit of a safe way to practice how to be safe in the world. On the flip side of that, I would say to judge a person and give them a trophy or cash or whatever it may be based on that passibility it's problematic for all sorts of reasons, right? And so it's a highly contested category – of why it existed then and why it still exists now.

How Did You Find Your Way to the Ballroom Scene?

Twiggy: I came to the ballroom 16 years ago in 2004. I was in high school. It was just after I had been asked to leave my church because of my sexuality and femininity. Basically they gave me an ultimatum that I butch it up and sing differently and act differently or, that I had to leave. And so I left and that was literally maybe two months or three months before I walked my first ball. And, at the time I danced at a dance studio and one of the only openly gay – I wasn't out yet – one of the only openly gay people in my high school also danced in that dance studio. Where I'm from, they have these competitive modeling competitions or model troupes, which are similar to balls, but actually they're…they're their own scene. Let's just say that. And so I had, you know, competed in those and walked in those since I was a child. But there's all sorts of people that walk those. And they're not necessarily, at least where I'm from, about gender or sexuality. In fact, a lot of them were tied to HBCU fashion shows and the groups of people who put on those fashion shows. The person who brought me into ballroom was Shisha. He would vogue in between technique classes. So we'd do ballet and modern, and then vogue. And I had no idea what voguing was, but because he had been dancing at the studio for so long, everyone else did. And so eventually we became friends and he said – I know you walk at the fashion shows and the model troops, you should just walk the ball. Little did I know the walk was, I mean, the style of form was totally different. I mean, it had similarities, but was totally different. That October I walked my first ball and, there was a format to balls, which I could explain, but basically, I got disqualified. Because of the style that I was walking was vastly different and not what it was supposed to be for the category. Anyway, two months later I joined the house. I came back, I walked, I won, and I've been walking ever since.

The Structure of Balls

Twiggy: These days, there's a person like a promoter, someone who's like really known and respected in the scene who can throw a ball, what we call it, throw a ball, or produce one of the balls. Or a whole house can throw a ball as a family. Typically that's to celebrate the house's anniversary or something like that. They come up with a theme for the entire event. And then they write categories that ask for a specific look for each competitor. And so, for example, I walk runway and let's say the ball's theme is a Christmas ball. So they might tell me to bring it like Santa. And so you get the information about the ball to start preparing your look. When you get to the ball and they get to your category, each competitor has to be scored by a panel of judges. These judges are esteemed people in ballroom, who've been walking for a while. They're either house parents or they're have a certain status in ballroom. So you come out, the judges read the category, or what look you're supposed to bring. And they score you on two things. Did you bring that look and are you executing whatever the category is? And the scoring has changed over the years, but pretty much now it's all or nothing.

The people who are not disqualified after they get through all of the scoring battle against each other two at a time, usually process of elimination until one person wins.

The Family Structure of Houses

Twiggy: So a bit about the family structure of a house, and how they are usually created. They're created by folks who are from the scene. Every house is structured differently. However, every house has the same sort of skeleton. And so there's founders that create the house. They either are the parents of the house, or they keep a position as founder in the same way a company would, right? So you can be the founder of X, Y, Z company, but you don't have to be the CEO, that's up to you. So similarly to that, people create houses and either they decide to be the overall parents, the overall mother and father, or they assign people to be overall mother and father. That means that you are underneath the founder, but you oversee the entire house. You are like the final decision makers other than the founders of the house. From that point, most houses have a structure where they have chapters based on location. And so I'll use my house, the House of Garçon, as an example. We have founders that are not the overall parents. And then we have chapters based on regions. So we have a New York City chapter, an Atlanta chapter, a Midwest chapter. And we even have internationals. And each of those has its own set of parents that oversee that area and lead the strategy and who's competing in that area. All of the members are the house kids, unless they hold a position. The house parents are responsible for everything from getting their kids ready to walk the ball, to making sure that their kids, you know, are housed and getting whatever medical attention they need or just mentally and emotionally supported or pushing them towards professional goals. And so, the parents are parents just like biological or adoptive parents or surrogate parents would be. and I think that's what draws so many people to ballroom.

Jama: When I'm thinking about exploring gender identity and expression – back in my day, there was no place to do that at all. And so it's striking to me that there exists this place where people could do that and that it was started decades ago. I'm wondering what do think made that possible? What made it possible that this space existed for people in what seems like a very nonjudgmental way to be affirmed and to be who they are. What makes it possible that that exists and how does it, because it's such a unique thing? Are there other places like that now?

Twiggy: That space exists for two reasons that, when I think about it, feel opposite, but are also very connected. It's like, because people need to survive and people need to feel loved, right? And so, **if you come from a family, whether biological or not, it's irrelevant, that doesn't accept you and you're seeking and searching for this acceptance, for this love, for this affirmation, and you don't get it, you make a whole new way of being. Like that's how ballroom was born.** You make a whole new way of being and a whole new way of existing in the world to fill that gap within yourself and for others. And so ballroom was born out of sort of this, this necessity to be celebrated and affirmed and to have a space to be oneself. And so it has perpetuated and replicated that in all of its iterations, from drag balls, all the way down to what's the newest version, which is the Kiki scene. And so it innately is that space. So that's the survival piece for me. The second piece around wanting to be loved is, is that, you know – I'll use myself as an example – I was ridiculed as long as I can remember for my femininity. Like, I mean all the way back to childhood. And when I came to ballroom, it was one of the first places that I saw femininity be celebrated, no matter who you are. Ballroom was a place for me – a person who was always told so much so that I was kicked out of my church for my femininity – that I could put on a heel and whatever and be comfortable and walking in category called runway. That is about me being feminine and literally bringing the room into an uproar. **It's that level of affirmation and celebration**, about what for some may be a performance and for others may be just me showing who I am, you know what I mean? And so I think it was created out of necessity, like that space was created out of a necessity and it has grown and it has survived all of this time and replicated itself and evolved, and has grown into this place where the exploration and discovery and celebration and affirmation of one's gender of one's sexuality and one's way of showing up outside to other people can happen.

Jama: I'm thinking of the celebratory nature of it and that in a lot of social work and social services, I think the language is a lot of times around like being inclusive and affirming and that's fine. I mean, that's better than being exclusive and judgmental. But that's not celebratory. And so the celebratory part of it really stands out to me. I'm wondering how have you seen the celebratory nature of ballroom impact young people outside of the scene?

Twiggy: This is just one example, but I would say it encourages a lot of my friends who, when I met them, were exploring their gender and didn't have anywhere to explore if they wanted to get in drags, if they wanted to transition, if they want it to go into any part of the journey of expressing their gender differently. It creates a space where, within the bubble of the scene at least, you can explore that in a way that you may not be able to do at all anywhere else. And then to also be connected to people and to resources too, if you do decide to move beyond exploration, then you can get that there. And so I would say for some of my friends, it was the only place that they felt comfortable and safe to even think about transitioning. They got affirmed and celebrated so much so that they were like, Oh, I can actually do this, can actually be who I am. So that's one example. A totally different example is **the way that you are celebrated in ballroom births so much confidence that it shows up in other aspects of your life**. Like, I would not be as professionally confident to speak to people, interpersonally, but also publicly, if I hadn't had the practice and positions of leadership within the houses I've been a part. So it, it has, at least for me personally, and I know for tons of other people, also impacted confidence and day-to-day interactions, and also competence and professional interactions, because of the celebration and the adulation.

Jama: So this book that we're working on is for social workers or people that are working in social services in order to provide people with the tools to be able to work with trans and gender expansive young people. And I'm going to say now in a celebratory way. I'm wondering if there's anything specific that you want to share that you think social workers and social service workers should know about the house and ballroom community, or should keep in mind when they're working with young people who are exploring or questioning their identities.

Twiggy: I mean, one thing that I've been curious about how to figure out, which is worth asking the question of, or pushing folks to also figure out is, **how do we use resources from the structures that already exist to empower and support this structure, which exists all in of itself**. And so, I used the example of host homes earlier, which has been happening in ballroom for deceased. How can some of those folks get resources to be host parents? So how do we get those resources to people in ballroom who have already created a structure that works for them, but don't have the support and the resources. So that's one thing I would push folks to ask the question and figure the hell out. I guess another thing would be to do the research on ballroom culture and educate themselves. **My goal is that in the same ways that social work students study other communities and scenes, they will study this**. Maybe a bit of that is happening now, but like for it to be embedded in syllabi all over the place. We're not there yet. So I would encourage folks to explore what that looks like. This is a community that has survived thrived, and now at this point is being elevated in the mainstream in a way that it has not before. What does it mean to be intentional about making sure it's in the canon in a way that isn't just passed down by words, which has obviously helped us to survive this long, but what does it mean to make sure that it's in the canon, and then in supporting young people directly? I think it's about understanding the value that being a part of a house or a family or house family can bring to a young person and the support that comes from that and the space that it provides for young people.

That doesn't mean get up and take yourself to a ball that you're not welcome to, but it does mean explore and ask the questions about what the young person is getting out of the experience and have them tell you what it is. You know, this is going to be a chapter in the book that will open the door, perhaps. But you still have to ask that person what it is, I think, because we all get something so different from it.

Jama: When you said making sure that this is in the canon, we should be learning about this community that has survived and thrived, and is now being elevated in this whole other way. I think there's a lot to be learned from the house and ballroom community as a whole. And then of course, individuals within the community. What are some things that you think social workers, but also the world more broadly, can learn, should learn, could learn from the house and ballroom community?

Twiggy: I mean, I say this all the time and at this point I say so often it feels cliché, but it really is not. It's just that the thing that I learned from ballroom is that you have the power to create your own reality. **When there was no space for us, we made a space. When there were no families for us, we created families. When there was no celebration for us, we celebrated each other**. And so we literally imagined and did and made the thing. And so, my biggest thing that ballroom has taught me and that I hope it continues to teach the world is that we have the power to create our own realities. Even when nothing exists, we can make something.

10 Trans Youth Are Our Future: Reflections from ARY on TGE Youth-Led Projects

*Aiyanna Horton, Aaron Kemmerer,
Justice Valentine, and Alex Wagaman*

If you have read to this point in the book, you likely already have a solid understanding of the barriers and challenges that have been put in place to make it incredibly difficult for transgender and gender expansive (TGE) youth in the United States to survive and thrive (Greytak, Kosciw, & Diaz, 2009; James et al., 2016). These challenges are compounded for TGE youth who live at the intersections of multiple marginalized identities. In our experience, the lives of TGE people are often problematized. There is a lot of focus on the challenges, the risks, the barriers. If you aren't yet familiar with what TGE youth have to face, familiarize yourself. It is essential to your ability to serve and support them. It will not be the focus of our chapter.

Despite all of the challenges, surviving is what TGE youth continue to do every day. The research literature calls this resilience – the ability to bounce back when you have faced adversity. And those who have studied resilience among TGE youth have found that spaces where they can explore their identities, live authentically, connect with other TGE folks, and engage in advocacy are all factors associated with resilience (Singh, Meng, & Hansen, 2014). But why should we focus on resilience as the end goal? Shouldn't TGE youth be able to thrive – sharing their talent and brilliance with the world? We think so! So, how might you – as someone reading this chapter who is invested in serving TGE youth, in supporting their resilience – also nurture and support resistance among TGE youth? How can you support the creation of spaces where TGE youth can imagine the world as it should be for themselves, their TGE siblings and the young people who will come behind them? We have learned a few things about this through our work with Advocates for Richmond Youth (ARY) – a Virginia-based, participatory action research team.

The evidence is clear that TGE young people need resources and support (Durwood, McLaughlin, & Olson, 2017; Grossman & D'Augelli, 2006; Kattari & Begun, 2017). The "how" is less present in the research. We need information from people who are building these spaces in real time to guide us on how to do this work. We need TGE young people who are living out the theories of queer world making and engaging in praxis every day to teach us what they need (Hereth & Bouris, 2020). That is what we have aimed to offer

DOI: 10.4324/9780429297687-10

in this chapter. Our work together has taught us that **peer support** and **youth-led community advocacy** are a powerful combination for TGE young people to build resilience, develop resistance skills, create spaces for nurturing, and gain valuable experience on how to make the world better for TGE people.

We want to define a few terms before we begin so that we have a common base of understanding. First, what do we mean by **youth-led**? A group or organization that is youth-led engages young people in organizing and facilitating the work (Ortega-Williams, Wernick, DeBower, & Brathwaite, 2020). That could be meetings or programs or direct action. The number of youth at the table is important (we prefer a majority youth) but it isn't just about numbers. In genuinely youth-led spaces, young people are able to resist co-optation, disrupt adult-youth hierarchies, and have true decision making power. This power goes beyond an advising role, or giving input on a decision that adults have made or will eventually make on their own. Adultism often shows up in complex ways when youth have power and authority. Adultism is the preference given to the voice and authority of adults over younger people (Bell, 2018). One way adultism undermines the work of youth-led groups is when adult leaders "grant" youth decision-making authority over decisions that they don't genuinely care about. In a youth-led effort, youth have a voice that holds substantial power at all levels of decision-making and adultism is dismantled (Wright, 2015).

What do we mean by **community advocacy**? We view advocacy as resisting decisions, processes, and structures that are harmful. Advocacy, for us, is working for change that relieves the conditions of people now and works for a better system of support in the future. Our approach to community advocacy resists adopting one agenda for all. Instead, we aim to incorporate perspectives and experiences that allow us to create a collective agenda. Community advocacy requires a group to take a stand, often rooted in an explicit set of values.

What do we mean by **peer support**? Peer support is when youth receive different kinds of support – tangible and intangible – from other youth. Peer support is based on relationships and the ability to connect with one another around a shared experience (Ortega-Williams et al., 2020). Peer support is important for TGE youth so they know that they are not alone. It also offers vital connection without the risk of harm because action is based in a deep, shared knowledge of experience. Trans Lifeline talks about this as key to their success as the only crisis hotline that will never engage outside resources (like police) without the active consent of the person (Trans Lifeline, 2020). In our team, peer support developed around a shared purpose (i.e., ending youth homelessness), and an unintended effect was that TGE youth had space and opportunity to support each other. Peer support creates opportunities to share and grow.

The combination of youth-led community advocacy and peer support creates a completely unique experience. They fortify one another. Together, they allow for power building and politicization. They support both self and collective care. Our ability to really see and be there for each other means that we are morally obligated to show up for each other in community.

Lastly, we use the words **collective** and **team** interchangeably to refer to Advocates for Richmond Youth. We are not a formal organization. We are a group of people who came together around a shared purpose and ended up building a network of young people based on a strong set of applied values that has been passed down through several "generations" of members. We do not have a hierarchy. We work for the collective.

The Beginning(s) of Advocates for Richmond Youth (ARY)

ARY was started as a participatory action research team focused on filling a gap in knowledge around youth homelessness in our community and a lack of engagement of young people directly impacted by youth homelessness at the decision-making tables. Alex, a university researcher, initiated ARY with the support of a transgender student and a student with lived experience of homelessness. This team of three worked to ensure that the first team re-cruited – 12 young people ages 18–24 – represented the groups who are most impacted by homelessness. TGE young people were prioritized for re-presentation on the team from its inception. We wanted to be sure our work supported and advocated for TGE youth. Because our origination as a team was crucial to the foundation that we built – particularly as a team that does youth-led community advocacy and peer support – we are going to tell a bit of our history here. Then we will share the core values that our team upholds, including how these values are lived out on our team. As we describe our values, we will outline some best practices for social workers and other helping professionals who want to know how to facilitate youth-led initiatives that engage in advocacy and peer support for TGE youth and young adults.

Reflecting on Our Beginnings

As we look back on our formation as a team, we recall key relationships that facilitated our connection with Advocates for Richmond Youth (ARY). Aiyanna remembers this vividly. She had been working on a project to de-velop safer sex education materials for TGE community members. Through this project, she met a social worker at the local LGBTQ+ community center, with whom she shared her experience of homelessness. The social worker heard about ARY forming and immediately thought of Aiyanna. The uni-versity researcher, Alex, who was launching ARY had been working with the same social worker on a project to increase access for TGE folks seeking shelter. The social worker was the *connector*. Through her relationships with both Aiyanna and Alex, she saw the value and mutual benefit of the con-nection between Aiyanna and Alex. As the safer sex education project ended, joining ARY was a way for Aiyanna to continue with her leadership as a young, transgender community leader. Alex knew that Aiyanna's presence on the team, bringing her experience as a Black trans woman, would shape the formation in essential ways. Reflecting on her experience, Aiyanna writes:

When I first was introduced to ARY it was an exciting and nervous experience to get to share and help other people with their experience of being homeless to be able to build from gravel into a foundation that we have built through our voices and hard work is amazing and to be able to be a black trans woman to have a voice in this journey has been a great journey. I was able to connect and share my experiences on national levels and teach and train people on my experiences and experiences of my trans brothers and sisters to learn and respect and be understanding of our journey. I remember when I was asked to be a part of a panel to speak to the police on trans experiences and what we face when we encounter them and how we felt being misgendered and misunderstood. I was able to travel to see the work of others to be able to bring back and share with the team. I was honored to be able to work with national organizations and be able to share my experience and work on amazing projects to help homeless youth has been something I will never forget and will continue to do to be able to show the world that we are here and we face the same as anyone else is just the beginning of the journey. I wouldn't change anything in the world. I've met the most wonderful people I never thought I would if I would have never stepped up and had a voice for change.

Aaron joined at the same time as Aiyanna – as an original member of the team in 2014. Regarding his connection to the team and the connections formed through the team, he writes:

I was job hunting at the library and I received a message about the meeting from R [transgender community member]. At that time, we did not know each other at all, but we had mutual friends online. All the days I had spent there at that library trying to figure out my housing situation, employment, or frankly where to go next after they closed that evening, then I showed up to the first meeting. I was so happy there was dinner and a small stipend at every meeting. I was completely unstable at the time – broke and brokenhearted. The regularity of our weekly meetings and the ability to open up and be honest changed the way I viewed myself in my own situation. I remember the power of us sharing our stories with each other and how much pain and healing was living in the same room together when we shared about houselessness, all the feelings it brought up, how losing home attacked our dignity, the unfairness of it! We coped together. We danced, laughed, and cried. People lost people and babies were born. Trans members of our group felt solidarity with each other and a real drive to keep showing up.

Justice came to the team several years later, in 2018. Justice writes:

In 2018, I was having a meeting with my caseworker, this person was with a community partner with Advocates for Richmond Youth. Afterward, we both went to an event for ARY (I don't remember what it was for). I talked to a couple of the advocates about my situation and how to receive help. A few months after getting housed and settled in, I went to ARY's drop-in hours to participate in a project and to learn more about them afterwards I went to a meeting and that's that. I felt safe in the space because of the work and care of the members before me and energized that we all wanted to end youth homelessness together. I have always felt that my insight was valued.

The connections that brought people to the team also fostered connections between team members, particularly among TGE team members, who formed and maintained relationships both inside and outside of the team's work together. This form of peer support was rooted in the purpose of the team – to conduct research and advocacy to end youth homelessness – and extended beyond the scope of the project. It became important for TGE team members to know that they had community and peers with similar identities on the team. The team served as a solid foundation of support for everyone and shattered our sense of isolation. Knowing that you are not alone in experiencing homelessness strengthened the team's understanding that we could work together to change our collective situation.

Values-Based Foundation

The set of values and guidelines for how we worked together set a tone of respect and support. These will be discussed in more detail later in the chapter, but the values established at the beginning of the team's formation provided a strong core that made it safer for TGE folks who joined the team later. The values did not emerge right away. They were formed over time and forged through experience with each other. We began by co-creating a set of agreements for how we would work and interact with each other. The collaborative agreement process was an opportunity for members to be upfront and clear about their boundaries – what they would and would not tolerate in the space and what they needed to ask of each other. These became a foundation – being read out loud and/or being posted on the wall each time the team gathered together. Through upholding and living into the agreements over time, some of the values that emerged included authenticity, confidentiality, joy, and humor.

The core values were protected by the original members during meetings. As new people came in, the original members welcomed them by modeling and reflecting these values. New members were oriented into the values through the meetings and activities the team did together, as well as the community agreement we had hand-written and visually hanging in our meeting space. New members also had space to add to the values and agreement. In essence, the core set of values was passed along as new members came and other members left. It was also a living document with room to morph and change in ways that were necessary to accommodate the diverse needs and experiences of team members over time.

Facing and Overcoming Obstacles

One of the important ways that ARY developed its capacity to engage in youth-led community advocacy and peer support was through facing and overcoming obstacles. These obstacles were experienced in the work that was happening within the team as well as during work that engaged outside stakeholders or community partners. The ability to step in and support one another when the obstacle presented itself allowed team members to center their relationships. Obstacles often provided opportunities to practice and enact advocacy.

One example of an external obstacle occurred during data collection for the first research study that ARY conducted. Team members were conducting a focus group with service providers to gain an understanding of the barriers they face in serving youth experiencing housing crises. Some of the service providers shared opinions and perspectives that framed young people as defiant and deviant – "having attitudes" or *wanting* to experience homelessness rather than stay in their family homes and follow rules. Some of the providers even resisted the idea that youth could experience homelessness. The team members who were facilitating called for a break. During the break, they found space to be together and debrief about what was happening – the fact that their own realities were being invalidated. They vented, shared their feelings, and validated one another. Then they completed the focus group. In the dissemination of the research findings, the team was able to highlight the damaging narrative that exists about youth among providers and to further emphasize the need for training. In response to the invisibilizing of youth experiencing homelessness, the team began advocacy work to expand the way that local stakeholders define homelessness, knowing that the narrow definition created barriers to recognition and community response. ARY pursued funding and partnerships to conduct regional training, specifically on youth homelessness and working with young people in an affirming way. The training took an intersectional approach – educating on the unique experiences of subpopulations of youth and emphasizing that youth can belong to multiple marginalized populations (e.g. immigrant, transgender, foster care experience), which offered a unique training experience in itself.

An example of an internal obstacle that the team faced was related to the diversity of the team. Young people on the team brought in a variety of experiences with and knowledge about LGBTQ+ people. Because the expectation of authenticity had been established from the beginning, LGBTQ+ identities and experiences were and are a prominent part of the discussion and visibility of the team, including TGE-specific experiences. It soon became clear that some team members did not know how to respect the TGE identities of other members. This was reflected through misgendering, having gendered conversations that sought alignment from folks who were perceived to align with that gender, and deadnaming (calling someone by their given name rather than their chosen name). TGE team members often spoke up in

response to support one another through these incidents. They also emotionally processed together privately, discussed strategies for communicating
expectations of respecting their identities and made plans to teach team
members for a deeper understanding of the harm of misgendering TGE folks.
The education and correction took time. They did not have the desired impact overnight. More and more team members stepped in to stand with the
TGE team members as accomplices in this process. Eventually, the culture
shifted to one of collective responsibility.

Both of these examples of facing and overcoming obstacles highlight the
value of having peers who can and will step in to support one another. The
value of having an outlet, determining together what boundaries will and will
not be crossed, and enacting strategies for interpersonal or community change
emphasizes the power that comes from a strong peer support network in
creating a foundation for addressing the inevitable conflict that will be faced
when working for change.

As social workers and service providers working with TGE youth, it can be
tempting to work in extremes: to avoid obstacles and barriers or to take them
on and address them without involving young people. It is our experience that
having a supportive environment in which barriers and challenges can be
faced and collectively addressed has the potential to build skills and capacity
to work on broader community advocacy. When social workers step in to
"handle things," they can disempower the group and send a message that they
do not believe in the capacity of the youth to address the issues at hand. This
is not to say that social workers and service providers should not intervene
when there is potential for harm. Assessing the difference requires trust and
opportunities for dialogue with the youth who are directly impacted.

Strategies for Building Connections

Connections and relationships are what brought most team members to ARY
and have kept many team members in the work, in some cases for years.
Connections are powerful roots. Relationship building was also an important
and valuable form of power building. We have learned that two forms of
connections are essential to intentionally nurture in spaces where TGE youth
are engaging in peer support and community advocacy: connections with one
another and connections to a broader network of stakeholders.

The Value of Connections with Each Other

Story sharing was one strategy that our team used early on in its formation to
build deep connections with each other. As we designed our first research
study, we realized that we would be asking other young people to share their
stories and experiences with housing instability and homelessness, yet we had
never shared our stories with each other in an intentional way. We knew that
we all had direct, lived experience but that was the extent of our knowledge.

So we decided to spend one of our meetings collectively answering the questions we had developed for our research interviews. The team was nervous. As previously mentioned, we had already experienced some challenges around affirming all identities on the team and we knew that some of our stories about homelessness were intricately interwoven with our identities. We spent intentional time talking about what we needed during the story sharing process – from the space, from each other. We decided to have certain foods that were comforting. We put a sign on the door to let people know that they should wait if they arrived late, so no one's story would be interrupted. We set guidelines about protecting each other's privacy and not questioning each other. We centered self-care so that each person felt comfortable doing what they needed to do to feel cared for.

The story sharing itself was a powerful experience. It allowed us to understand our connection to each other and the issue our team formed around more deeply. It also allowed us to recognize and understand the incredible variety of experiences. Story sharing built a level of empathy across identity groups that had not been present in the team before. Four years later, the founding team members still remember the experience. Story sharing was a tool to begin building strong roots among new team members while also building research knowledge on the diversity and complexity of experiences of youth homelessness in our community. Our team designed another qualitative research study in which some ARY members decided to participate. The stories were collected through interviews conducted by team members – all young people with lived experiences of housing instability. The stories were transcribed and then collectively analyzed by the ARY team to identify themes. To present the themes to the broader community, ARY worked in small groups to develop audio stories that included quotes from the transcripts, poetry, analytic reflections, and composite stories. These were audio-recorded and mapped onto the Richmond community using GPS coordinates of locations that had symbolic or other meaning to the team. Figure 10.1 shows a screenshot from the website showcasing the culminating project, *In Our Voices!: Exploring the Diversity and Complexity of Youth Housing Instability in Richmond, VA*. Readers can find the story map at the following URL: http://righthereonce.org/audio-map/#in-our-voices-advocates-for-richmond-youth

The Value of Connections with Other Stakeholders

Building a Local Network

Early on in our work together as a team, we learned that we each brought a number of important connections into the work. During one meeting, we decided to map out on flip chart paper all of the key people who we knew as a team. We went through each important sector involved in ending youth homelessness, including education, mental health, medical care, workforce, LGBTQ+ services, etc. As we went around the room writing down our

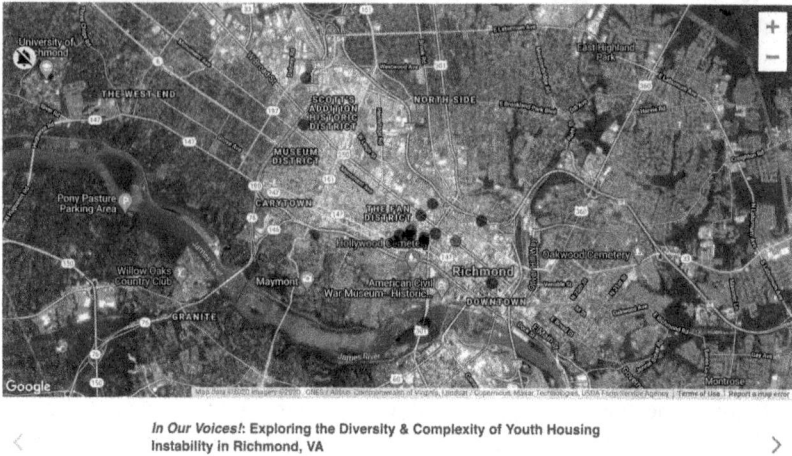

<

In Our Voices!: Exploring the Diversity & Complexity of Youth Housing
Instability in Richmond, VA

Figure 10.1 Screenshot of ARY's *In Our Voices!: Exploring the Diversity and Complexity of Youth Housing Instability in Richmond, VA.*

connections on flip chart paper, we began to visually see the many people we knew: folks who supported us, who partnered with us, or who engaged us in services. Everyone on the team knew someone who we could leverage for access to an organization or system that needed to be involved in the work to end youth homelessness. This was a powerful acknowledgment and an opportunity for us to recognize the power we hold. Many of us were nervous about engaging in organizing that supported base building for a community-wide effort to end youth homelessness. But when we looked around and saw who we knew we could count on to show up for us and who we could ask to bring others along, the work felt possible. Throughout this process, we always talked in-depth about the partners and organizations we brought to the table. We would not compromise our values, including being openly and explicitly trans-affirming. We knew that some partners may not be ready or willing or equipped to practice this with us. Our values were not up for negotiation or compromise.

After the first research study that ARY completed, the team was asked to work on developing training for service providers and stakeholders in the region. The training built on the network described above along with the networks of our training partner organizations to bring together an array of direct service workers, program managers, policy advocates, and others together to learn about youth homelessness and youth-affirming service delivery. ARY used three key strategies in the training to establish clear expectations for trans-affirming youth services in the community. Using these strategies helped us to use the training for broader advocacy. The first strategy was to center the needs and experiences of LGBTQ young people with an emphasis on trans-specific practices that organizations should be using. ARY team members developed tip sheets for select populations that are disproportionately represented among youth experiencing homelessness and engaged in rotating break-out sessions with training participants to educate them. The rotation structure made sure that every training participant heard about every population and began to think about the impact of homelessness on youth who hold multiple marginalized identities, such as undocumented TGE youth. The second strategy we used was to center our direct service worker workshop on a case study involving a transgender young person seeking services. Volunteers role played and received feedback on their application of the practices they had learned about in the population-specific break-outs earlier in the training. This opportunity gave training participants a chance to see the role play modeled by ARY team members and to practice using affirming language, pronouns, and more in an open learning environment. ARY team members gave positive reinforcement. Training participants acknowledged their own misunderstanding and limited knowledge. Service providers were able to look to the youth as the experts/teachers. The third strategy that ARY used in the training was to facilitate a mapping exercise through which all training participants put themselves in areas of expertise and then drew connections to others in the training with whom they wanted to connect. This allowed participants to see each other as resources for learning how to better serve and support youth experiencing homelessness. The strategy for building connections outside of the team established a network of people with whom ARY was able to facilitate collective goal setting and momentum towards ending youth homelessness.

Transgender Community Connections

It is important to acknowledge that ARY TGE team members did their own work to build and nurture trans-specific connections in and with the community. This ensured that TGE voices were present in the work that happened within and outside of the team. It also created space for TGE ARY members to advocate with other trans advocacy groups and build power that supports cross-issue advocacy. One example of this was a listening session with local police that was organized by the local chapter of SONG (Southerners on New Ground), ARY and other TGE community leaders. The issue of police violence and TGE community members kept coming up across multiple organizations. The listening session was an event that facilitated listening on the part of the police and sharing on the part of TGE community members (including an ARY team member) about interactions with police. The event was hosted by a local LGBTQ theater and included information booths staffed by local trans-led or focused organizations that facilitated questions and discussion with law enforcement officers in attendance. The alignment of purpose that occurred in this event facilitated future partnership opportunities in the years following. This event also put ARY on the radar (gay-dar) of trans-led organizations as a group who was doing important work.

National Connections

Lastly, the national connections that ARY established through its work created a force of confidence and resources within the team that enhanced the
peer support and youth-led advocacy we had already been doing. Early in our
work, Alex, Aiyanna, and Aaron were invited to participate in a national
convening with True Colors United, an organization working to end youth
homelessness with an emphasis on LGBTQ+ youth. Our first attendance
turned into multiple years of ARY team representation at the national con-
venings, representation among youth selected from across the United States to
work with True Colors, presenting workshops and conferences, and working
on a national research agenda. There are a number of ways that our participation in True Colors held value for ARY. We also want to highlight some
of the ways that national connection fortified us in our local community. First,
traveling is a bonding experience. Having concentrated time together to work
and enjoy each other's company fortified our relationships. It freed us up to
dream about the future of our work and what we envisioned for youth in our
community. Fun and joy are essential for sustainability. Time to laugh together and experience new things together cannot be underestimated.
Second, we met other TGE youth leaders from across the country who are
doing this work. The network for peer support was expanded. Many of these
groups were further along in their journeys than ARY. So, we were able to
learn from their experiences, feel affirmed in our common challenges, and
know that we could call on them when we needed to. Seeing other people and
groups making change and having an impact fortified our belief that change
was possible. And finally, we learned. We learned *so much!* We learned from
national experts about things that could strengthen our work. We learned
language to apply to the thoughts and ideas we had been exploring but didn't
have a knowledge base for. Most importantly, we learned that we were not
alone. There is so much power in that.

Building a Base of Values to Guide the Work

In the following sections, we will outline the set of values that guide and
ground ARY's work. In addition, we provide detailed information about each
value and best practices that have supported our embodiment of these values.
We hope this will be a practically useful document for social workers and
youth involved in community organizing and social change efforts. Our values
and best practices were developed over time and through experience. In many
ways, this is still a "living document," just as our hand-written group agreements were. A combination of challenging and successful moments shaped
these values. The most polished stones have usually been through a rock
tumbler. See Figure 10.2 for a graphic explanation of ARY's values.

We value being clear and consistent about the principles that ground the
ARY collective and our work to end youth homelessness. In order to thrive,

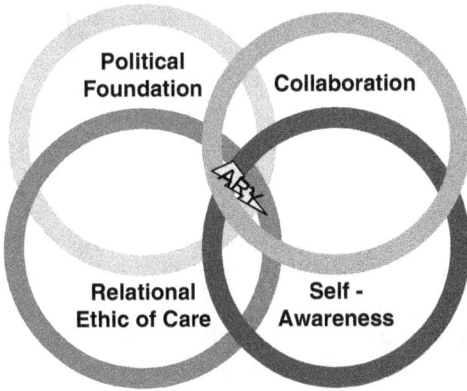

Figure 10.2 Venn diagram of ARY values (political foundation, collaboration, relationships and care, and self-awareness). Values are non-hierarchical and nonlinear on purpose – each is a critical and important piece of the puzzle!

youth collectives must remain grounded in a political foundation that embraces intersectional politics. An intersectional analysis is vital to ending pervasive socio-political issues, such as youth homelessness, where vulnerable individuals often hold multiple marginalized identities and face increased barriers to employment and housing. This lived experience is central to community organizing and social change work, particularly for TGE youth populations because of the social systems we live under (i.e., misogyny, heterosexism, cis-sexism, anti-Blackness, and racialized capitalism). An intersectional politic inherently focuses on the varied lived experiences of those surviving at dangerous intersections of multiple systems of domination. Thus, the work of effective community organizations (such as ARY) causes collaboration on power shifting strategies, emphasis on collective power, and commitment to shared purpose.

Being Clear about Our Intersectional Politics

We explicitly work from a place of dismantling all systems of oppression and believe we can dismantle no system in isolation. The very nature of the social problems we seek to solve (i.e., public policy, housing instability, and youth mental health) calls for an intersectional political strategy.

Using Narrative to Understand the Variety of People's Experiences

Intersectionality also informs the decision to use a narrative in our organizing efforts. Using narrative in ARY's collective has proven essential to understanding each person's lived experience and examine trends among experiences of marginalization. The direct experience of housing instability challenges dominant paradigms that rely on stereotypes and myths, so centering individual and collective narratives of young people is a power shifting strategy. Practicing storytelling and counter-storytelling as techniques help to build understanding across group members and collaborators.

Embracing Power-Shifting Strategies

Groups like ARY should incorporate practices that place youth in genuine decision-making roles (avoiding tokenizing or "for show" positions). We also recommend inviting youth to train, teach, and lead service providers who serve TGE youth. We believe strongly in autonomy and youth-led space – sometimes this looks like youth facilitating meetings and planning agendas; youth leading small groups of service providers and community members. Sometimes it looks like the steps that adults take to support the youth (like facilitating logistics around meeting space and transportation). Often, it also just looks like adults (especially service providers and policymakers) taking a step back, putting on their listening ears, and respecting autonomous youth activity. Facilitators should remain mindful of the physical configuration of meeting space and those seeking to shift into practices to increase youth autonomy should ask themselves questions like "Where are the meetings located, in the city or county? Are buildings accessible? Is the physical meeting space welcoming and comfortable for youth? How is the physical meeting room arranged?" Each youth-led group must make unique decisions to fit their context. ARY prefers circular tables over "head of the table" meetings, buildings accessible in their design for persons with disabilities and accessible via public transportation lines, and meeting locations central to collective members. Post-COVID-19, virtual meetings should always be an option. These logistical factors influence a shift in power dynamics of public forums and the accessibility of gathering space.

Committing to a Shared Purpose

ARY continuously re-centers our work on the shared purpose of ending youth homelessness, which strengthens our work and keeps us focused. Moving work together as a unit leads to more cohesive outcomes. When we affirm our commitment to a larger purpose by centering meetings on the mission (in our case, ending youth homelessness) we see this as a practice that not only addresses a practical problem but strengthens our connection to one another. Various community members become engaged in social work larger than themselves and feel connected to one another across race, class, gender, and sexuality. Affirming our commitment to a shared purpose facilitates a spirit of connection and collaboration.

Collaboration

We value working together. All the youth advocates and our community partners have a responsibility to nurture our working spaces so we can have a cohesive movement toward ending youth homelessness. Some practices that encourage this collaborative environment are creating a welcoming environment, maintaining open educational space, and facilitating a culture of accountability.

Creating a Welcoming Environment

The original team took on the responsibility to make others who came on board later feel comfortable and welcome. New members often came into ARY with trauma histories – sometimes there was an initial difficulty opening up to share or difficulty adapting to group norms. Older members and people who had been involved for longer engaged new members in conversation and built connections to ensure new folks felt welcome and willing to return. ARY members are always verbally acknowledged when they enter the team's space as an expression of the value that each person holds. We are happy to see each other and we work to not take for granted what it might have required for someone to be present. ARY members bring their whole selves to the workspace. Sometimes that means having children in meetings or sharing something difficult that happened that day. Also, ARY eventually created a graduation celebration for people who aged out of the group. Alumni continued involvement by offering time or resources when ARY held a big event or expressed a need for support.

Creating a Space for Learning and Teaching

Everyone has expertise in their own housing experience and their own gender journey. Providers have the experience of knowing how to navigate through systems to accomplish our goal of ending youth homelessness. Youth have the first-hand experience going through the homelessness system and also their lived experiences of marginalization and hardship (i.e., being in foster care, being TGE, or being a parent). We have learned that there are some essential aspects of creating a respectful space, including accepting being wrong, avoiding shame, continuing learning of participants who don't "get it right," and encouraging an open and affirming learning environment. Our political foundation urges us to create an environment that encourages critical questions in the discussion. No one should be silenced.

Building Accountability Culture

In ARY, we believe that conflict can strengthen our bond rather than weaken it. By creating an "accountability culture" we are proactive about conflict resolution before any conflicts occur. Conflict is inevitable. We recognize that conflict is not the same as perpetuating oppression. So we embrace working through conflicts appropriately. We also appreciate the importance of belonging and communication to matters of accountability – at ARY we have strived to stay connected and complete our work by checking in with each other through texts, meeting up after/between weekly meetings. These communication practices can offer a sense of social support and accountability. We strive to be clear about group norms, promoting what is (or denouncing what is not) acceptable in our meeting space. For example, we will not accept racist or homophobic language in the space. (Period!) We appreciate the value of constructive criticism and reject perfectionism because it is a value of white supremacist culture. We expect to hold one another accountable through "calling in," (*a private acknowledgment of harm*) as opposed to cancel/call out culture (*a public shaming*). When someone makes a mistake, crosses a boundary, or gets involved in a conflict, they have an opportunity to grow, recover, make amends, and communicate. One model for framing conflict-resolution statements is "When you did x, it made me feel y because z. What I need is w." See Figure 10.3, which graphically displays this communication model for conflict resolution.

ARY solidified group accountability norms through behavioral modeling and refusing to exclude people from the space when they share a genuine commitment to ending youth homelessness. Regular debriefing strengthens accountability norms as a group analyzes the outcome of collective actions. Sometimes coupling the use of self-reflection/self-critique with group reflection/group critique better situates individual members in the collective context. For example, members might use the following questions to prompt critical dialogue in the group: What is one thing you did well in this meeting? What is one area of growth for you in this meeting? What is one thing the group did well in this meeting? What is one area of growth for the group after this meeting? The spirit of collaboration directly connects to our next value, which highlights relationships and care.

Relational Ethic of Care

We value our members and partners as whole people. Perhaps one of the most salient values that emerged from organizing within ARY was our prioritization of relationships and care. The work to end homelessness is hard,

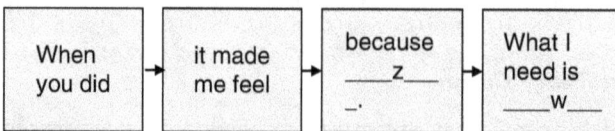

Figure 10.3 Communicating about conflict.

so we need to be thoughtful with each other while maintaining the integrity of the collective.

Establishing a No Throwaway Culture

We do not dispose of people. For ARY this looks like holding each other accountable, not throwing each other away. We engage in challenging conversations when necessary but never threaten to end relationships. We practice prioritizing funding and stipends for youth – we know that limited funding supports our projects. Thus ARY members understand external demands that other members face around jobs, childcare, and housing. For example, when a member needs to step away due to new employment or family changes, we welcome them back when they are available to take part.

Honoring the Complexity of Human Relationships

Members of the collective hold high regard for interpersonal relationships (friendships, working relationships, and mentorships). We recognize that youth have complex relationships with each other, adult mentors, and external community members. For example, there are ARY team members who have received services and support from organizations. Team members use these previous relationships and connections to build organizational relationships that support ARY in achieving its goals. ARY team members elevate their relationships to bridge the gap so ARY can achieve our mission of ending youth homelessness. In ARY, we discourage the compartmentalization of relationships. We encourage youth to build platonic relationships outside of working relationships while practicing healthy boundary-setting. Even though friendships are born organically, group facilitators can encourage this relationship-building process by providing social space for people to gather and work outside of regular meetings. Deeper relationships allow us to learn more about ourselves, our colleagues, and neighbors on the team. They allow us to show up more authentically. As we learn more about members and partners, we can communicate more effectively and strengthen the integrity of our practice together.

Practicing Thoughtfully with Each Other

Surviving multiple systems of oppression, the world is hard on all of us already. Why should we be that way with each other? We consistently center each person's inherent dignity and humanity. One very helpful practice is the use of check-ins at the start of each session. This practice encourages members to share about their daily lives and relate across differences. We are adamant about our respect for confidentiality. One significant group norm around confidentiality that we hope you will practice with is: "take the lesson, leave the details." We will not repeat personal details shared in a meeting space with outsiders, yet we can grow from listening to the stories of other members and communicate about our own growth journeys.

Building Community

We know several practices that effectively facilitate community building. The first and most important (to us) is food. Not only does the practice of serving food encourage a sense of togetherness, but food also helps members work productively. No one can do good work on an empty stomach. It is important to ask about and consider folks' dietary restrictions and allergies ahead of the meeting. Also, we prefer to provide high-quality nutritious foods when organizing youth who have experienced housing/food instability. We like comfort food, but not just snacks. Youth might depend on that consistent meal, so we encourage serving a full breakfast, lunch, or dinner (and all three for all-day events). Now that most meetings are virtual, we also encourage eating during virtual meetings (esp. lunchtime). We never ask people to bring their own food, which can highlight class differences among people in the room.

We also recommend offering space before and after meetings for people to socialize and exchange contact information. Trans-centered youth groups benefit from having this unstructured social time, and it fosters a sense of connection among a group suffering from high rates of isolation. ARY additionally sought to activate and partner with other community groups toward common goals. For example, we often used the building space of community organizations who offered their conference rooms. This not only mutually strengthened the organizational commitment to ending housing instability among young people but also led to ARY acting as a bridge between often siloed social change efforts. For example, we held meetings at the local LGBTQ+ youth center and also at an organizational office that supports efforts to end homelessness. This led to increased connectedness among ARY members, LGBTQ+ leaders, and members of housing organizations.

A youth-led organization might receive invitations to broader community events. Engaging with these events supports our work and allows us to serve simultaneously. Through representing ARY (i.e., youth speaking on panels or tabling at community fairs) we can engage new youth members in the work to end youth homelessness. These events also raise awareness of our work and empower youth to speak their truth in community spaces dominated by adults. Events provide a service opportunity for the youth, which fosters a sense of leadership and purpose. We also listen to feedback from community members and build with community partner organizations.

Practicing Self-Care and Collective Care

We have learned that it is vital to take care of ourselves and each other. ARY strives to create a working environment that accepts the often limited personal capacity of each member. Because ARY encourages members to build relationships beyond the confines of "the work," we can check in about personal capacity. Does a member face challenges with making rent or bills this month? Does one of our members need extra support with childcare or transportation? Again, at every meeting, we serve a meal. We cannot emphasize the importance of food enough! Food sharing is not only a community-building practice, but an act of collective care. Communal meals nourish folks on physical and spiritual levels. We know focusing on our work is more challenging when on an empty stomach or facing financial stress. ARY is a collective grounded in ending youth homelessness, so we seek to prevent and remedy housing instability and food insecurity among our members through collective effort and support. Many members (and supportive adults as well) share resources among one another and practice mutual aid. We take a harm reductionist stance, especially related to substance use and mental health concerns – although we do not condone active substance use in the meeting space, we do not ostracize people from community involvement because of their coping patterns. Our work focuses on youth with experiences of housing instability. These experiences require us to build in extra care and sensitivity in the space. Youth are making themselves vulnerable by showing up and speaking about their story. We are transparent about when a story we share might include triggering aspects. We know how powerfully healing sharing our trauma experiences can be and the ARY collective honors the bravery of that action.

At the same time, we are not defined by our suffering. To align with respecting our members as whole people, we also prioritize having a good time with each other! Our meetings often include celebrating accomplishments such as graduations, new employment, and birthdays. There is laughing, singing, and dancing! We share plenty of moments of joy.

Self-Awareness and Reflection

We value a deeper understanding of ourselves through intentional process of reflection/action. We know our strengths and our limits. We know our potential, yet we accept being wrong sometimes. We are TGE and still make mistakes about gender – no one is perfect, but we can strive to do better. And we can strive to know ourselves as intimately as possible. Self-awareness and reflection are important to normalizing trans identities and dismantling transphobia. Through reflection, we can change our thoughts and behavior. Through self-awareness we can bring our whole selves to the collective table.

Accepting Being Wrong

We accept that we don't know it all – especially not individually! One major component of organizing a youth-led space is accepting that we don't have all the answers. We will make mistakes. The initial mistake says less about the person than their response to that mistake. This is especially true for folks who are seeking to dismantle oppressive systems (particularly transphobia) in organizing spaces. Adult service providers (especially those who hold race and class privilege) must become comfortable being course-corrected, especially if the criticism is coming from a young person. We have realized that the more we normalize the criticism and accountability process, the more we move towards the normalization of TGE youth experiences.

Normalizing Trans Visibility / Dismantling Transphobia

We have a few key ideas about best practices to facilitate the normalization of trans visibility in youth-led organizations. First, we ask all people involved to critically examine your beliefs about TGE people and why/where you may hold rigid beliefs. How were you raised and socialized around gender norms? What do you believe about how gender 'should' be? How do race, gender, and class intersect for you personally? What beliefs are you required to unlearn to serve a collective with a shared purpose? *On a practical level, we urge social work practitioners to begin all meeting introductions with our names and pronouns and respecting pronouns in meetings and beyond.* We encourage practitioners to celebrate diverse gender expressions – we prefer "gender expansive" over more limiting terms for gender diverse populations. We express a celebration of diverse genders through talking positively about gender-affirming behavior (i.e., gender expression through wardrobe and name changes, hormone treatment, and gender-affirming procedures, etc.). Practitioners must recognize that medical interventions are not the only path towards trans-ness.

We must intervene when we see transphobic behavior – in ourselves and interpersonally. Actively correct people on pronouns and names! The onus of responsibility is not on TGE people to correct transphobic behavior. When corrected on pronouns, the most caring reaction is usually to thank the person for their effort to facilitate mutual respect in the space, correct yourself, and move forward with the meeting. *Transgender and gender expansive folks exist* and our wellbeing is important. While we support the effort to abolish gender(!), we also recognize that not all practitioners are "there" yet and want to emphasize harm reduction – we strive to improve conditions for TGE youth on a material, daily level. Thus, we encourage social work practitioners to think critically about their interactions with TGE youth in clinical and community practice settings, even if those spaces are not "radical" or open about trans identity.

Being Our Whole and Authentic Selves

Honesty is a key value within ARY. We must be honest if we are to speak truth to power. Showing up as our complete selves helps us to build a more authentic collective space. We practice radical honesty with ourselves and one another, even when that truth might be painful. We strive collectively to make the group space emotionally safe enough so that people can be vulnerable, thus more authentic.

All Four Areas Are Important!

"The journey is just as important as the destination." – Elaine, founding ARY member

We are consistently reminded of this motto, which highlights the importance of process over "product." Our ethical values outlined above require us to recognize the value of our relationships with each other (as individuals, friends, and advocacy partners) These relationships ebb and flow into our relationship with the work we embark on together. To remain purpose-driven, we tend to re-center our mission to end youth homelessness. One important practice that supported a process-focused environment was assigning a member to the "temp check" role at each meeting to remind the group about the importance of process, slowing down, and centering member's feelings.

Conclusion

In this chapter, we hoped to provide some background about ARY, how our collective developed, and the values that have sustained us. We must say: our suggestions for best practices developed over time and are specific to our process at ARY. With near certainty, we can assert that each youth-led collective or team will require its own unique process for formulating values and establishing practices. These are practices that worked for us and we hope this chapter will be a useful tool. At the same time, we know there are no "cookie-cutter" solutions for creating spaces for TGE youth to engage in community advocacy and peer support. Thus, we urge all readers to think deeply about which practices might be most beneficial for their specific organizing effort, apply them, experiment, and go back to the drawing board as often as necessary. When folks remain committed to a political foundation that values the lives and well-being of TGE young people – and, more importantly, when folks are committed to each other – the outcomes will reflect those commitments. Here, we reaffirm our commitment to continued learning. Actually, collaborating on this chapter contributed to our growth and strength as a team. We can only hope this overview of our work supports your efforts towards liberation and safety for all transgender and gender expansive youth.

References

Bell, J. (2018). Adultism. In B. B. Frey (Ed.), *The SAGE encyclopedia of educational research, measurement, and evaluation*. Thousand Oaks, CA: SAGE Publications, Inc. doi:10.4135/9781506326139

Durwood, L., McLaughlin, K. A., & Olson, K. R. (2017). Mental health and self-worth in socially transitioned transgender youth. *Journal of the American Academy of Child and Adolescent Psychiatry, 56*(2), 116–123. doi:10.1016/j.jaac.2016.10.016

Greytak, E. A., Kosciw, J. G., & Diaz, E. M. (2009). *Harsh realities: The experiences of transgender youth in our nation's schools.* Gay, Lesbian and Straight Education Network (GLSEN). Retrieved from https://files.eric.ed.gov/fulltext/ED505687.pdf

Grossman, A. H., & D'Augelli, A. R. (2006). Transgender youth: Invisible and vulnerable. *Journal of Homosexuality, 51*(1), 111–128.

Hereth, J., & Bouris, A. (2020). Queering smart decarceration: Centering the experiences of LGBTQ+ young people to imagine a world without prisons. *Affilia, 35*(3), 358–375. doi:10.1177/0886109919871268

James, S. E., Herman, J. L., Rankin, S., Keisling, M., Mottet, L., & Anafi, M. (2016). *The report of the 2015 U.S. transgender survey.* Washington, DC: National Center for Transgender Equality. Retrieved from https://transequality.org/sites/default/files/docs/usts/USTS-Full-Report-Dec17.pdf

Kattari, S. K., & Begun, S. (2017). On the margins of marginalized: Transgender homelessness and survival sex. *Affilia, 32*(1), 92–103. doi:10.1177/0886109916651904

Ortega-Williams, A., Wernick, L. J., DeBower, J., & Brathwaite, B. (2020). Finding relief in action: The intersection of youth-led community organizing and mental health in Brooklyn, New York City. *Youth & Society, 52*(4), 618–638. doi:10.1177/0044118X18758542

Singh, A. A., Meng, S. E., & Hansen, A. W. (2014). "I am my own gender": Resilience strategies of trans youth. *Journal of Counseling & Development, 92*(2), 208–218. doi:10.1002/j.1556-6676.2014.00150.x

Trans Lifeline. (2020). Why no nonconsensual active rescue? In E. Dixon & L. L. Piepzna-Samarasinha (Eds.), *Beyond survival: Strategies and stories from the transformative justice movement.* Chico, CA: A.K. Press.

Wright, D. E. (2015). *Active learning.* New York: Routledge.

11 It's Like Church Without the Hurt: Trans Youth of Color and the Black Joy Experience

A Conversation with Jonathan Lykes

Jonathan Lykes and Jama Shelton

Introduction

Much of the research literature about trans and gender expansive (TGE) youth examines risk factors in an effort to reduce mental and physical health disparities. This is indeed important knowledge for social workers to possess. However, it is equally if not more important that social workers are able to utilize a strengths based approach in their work with TGE youth. A strengths-based approach centers an individual or community's resources and strengths rather than problems and risks (Saleeby, 1996). If social workers base all of their methods of engagement of and collaboration with TGE on only a risk reduction model, they may miss the opportunity to support TGE youth in further developing their strengths and strategies for resistance. Social work as a profession has moved beyond the tolerance model of TGE identity into identifying ways to support and affirm TGE people. I suggest that social work needs to take this one step further, and actively celebrate TGE youth. This idea of celebration brought to mind the work of social worker Jonathan Lykes, the curator of BYP100's freedom song and chant album, "The Black Joy Experience," helping to teach holistic energy through the Black radical tradition.

Jama: How would you describe the Black Joy Experience?

Jonathan: So to me, the Black Joy Experience is what I would describe as the spirit work of this time. I think as queer, trans, GNC (gender nonconforming) folks, we have been alienated and excluded from many types of spiritualities over our lives, from rejection from the church and rejection from many of our biological families. So to me, black joy experience is kind of a rejection of that and a declaration to say, we should have access to tap into our spirits. So I would describe that as the ability to experience joy, liberation, love, community, even in the midst of navigating white supremacy, systemic oppression, intra community harm.

    I think that in many ways we have to demand and declare joy for our lives. And so the Black Joy Experience is about using our bodies and our spirits, but usually through the pathways of cultural

DOI: 10.4324/9780429297687-11

production, creating. We are here on this earth to create, and through the idea of creating family, creating meaning, re-creating our bodies, creating music, creating culture, through that process, it allows us to experience liberation and build systems of liberation through this radical declaration of joy.

So the Black Joy Experience literally is a musical compilation of freedom songs and liberation chants, but it is so much more than that. **I would think of it as the spirit work of this time.** We did a session at allied media conference about two years ago, and when we do these sessions, it's like the creation of chants in real time, it's singing the music, but it's also having conversations about what does joy mean to us, where do we find community? And towards the end of that conversation, someone was like, **"Wow, this feels like church, but without the hurt."**

And that is exactly what we're trying to do. That's exactly what we're trying to accomplish. We are trying to build spaces for folks to return to a type of spirituality that I think is woven into the black radical tradition, but more recently, and historically, queer and trans folks have been alienated from those spiritual spaces that many folks throughout the black radical tradition have leaned on in order to fight for liberatory efforts in the world, but also just to get your spirit free.

So the Black Joy Experience is this declaration that **we deserve this space just as much as anyone else.** And this is our ability to be free, to be liberated, even in the craziest, most depressive moments of our ancestral lineage, even in the craziest, most depressive moments of society, even when things... I don't know, I think a lot about grieving and navigating death in 2020, but **black queer and trans folks throughout history have always had to deal with just higher levels of grief and higher levels of death.** Look no further than the average lifespan of a black transwoman in any American city. So the Black Joy Experience is the ability to even experience freedom and liberation, even in the midst of all of that.

Jama: You mentioned that queer and trans people have also traditionally been, or historically been excluded from spaces like this, even when they have existed. How do you make sure that queer and trans people are included in this work?

Jonathan: So first, I think that within our communities, we have traditionally created spaces, subcultures, families, and they look different depending on where you are in the world and what city you're in. But we have created radical spaces that are radically inclusive, not only for black and brown queer and trans people, but for everyone. So I think it is just a glimpse into the history of these spaces that allows us to reaffirm that we've always been the most welcoming and most inclusive, and always been the most accepting across identity spectrums. So that's one, just the fact that because of the identities that these communities hold, and the external oppressions that we're all navigating together that forces the space to be inclusive.

I think as we look up now in a world of 2020, where we're navigating one of the most probably difficult times in many of the millennial or gen Z-ers' lives, so navigating the largest economic depression that we've experienced in our lifetime, navigating one of the worst pandemics of our lifetime and still navigating the devaluation of black life. **I think we have to look to black feminist thought and the teachings that came before us that allow us to center our identities in these radically inclusive spaces.** When I think about inclusion, it takes me back to the writings of the Combahee River Collective, and Barbara Smith.

When I think of inclusion, and when I think of just the spaces that I've been a part of... inclusion just feels like a necessity because of... We are creating systems in our own worlds that are responding to the broken systems externally. So that if a black transwoman or black queer person isn't allowed to go into a homeless system in Brooklyn without experiencing more harm.... Gay families on the South side of Chicago become these inclusive spaces, these systems unto their own, that are holding all of these people. So in many ways it's inclusion by necessity, because we're all in this together. Like we're all experiencing these multiple levels of oppression, and the response of white supremacy together. So in response to that, **we're creating these spaces in order to hold each other, in order to include each other radically in those spaces, and to make sure that we're not recreating problems of the past.**

Now that that dynamic only exists with like intra, within gay families, within ballroom community, where like folks are holding similar identities. **The problem comes when we open that door to larger movement spaces, or to larger radical spaces. And then not everyone is included, to be quite honest. There is still what Cathy Cohen would call secondary marginalization, where hurt people are hurting people.** So I don't know, part of me is like inclusion by necessity, because we were all trying to survive together in this world that are sharing and holding these identities. And the other piece of me is saying we're still navigating rejection and harm, and struggling with making sure that we can all include each other in this world, particularly when the space is opened up and you have people holding more complex identities.

So what does it mean even within the house and ballroom community? What does it mean even within radical queer and trans organizing spaces for folks to have an analysis on disability justice? **How do we make sure that we are not holding space and time and care only for certain people and then forgetting and leaving others out?** So when I look across to these radical projects, it's like inclusion by necessity because we have to, and once we brought in the space, it complicates the issue more and more. I don't feel like totally articulate on that point, but I'm trying to balance those two dynamics.

Jama: That makes a lot of sense, actually. So I'm wondering how you got to Black Joy Experience?

Jonathan: The origin story?

Jama: When did you know that joy was the thing that was missing? How did you know that was an important perspective? So maybe the origin story, but I guess I'm curious about maybe even you as an individual person, you're a social worker by training, right? Involved in the movement for black lives and BYP 100. Where do those things intersect or inform the Black Joy Experience?

Jonathan: Yeah. Good question. So the Black Joy Experience, I think in its current form comes out of the first day that Dr. Cathy Cohen brought together the 100, Black Youth 100. This was July 2013. And it's like we're often struggling with these dualities. So 100 young black people are in a room together, and we get the news that the Zimmerman verdict is about to be released in real time. And we're standing in a circle and Zimmerman gets declared innocent when he so clearly murdered Trayvon Martin. And that became like one of those Kairos moments of, I'm supposed to be in this space with these people right now, stars aligning, in order to respond to this generational moment that we're all living in.

I locate the origins of the Black Joy Experience in that moment of pain, because there were several people in the room that day that responded to that moment of pain, with our value of holistic energy. How do we shift energy in moments of deep grief, deep pain, deep trauma, how do we shift energy so we can come to those collective spaces with our full selves to do the work, to be transformed in the spirit of the work.

So I locate birth of Black Joy Experience and kind of this new generation, this concept of holistic energy or what some folks might call the holistic turn up. **I locate it in that moment, July 13, 2013, sitting in a room with 100 young black radical youth experiencing extreme pain and extreme harm in this generational moment.** But we were only able to respond in that moment, shift the energy in that moment, cultivate our own holistic energy in that moment because folks had ancestral knowledge and had tapped into the tradition that came before us.

So much of the Black Joy Experience is rooted in the history of Marian Wright Edelman's freedom schools. Much of the Black Joy Experience is a cultivation/ reiteration of Sylvester and Nina Simone and the SNCC Freedom Singers. So in many ways we were trying to re-conjure up what our ancestors had already leaned on for them to survive in this world. So much about the black joy spans for our generation is locating it in this generational moment, in this movement moment, which is just like, not like any other moment that has ever existed, with social media and the fact that there will be no jobs at some point, because AI is completely taking over, the fact that there are these apps that we sit on 24 hours a day that are watching our every move. Like the level of surveillance and kind of Big Brother watching, and just cultural shifts that exist, like **there hasn't been a 2020 before.**

So given that dynamic, it was about **how do we utilize the tools of our ancestors?** How do we utilize the dynamics? The spirit work is kind of just like what I keep going back to. How do we utilize this idea of holistic energy? And then going back to, how do we utilize our ability to create? **No one creates like black and brown queer and trans people.** And whether that is a response to our oppression, whether that is just a cultural formation rooted in collectivism of the history of the traveling griots in Africa, of storytelling and sharing lineage, wherever you want to route that into, the Black Joy Experience is rooted in kind of leaning on those ancestral tools in a world that is just ridiculous. In a 2020 world where we are trying to navigate just things we've never seen before in society.

It's needed now more than ever. **It's going to be a requirement for us to utilize radical joy as a mechanism to experience freedom and love and community**, but then like joy plus cultural production allows us to think about the future in radical ways. It's going back to spirit or this idea of church without the hurt, this concept of faith. **The ability to imagine things that don't currently exist, the ability to dream up worlds that we can't see around us**. And I think that gives us incredible hope to not only make it through the grief of today, but it gives us hope to believe in the next thousand generations of our lineage, of black queer and trans lineage that we are fighting for, that is on the line right now. Yeah, that's the Black Joy Experience.

Interviewer: I'm teaching organizing this semester, and I was just talking to my class this morning about Emergent Strategy and Pleasure Activism. And so, many of the things you are saying resonate a lot. And the idea that if we don't have the ability to dream our way forward and imagine our way forward, then where are we going to go, right?

Jonathan: Absolutely.

Jama: There's an idea I hear from social work students a lot, because I try to infuse creative projects or arts-based learning into the classroom. And a lot of times, social work students say, "I'm not a creative person. I'm not an artist." And I think, "You wouldn't be in this, you wouldn't be an organizer if you're not a creative person." There's just no way. You just haven't... You're not owning it, or you haven't tapped into it but it's there!

So, what I thought about when you were talking about being able to shift energy, and how it emerged out of this particular moment of pain in the room with this particular group of people. And being able to shift the energy into a different direction, to be able to do work, reminded me of this conversation I was in at a social work research conference where folks were like, "Stop telling me that my job is to help Black youth cope with what it is to live in this super white dominant racist world. We need to stop talking about it that way in social work. Our work is not only to strengthen coping mechanisms, we need to change the systems that do this kind of harm." And so my question is, with the concepts you're enacting through the Black Joy Experience, do you see ways to kind of map that onto or translate into something for social workers who are working with black queer and trans youth?

Jonathan: Yeah, absolutely. Number one, I think that the Black Joy Experience challenges the world because **the Black Joy Experience isn't just for black people, I think it's for everyone**. But it challenges the world to demand that... Really move away from this dynamic of helping. **Helping never helps**. If we cannot get to the roots of understanding that all of our liberation is tied up into each other, is woven into each other, that our destinies require all of us to come to the table, to shift power dynamics, to not reiterate them, to not re-declare them onto each other, but to undo them, to untangle them, and to respond to past harms in order to experience joy in the present. If we're not declaring that, moving away from the helping dynamic or savior dynamic, then we are perpetuating harm. And we are perpetuating dynamics in our society that just doesn't help the core of the movement.

There's this chant created by Mary Hooks in the Black Joy Experience called The Mandate. Can I remember it? The first piece goes, the mandate for people in this time is to avenge the suffering of our ancestors. And then it ends by saying, and to be willing to be transformed in the service of the work. And **that piece of transforming yourself before trying to come and insert your piece on another community, I think is just the lesson that social workers have to pick up at mass**. The other piece is just this concept of principled struggle and moving away from dynamics of politeness, white, dominant cultural characteristics of being afraid of conflict. It is the conflict, it is the struggle. Those things are a condition for us to reach liberation with each other. **It is the conflict, it is the struggle that allows us to get to liberation together**.

So I think a lot of times social workers, because there's this dynamic of, Oh, I'm humbly entering into this other community I'm not a part of, and I'm going to help these folks. Like anyone even has the ability to do that. One, it's paternalistic, one, but this shying away from the conflict and the struggle that is required for us all to grow and to be willing to be transformed together. If the goal is to transform the world ultimately, there's this transformation that I think a lot of people who are benefiting from the current dynamic and power structures of the world are uncomfortable with.

So I think my last thing to social workers is just like, fuck the status quo. We are way... And I get it. There's this illusion that we're benefiting, or that some folks benefit from the status quo, so they want to hold on to that privilege. **But even the white cis woman that is the most common social worker that we interact with is losing under the structure of the world right now.** The fact that in order to inherit whiteness, there's this sacrifice of culture, culture being creation, creation being how we're all going to get free. It's just not worth it. **So give it up, give it up, reject the status quo and be willing to be transformed in the service of the work.**

I think it's, 2020 probably more than ever before, it's becoming more and more clear that this is not sustainable. The fact that so many social media viral moments and social media, which is probably one of the most shallow places I've ever been forced to interact with. But this year in social media we were hearing the social contract is broken. That moment, that viral moment of seeing us trying to renegotiate a social contract with society, with our government, it is clear that how society is structured in this formation is not sustainable and won't last.

So those who are at the front lines of marginalization are not only the most prepared to leverage our experiences, our identities in order to create something new, but all of us who are in this field trying to be in principled struggle with folks who are at the front lines, **it is even that much of a greater requirement that we give up this privilege,** and that we kind of dig deep into this current fight against all the things you could call it, cis, hetero, patriarchal, racial, capitalism, whatever you want to name it as, it could be all of the things. But one thing that we know, it's not sustainable, and it's going to be a requirement to dig down and create something new. Billionaires are trying to go to Mars and just leave us here. So, yeah.

Jama: Right. 2020, here we are. Is there anything else that you want to just make sure you say that we didn't talk about, or I didn't ask you about?

Jonathan: Anything else I would add… Just this piece about, and I name this often, as we're creating new systems, those systems exist in contestation. **When I think of new systems or alternative systems or systems of liberation, they exist in contestations to systems of oppression. So there has to be a breaking point where we decide, how do we resource the informal, non-traditional, non-government systems that literally people are creating in order to survive in real time?** Yeah, I think that's important to name, that our resources are still investing in harmful systems, or systems that were made to harm. So as we think about centering joy and centering creation, and even as we think about going back to pleasure activism, even like our erotic truth and understanding our bodies better, so we can then juxtapose that pleasure and that fullness with everything else in the world that deems us not full, that deems not full in our humanity, **we have to find ways to resource these systems of liberation that cultivate our Black Joy Experiences.**

For more information about Black Joy Experience, visit www.liberationhouse.org/black-joy-experience/

For more information about BYP 100, visit www.byp100.org

For more information about the Movement for Black Lives, visit www.m4bl.org

Reference

Saleeby, D. (1996). The strengths perspective in social work practice: Extensions and cautions. *Social Work*, *41*(3), 295–305.

12 Existing Outside of Gender: Autism and Gender Identity

A Conversation with Liliana Valvano

Liliana Valvano and Jama Shelton

Introduction

"To understand a person who is neurodiverse, a neurotypical person needs to leave the comfort of their own social position and view from the inside out, from the neurodiverse person's perspective" (Ehrensaft 2018, p. 4080).

In the same way that trans and gender expansive (TGE) people are often pathologized within mainstream social systems and experience harassment and discrimination from peers and community members, autistic people are frequently viewed through a deficit lens and experience widespread marginalization. Autistic activist Lydia X.Z. Brown explains:

> In the rush to affirm the validity of trans identities and experiences, trans movements frequently practice disavowal of neurodivergent and other disabled people. The common refrain, 'Being transgender isn't a mental illness, so there's nothing wrong with us!' results in real harm to all people with mental disabilities, but especially those of us at this intersection. (Brown, 2016)

Minimal social work literature examines the intersection of autism and TGE youth identities, yet some existing research and community based knowledge suggests that many autistic people identify as what we may label TGE. The following conversation with MSW student Liliana Valvano explores this intersection and provides several examples of ways in which the social worker (and the social work profession at large) can and should work to undo the societal valuing of certain ways of thinking and being over others.

Jama: Can you start by introducing yourself and telling us a little about yourself and why you're interested in contributing to a book about social work practice with trans and gender expansive youth?

Liliana: Sure! I am a queer and autistic student at Silberman getting my master's in social work. I think it is really unfortunate that in a field that does so much work directly with the disabled community, there are very few disabled folks doing the actual knowledge production.

DOI: 10.4324/9780429297687-12

It's really important that we emphasize listening to the voices of people within the disabled community. People, rightfully so, would be really dissatisfied with an ethnic studies program with all white professors, or a critical gender studies program with all cis/het men professors. I think we have to be equally critical when we have no openly disabled or autistic folks teaching about disabled and autistic life.

I'm really interested in bringing that in. I am especially interested in centering the autistic experience, because often when we're talking about disability there is a centering of physical disability and a decentering of cognitive disability. We are much more likely to give credit to the voices of physically disabled people because there's this really terrible and ableist mentality that "their minds are still intact, even though their bodies are not." However, autistic folks are almost never allowed to speak on autistic issues. We almost always see caretakers or service providers speaking. I think it's imperative for actual autistic folks to be speaking on the issues that impact us and speaking to the people who will be working with our community.

Jama: Yeah, I totally agree. I'm wondering if you have thoughts about why it is that autistic people are rarely asked to speak about their autism experience.

Liliana: **I think that centering autistic voices in autism discourse would demand a complete restructuring of how we think about not only disability, but the entire hierarchical value system that we subject people to in this country**. This would essentially demand a rethinking of capitalism – capitalism values abled people while disabled folks are perceived as disposable. We have a lot of very, very profitable systems impacting autistic people that are run by non-autistic people. Most prominently, we have ABA (applied behavioral analysis), which the autistic community largely and emphatically rejects. ABA is widely practiced throughout this country and is extremely profitable to the non-autistic people practicing it. If autistic voices were actually elevated, it would force a deconstruction of many of the non-autistic run autism service industries. Thus, non-autistic people have a lot to gain from silencing autistic voices so they can continue to profit off the community.

And then there's the social element, right? Our society still has this conception that the voices of cognitively disabled folks are less credible. People who are under the umbrella of intellectual disability, which is a portion of the autistic community, are especially subject to this perception. We have laws that cement that. Folks with cognitive disabilities can have their children taken away because they're seen as not able to parent simply because of IQ levels. **I think generally there is still an idea that autistic people don't know enough about their own experience to**

credibly speak about it. There is also a lack of acceptance for the way that autistic people may need to communicate. There are non-speaking autistic folks who have written entire books through augmentative and alternative communication (AAC), but sadly many non-speaking autistic people are denied AAC, and thus denied the ability to communicate at all. Additionally, spaces like academia and higher education, which are unfortunately often required in order for one's voice to be given credibility, are very inaccessible to autistic folks not only in the way they are structured, but also because of the way K–12 education holds autistic folks from pursuing higher ed. Traditional workplaces are often inaccessible, ruling out that space for autistic folks to have their voices heard. Getting into the field of policy-making is also often inaccessible, so autistic people are unable to have direct influence on policy which impacts them. **Essentially, we are put in a place where our voices can't be heard because we don't have access to the social and tangible structures needed to elevate one's voice**.

Jama: You said earlier that to center autistic voices would demand a restructuring of the entire hierarchal value that we give to people in this country. I think the same is true for trans people. To center the voices of trans people would require that we also dismantle structures and systems that cause trans people harm. Since this book is specifically about working with trans and gender expansive youth, I'm wondering what can you tell us about autistic trans and gender expansive youth?

Liliana: There's a lot of research being done about the significantly larger population of trans and gender nonconforming folks within the autistic community in comparison to the non-autistic community. So, essentially autistic folks are more likely to be trans than non-autistic folks, which is a really interesting thing to be published in empirical research because the autistic community has known this for some time. So on one hand, it's like – yay! Finally, this is being incorporated into empirical research! On the other hand, within the community, we're like, yeah, we've been saying this for years. A lot to say here on the way community wisdom isn't seen as a valid form of knowledge until it's put into an academic study... But anyway, I think there's a lot of really interesting overlap between the autistic experience and the trans experience, and the autistic experience of gender.

The autistic community has conceived this idea of a gender or a gender identity known as autigender. I preface in defining this term with the fact that if you asked 10 nonbinary people to explain what being nonbinary means to them, you'd get 10 different answers. Similarly, autigender means different things to different people.

I will try to give an explanation that incorporates the many voices I've heard within the community as well as my own experience. But generally, autigender is this idea that autism inherently impacts the way that people experience gender.

There's a lot of facets of that. **We can start by recognizing that being autistic is quite literally one's entire neurology, it's how one's entire brain works. Given that, an autistic person's perception of everything is going to be through the lens of an autistic mind. So, an autistic person's perception and experience of gender is also going to be conflated with autistic cognition and perception**.

Autistic people tend to struggle to pick up on social cues and norms, both interpersonally but also societally and culturally. And so when we think about normative gender, it is largely about normative social roles and social cues, right? And they're very pervasive. Cisnormative gendering is not just about how one adorns their body with certain clothes. It's how one sits, how one speaks, and how one expresses and processes emotion. So, with that in mind, some autistic folks struggle to pick up gender cues and gender norms and thus their gender identities tend to then be "autistic" in that they tend to be informed by the missing social cues. Performing normative gender requires a keen adherence to social cues, and therefore, autistic people experience gender really differently.

Another interesting part of the connection between autism and gender can be highlighted by the very controversial "extreme male brain theory." This theory emerged in the 1990s largely through the work of researcher Simon Baron-Cohen, and posited that autistic cognition tends to align very heavily with "male" cognition. The most significant part of this theory focused on the way that autistic people tend to systemize rather than empathize. It is important to recognize that the experience of being autistic is not monolithic, and that leaning toward logic rather than emotion is not the experience all autistic people, but is that of many. A lot of people also argue that theories like this are part of what prevents people who are assigned female at birth from receiving autism diagnoses. Regardless of the flaws this particular theory has, it is important to note that many autistic traits – such as a lack of adherence to social norms and a propensity for being very logical to the point of difficulty understanding abstract and emotional ideas – are elements of cognition and processing which are heavily cisnormatively gendered as "male." This can create an interesting gender experience for people who are assigned female at birth and have an autistic mind deemed by a cisnormative society to be "extremely male."

There are also many aspects of being autistic that influence the way that one physically presents. For example, sensory issues may influence the way somebody might dress or style their hair. Both of these things are extremely gender-codified. Autistic folks might dress in a way that is purposefully comfortable and conducive to their sensory needs which may not align with a normative gendered presentation and thus creates a gender non-conforming appearance.Generally, a lot of autistic people explain that they just don't get gender. It doesn't make sense. It doesn't feel like it's built for or applies to us. And so therefore we often feel like **we kind of exist outside of gender and instead we do what feels right socially and physically for our bodies and our minds, which often does not fit a cisnormative standard of gender**.

Jama: Are there other things based on your experience working in the community that you think would be really important for social workers to know, or to do when working with autistic trans and gender expansive youth?

Liliana: There are a lot of thoughts that come to mind. I think it's important to note that a lot of trans experiences have overlap with autistic experiences. Being autistic is an identity that folks also have to sort of "come out" as, and are constantly "coming out" as. This "coming out" oftentimes carries a lot of similar risks to coming out as trans. There are so many legal and social risks of being openly autistic. Openly autistic people fear workplace discrimination, fear not being seen as competent enough to have agency, and fear state violence such as police brutality, institutionalization, forced sterilization, and having their children removed. These things are terrifying. There are laws in place that actively discriminate against cognitively disabled folks. Even though we have the Americans with Disabilities Act (ADA), we also have a whole lot of laws that regulate what cognitively disabled folks can and cannot do. Social workers working with trans and autistic people need to have a baseline familiarity with laws that impact both communities. There are specific regulations that permit social workers to break confidentiality in ways that they couldn't with non-autistic folks because autistic (and cognitively disabled folks) are viewed as a more vulnerable group similarly to children. A lot of infantilization to be unpacked there… There are also laws in some states that assert that cognitively disabled folks cannot consent, meaning that technically, sexual interactions where one or more partners are autistic can be considered a non-consensual act under law. And what that translates to is a lack of marriage equality for autistic folks, because especially in group homes, often cognitively disabled folks, intellectually disabled folks, and autistic folks are not allowed to be romantically involved, get married, or cohabitate in order for the group home to avoid potential consent-related legal liability. There is a social aspect coming out as autistic, which can often lead to being socially outcasted and put in harms way in the same way that coming out as trans can.

Many autistic people attest to the experience of trying to find a therapist and having a number of therapists refuse to even do a consultation because the person is autistic and the therapist claims to "not treat autism." Autistic people seeking mental health treatment are not looking for "autism treatment." This idea that autism is a pathology and that clinicians cannot work with autism because it needs to be treated is really apparent. It is already difficult for trans youth to find a trans-affirming therapist, but trying to find a trans *and* autistic affirming therapist is nearly impossible. This search becomes even harder if the youth has additional oppressed identities. That's a clinical example, but in the larger world of social work, I think that autistic people are not given credibility and agency in the same way that non-autistic people are.

When autistic people express literally anything, it is immediately called into question because autistic folks are not seen as credible voices to speak on their own experiences. So autistic folks are often not taken seriously when they express queerness. Some people even believe that autistic and cognitively disabled folks cannot be queer or trans, especially autistic folks who are non-speaking or have a co-occurring intellectual disability. This is largely because of the infantilization of autistic folks.

It is also important for social workers working with trans and autistic youth to recognize that parents of autistic youth may be far more involved in their child's life, and in turn, the child may be given less independence and space than a non-autistic child. Because of this, if the parents are not accepting of trans identities, the child will have far less space to explore and express their identity and might be more likely to being subject to transphobia in the home.

Working with autistic folks means completely deconstructing our ideas of the way that we value minds, right? We have to deconstruct ideas of intelligence and ideas of what makes someone credible and valuable. It's really important for social workers to just be aware of ableism as a systemic form of oppression. And the baseline of that is to be aware of ABA as a traumatic experience. I'd like to imagine that is the bare minimum, but there are so many social workers who advocate for and support the use of ABA, and gaslight survivors who express trauma from ABA. In being a trans and autistic affirming, a social worker must recognize the systemic oppression, but also – and this is important – recognize the joy and the comradery and the pride that exists within both communities.

A medicalized model focuses on "overcoming" perceived limitations and shortcomings of autism. Moving into a social model of disability in regard to autism means recognizing the systemic oppression, and also recognizing the pride and the fun and the community that comes with being autistic. It is important for social workers to understand that both trans and autistic identities, which often are mutually informed, are things that come with suffering due to discrimination and oppression, but also come with so much pride. It's so important for social workers to not only encourage pride in queerness, but also encourage pride in being autistic. Being trans and autistic is something to celebrate.

References

Brown, L. (2016, June 22). *Gendervague: At the intersection of autistic and trans experiences.* Retrieved from https://www.aane.org/gendervague-intersection-autistic-trans-experiences/

Ehrensaft, D. (2018). Double helix rainbow kids. *Journal of Autism & Developmental Disorders,* *48*(12), 4079–4081. Retrieved from https://doi-org.proxy.wexler.hunter.cuny.edu/10.1007/s10803-018-3716-5

13 Mental Health Supports for Trans and Gender Expansive Youth

Meghan Romanelli, Leah Abay, and Kelly Ancharski

Introduction

An estimated 355,600 youth between the ages of 13–24 in the United States (US) are transgender (trans; Herman, Flores, Brown, Wilson, & Conron, 2017). Experiences of discrimination and social exclusion may expose trans and gender expansive (TGE) youth to stressors that elevate their risk for mental health (MH) concerns relative to their cisgender counterparts (Tan, Treharne, Ellis, Schmidt, & Veale, 2019). Research shows, for example, that TGE youth have increased rates of depression, anxiety, and attention deficit disorders (Becerra-Culqui et al., 2018; Chodzen, Hidalgo, Chen, & Garofalo, 2019). Another critical issue for social workers' immediate consideration is TGE youth's increased risk for suicidal ideation and attempted suicide (di Giacomo, Krausz, Colmegna, Aspesi, & Clerici, 2018; Hatchel, Polanin, & Espelage, 2019); past-year prevalence of attempted suicide among trans youth was 35% (Johns et al., 2019), which far exceeds the national average of 8.9% among all US adolescents (Ivey-Stephenson et al., 2020). Not only is access to MH care necessary to identify, monitor, and treat MH symptoms (Burgess, Tran, Lee, & van Ryn, 2007; Romanelli & Hudson, 2017; Substance Abuse and MH Services Administration SAMHSA, 2012), but access affirmative care, more specifically, is associated with better MH outcomes for trans care-seekers (Kattari, Walls, Speer, & Kattari, 2016).

Barriers to Affirmative Treatment

Significant barriers to affirmative care, however, may typify the care-seeking experiences of TGE youth. Common barriers include discrimination and rejection from services, poor treatment and provider insensitivity, problems with the physical environment and climate of services, issues with the availability and appropriateness of services, and lack of providers with trans competence (Stotzer, Silverschanz, & Wilson, 2013). Furthermore, trans care-seekers have often experienced more than one of these barriers or multiple forms of discrimination throughout their care-seeking histories

DOI: 10.4324/9780429297687-13

(Romanelli & Lindsey, 2020). Multiply marginalized TGE individuals, such as TGE people of color, poverty-impacted TGE individuals, and TGE with MH diagnoses, are at increased risk for receiving discriminatory care in the health/MH systems (Kattari, Bakko, Hecht, & Kinney, 2020; Romanelli & Lindsey, 2020).

Trans Pathologization in the MH System

It is also important to acknowledge the historical context through which stigma towards TGE individuals has established itself in the MH system (Drescher, 2010). A history of mistreatment, vulnerability, and pathology characterizes many TGE care-seekers' interactions with the MH system. The role of the MH professional needs to be reconceptualized to minimize a (potentially) pathologizing process for TGE youth who use or want to use MH services. For many TGE youth, MH professionals – including social workers – are viewed as "gatekeepers" to hormones or pubertal suppression (Gridley et al., 2016), i.e., we hold power to deny or grant access to formal institutions and physical/emotional care. This creates a barrier to self-actualization for those TGE youth who have a goal to transition via psychological scrutiny (i.e., application of a gender dysphoria diagnosis; Lev, 2009), and further, this can compound stress for TGE youth with MH concerns. Further, the perspective that TGE youth interact with MH services solely based on their gender identity or transition-related care creates a pathologizing system and erects a barrier to services, restricting care-seeking for other potential issues (Sperber, Landers, & Lawrence, 2005; Shipherd, Green, & Abramovitz, 2010). Here, the emphasis remains that social workers serve only as gatekeepers and that they are professionals who "dislike" TGE youth (Gridley et al., 2016), rather than clinicians who can promote emotional wellness.

Best Practices for Working with Trans and Gender Expansive Youth

In addition to identifying barriers to care, it is critical that we also examine the ways in which social workers can make their practices more accessible for TGE youth, with consideration for both logistical and functional accessibility. This section highlights the critical role of identity within the therapeutic process for the social worker and client, ways to reduce barriers to MH care by enhancing your services' approachability and acceptability, formal and informal methods of MH care for TGE youth, and steps to consider throughout the different stages of therapy.

Clinician Identity and Power Relations

The idea that social workers must remain "blank slates" to be clinically effective has evolved. Instead, the focus has transitioned to how our identity is infused within MH care and our relationship with our clients (Dewane, 2006). The role of identity is grounded in culture and value systems, thus shifting and shaping how individuals share meanings, norms, beliefs, and ideas (Constance-Huggins, 2012). Before being able to guide a client through MH care, social workers must grapple with, question, and reflect on our identities.

Our identity – sociocultural, political, ideological – influences, imbeds, and transforms how and why we operate as social workers. In order to build relationships and work alongside TGE youth, we must first confront our implicit bias and strive to unlearn and learn our identity and imbedded power as a professional imperative. Critical to self-care and anti-oppressive social work is accountability to those served. Through reflection and accountability, we seek to reduce gatekeeping of social services, identity, and community (Fisher-Borne, Cain, & Martin, 2015).

For TGE communities, identity exploration is a process that spans the life-course. Trying to figure out within a binary sociocultural system what it means to be a "man," "woman," or nothing or somewhere in-between, is a continuum between defiance and euphoria (Kuper, Wright, & Mustanski, 2018). As gender is believed by dominant culture and the status quo to be natural, unchanging, and innate, this directly contrasts the lived experiences of TGE communities (Levitt, 2019). To hold space for this exploration, social workers must first question their positionality and begin to unrestrictedly signal to clients that gender fluidity is valid, powerful, and transformative (Austin, 2017; Pryor & Vickroy, 2019). This will be explored throughout the chapter and especially in the section *Infusing Macro-Understanding of Barriers to Care and Identity Complexities.*

Accountability and Humility

In moving away from the concept of "cultural competency" toward accountability and humility, clinicians must engage in critical self-awareness, utilizing a more curious, compassionate, and critical framework for working with TGE youth. We are called to challenge the inherent power dynamic presented in the therapeutic relationship – the differential and influence afforded to the clinician via education, employment, socioeconomic status, and in some cases, whiteness and cis-privilege (Boyd, 1996; Butler et al., 2003; Fisher-Borne et al., 2015; Tervalon & Murray-García, 1998). The accountability and humility we are striving for in working with TGE youth, however, will not happen in one class, one training, or one workshop. Shifting cultural norms requires increased self-awareness and ongoing education for social workers. Supported by The Code of Ethics, Competency 1.04, to ensure no harm be done to the client, it is our responsibility to go beyond competency to humility, recognizing the power of language – further detailed in *Terminology* – and its effects on MH and gender identity (National Association of Social Workers [NASW], 2017).

As social workers, we are encouraged to continuously gather information about ourselves and our clients while acknowledging the multiple layers of each of our identities (Fisher-Borne et al., 2015). Listening and modeling the language our clients use denotes to the client that you are not only actively listening, but also invested in understanding their complete identity. This concept of creating space leads us to another important aspect in moving toward accountability and humility: continuing education and lifelong learning.

The Code of Ethics, Continuing Education and Staff Development 3.08, states that social workers must be informed by new knowledge and research through lifelong learning (National Association of Social Workers, 2017). Continuing education will benefit the ability of the clinician to complete their job more effectively while reducing the emotional labor that TGE clients may have experienced in other therapeutic and social situations. Although our clients may be some of our best teachers, it is not their job to educate us. In fact, research has shown having to educate providers is correlated with poor MH outcomes among trans care-seekers (Kattari, Bakko, Hecht, & Kattari, 2020). Rather, it is our professional responsibility to center their experiences and to remain mindful when working with clients who hold marginalized identities. This is essential to uphold when working with TGE youth, as they likely must continually educate others in their lives, like parents, teachers, coaches, and peers.

Use of Self and Building Relationships

Acknowledging our identity and power allows us to know ourselves and the client better. When knowledge and experience are shackled by history, culture, and social systems, the scope of intervention and evaluation of identity and MH must incorporate not only biological and social factors, but also the impact of socialization and the status quo on individual development (Dietert & Dentice, 2013). We have all confronted gender identity and roles; we have all been socialized within the gender binary. Regardless of our gender identity, social workers must unravel the complexity of our identity, not only to relate to the TGE youth we are working with, but to radically shift the social order of white supremacy that reinforces a hierarchy of identity domination and subordination (McLaughlin, 2011).

For clinicians, we cannot work to understand the experiences, trauma, and/or oppression of a client in relation to their identity without reckoning with our position in the gender system. For example, when working with TGE youth, we must not reproduce the binary structures that increase marginalization and isolation (e.g., believing gender/sex are fixed, misgendering, assuming pronouns, and reducing MH conditions to transness; Strauss et al., 2017). There are a multitude of ways we unpack and unlearn these oppressive systems and our relation to them. Along with the appropriate use of supervision, an examination of countertransference may aid in this process.

Importance of Supervision

Supervision is a place to explore, reflect, and ultimately learn about ourselves and the therapeutic process. Through critical thinking and analysis of core beliefs and values, supervisees and supervisors can begin to unpack their identities and how their internal biases influence their roles as social workers. Supervisors can create a parallel process by acknowledging power dynamics between themselves and supervisees. This further strengthens the supervision relationship. The parallel process is often replicated within clinician-client sessions. Relational safety – space to raise questions, confront biases, and challenge points of view – is foundational for all supervision, but is key if/when either party requires additional TGE-related resources (Hernández & McDowell, 2010).

Countertransference

Countertransference can be an incredibly constructive tool in the therapeutic relationship. However, failing to recognize our own emotional responses during sessions decreases treatment effectiveness. Countertransference is more than concealing our emotions, but an active and ongoing process of working through our own responses (Agass, 2002). In working with TGE youth, awareness of internal gender binarism is crucial in unlearning potential oppressive behaviors and language. In questioning our internalized binarism, social workers can begin to decenter themselves, concede power, and cultivate a relationship with the client holistically and honestly.

  Questions to Consider
- When did you first think about your gender/sex?
- What sociocultural signs do you remember about gender cues growing up?
- How have you thought or not thought about your gender identity?
- What is assumed to be natural, essential, unchanging about sex/gender?
- Has sex/gender been discussed in supervision? Why/why not?
- How can you utilize your positionality within the therapeutic process and in supervision?

Reducing Stigma and Pathologization

Transness has traditionally been outlined and viewed as a MH "disorder," and in order to access to hormones, pubertal suppression, and transition-related care (if fitting with the goals of the TGE youth) – especially with insurance coverage – people of trans+ experience often need a formal diagnosis, as relatively few practitioners provide gender affirming care under an informed consent framework (Coleman et al., 2012). The tension of engaging in oppressive systems as a pathway to liberation and social validation primes

MH care clinicians as gatekeepers. Through transparency, psychoeducation, and client-focus engagement, social workers can begin to dismantle barriers to care.

Acknowledging Professional and Sociocultural Gatekeeping

When working within a system that abides by the medical model, emphasis is placed on the clinician to diagnose symptoms, claiming "medical necessity." This further enacts the power dynamic between client and clinician – and perhaps also the fields of medicine and social work – through gatekeeping access to MH services. The structure of the medical model continues to pathologize clients through simplifying their symptoms to fit within the Diagnostic and Statistical Manual of Mental Disorders-5 (DSM-5) criteria followed by a treatment plan to eradicate those symptoms. Diagnoses and treatment plans are then presented to insurance companies in order for clients and clinicians to be reimbursed for care.

It is imperative that we move forward with transparency and disclose the flaws within the current systems by sharing with the client *why* we have concluded this diagnosis and treatment plan. Not only will this process acknowledge that sociocultural gatekeeping exists, it also informs the client about the systems that work to oppress their identities. The problem lies within the systems and societal discomfort, rather than within the TGE youth.

A common diagnosis for TGE youth is "gender dysphoria." In the DSM-5, "gender dysphoria" is defined as "a marked incongruence between one's experienced/expressed gender and assigned gender" (American Psychiatric Association [APA], 2017, p. 215). On one hand, this diagnosis may permit access to hormones, pubertal suppression, gender-affirming surgeries, and document changes (Coleman et al., 2017). Conversely, "gender dysphoria" has drawn criticism because the "clinically significant distress or impairment in social, school, or other important areas of functioning" is not psychological, but external (American Psychiatric Association, 2017, p. 215; Davy & Toze, 2018). Gender identity development is not an internal struggle, but a consequence of hetero/cis-normativity. Furthermore, to be trans, one does not need to have "dysphoria" or desire medical transition. While we may not be able to radicalize the insurance processes or diagnostic institutions, we have the opportunity to divulge to the client the failures of "gender dysphoria," as well as the access afforded due to an official diagnosis. This may alleviate feelings of internalized shame.

Queering Therapy

In an effort to move away from binary ideas of public and private modes of operating and receiving MH care, we highlight institutional forms of therapy (i.e., traditional care), compared to community care to cultivate a more robust awareness of the myriad of social support networks available or relevant to TGE youth. Combined, both support systems are able to foster resiliency (Noltemeyer & Bush, 2013), ease isolation, and bolster an understanding of self. The formal and informal nexus of MH care is an articulation of systems theory and the biopsychosocial model espoused by social work.

When we "queer" therapy, we commit to subverting elements of rigid social norms within larger feminist and anti-oppression advocacy (Hardy & Monypenny, 2019; Sullivan, 2003; Turner & Maschi, 2015). The focus of MH must include a true biopsychosocial assessment in order to support and bolster all pathways and relationships with the trans experience. Through community care, we can frame MH care as a process of merging traditional therapy and formal/informal networks. Redressing MH support through a queer perspective will embolden a more encompassing approach to civil society, resiliency, and trauma-informed care.

Traditional MH Care: Institutional Psychotherapy

Formal therapy and MH care offer standardized treatment and can facilitate increased access to other sociocultural and legal services. Traditional MH care is the usage of institutional psychotherapy, administering of direct counseling, and coordination of care. While a typical role for MH service providers often falls into gatekeeping access to medical transition, TGE youth seek MH care for a variety of reasons and present with many of the same issues as cisgender youth, including anxiety disorders, depression, substance abuse, life changes, and relationship difficulties, which can be peripheral or unrelated to gender dysphoria (Shipherd et al., 2010; Bockting et al., 2013). While there is movement for clinicians to become trans-affirming advocates through a partnership of opening doors for TGE youth and increasing transparency, accountability, and use of self, traditional care for the TGE community has repeatedly reverted back to the medical model (Coleman et al., 2012).

It is imperative that we reevaluate how the conventional therapeutic process or standardized interventions may or may not apply to TGE youth. Most evidence-based interventions are designed for and tested against white, cis, non-disabled individuals, and not the trans community (Reisner et al., 2016). Ascertaining the rationale for seeking MH care will provide parameters for traditional care and selected intervention(s). Moreover, engagement and relationship-building are essential in establishing trust and continuity of care (Singh & Dickey, 2017). Within formal therapy, social workers need to recognize the vast array of experiences within TGE communities. Transness is not dependent on or isolated to suffering. In depathologizing transness, MH care and social workers must remember that trauma and "dysphoria" do not equate the trans experience.

Evidence-Based Adaptations for TGE Youth

While few models have been designed specifically for trans youth, some individual and group therapies have been adapted to address the specific experiences of TGE communities. Cognitive Behavioral Therapy (CBT), or Trans-affirming CBT (TA-CBT), has illustrated an effective connection in reducing anxiety symptoms (Craig & Austin, 2016; Busa et al., 2018). Although not yet tested via Randomized Controlled Trial, the eight-module pilot study of the affirmative cognitive behavioral coping skills group intervention (AFFIRM) demonstrated a reduction in stress and depression, as well as increased coping and feelings of acceptance. Within AFFIRM, Craig and Austin suggest setting the stage of formal therapy by explicitly disclosing that providers are trans-inclusive, standardizing gender-neutral language, validating lived experiences and identity, and calling attention to how anti-transness/systematic oppression impacts overall well-being (2016). Other interventions or guidelines for MH care seek to tailor modalities to the individual situation, needs, goals, and desire for therapy (Edwards-Leeper, Leibowitz, & Sangganjanavanich, 2016; Mizock & Lundquist, 2016; Singh & Dickey, 2017).

Another body of literature centers on group therapy interventions aiming to decrease social isolation for LGBTQ youth. As with individual therapy, though promising, there is limited evidence of effectiveness. Wilkerson and colleagues outline training, group formation processes, and overarching themes that emerged within the program, Hatch Youth. Within these three 1-hour sessions, meetings were structured with social time, psychoeducation/consciousness-raising, and peer support (2017). Participants who attended between one to six months reported more social support, and this increased inclusion was associated with reduced depressive symptoms (Wilkerson et al., 2017). Likewise, other literature analyses the benefit of GSA or school-based clubs on improving acceptance and decreasing bullying, marginalization, and victimization (Heck, 2015; Kuff, Greytak, & Kosciw, 2019). Overall, increasing resource availability, improving social support through community development, and bolstering identity-affirming spaces are critical in providing traditional MH care to TGE youth.

Community Care: Networks and Family Formations

To survey the lived experiences of a client, social workers must emphasize the value and protective nature of community care. Community care is the process, action, and motivation of creating mental, physical, and social health, healing, and sustainability not just for the individuals, but for and by the whole community. For the broader LGBTQ+ network, safety, acceptance, resource sharing, community organizing are strengths rooted into queer culture that enrich mental and physical health (Austin, 2017; Hudson & Romanelli, 2019).

COMMUNITY DEVELOPMENT

A wider tie to history serves as a bond for connecting expressions of gender, queerness, and community. It is essential to view an association with trans history as a possible means for TGE youth to relate to a larger sense of purpose. Due to the prolonged isolation of transness from normative family and community structures, the queering of community developed within distinct social venues (i.e., kiki ballroom, public open spaces, and bookstores, through media/organizational membership, activism/advocacy participation, and the development of chosen families; Balestrery, 2017). The dismantling of normative family and community structures throughout trans and queer historical narratives continues to allow TGE youth to discover a sense of self in relation to others within a system of support.

Linked to community is the development of self and identity within social interactions and support networks. For sexual and gender development, a connection to aspects of trans and queer culture is a core feature of constructing identity within a sociocultural value system that differs from heteronormative culture (Levitt, 2019). Self-acceptance, especially for TGE youth, is a perpetual practice. In negotiating a sense of self with environmental stressors and heteronormativity, TGE youth are forced to decipher their identity in relation to systematic oppression. Finding sustaining and coherent identity, security, belonging, and valuing of sexual and gender diversity are critical in cultivating authenticity and acceptance (Austin, 2017; Levitt, 2019; Russell & Fish, 2016). Early and regular association with other TGE individuals and communities may impact positive identity development, reduce isolation, and decrease MH conditions (Austin, 2016). As social workers, we must acknowledge the positive impact of MH care outside the therapeutic relationship. Beyond community resource sharing and providing group therapy, we must evaluate various associations in school, peer networks, and within (formal or informal) queer organizations in order to outline all the factors influencing TGE youth wellbeing. We can catalyze upon community strength to encourage and empower existing protective systems (Higa et al., 2014).

CHOSEN FAMILIES

An incredibly vital aspect of community care, particularly for TGE youth, is the development of chosen families. Social support and approval surface from relationships extending beyond the parent-child dyad. Because of exclusion and prejudice faced by TGE youth from birth families or sociocultural value systems, the chosen family for trans communities can counteract disapproval, isolation, and chronic stress to produce resilience (Budge et al., 2013; Pflum et al., 2015). Chosen families are defined as a group of people who are emotionally close and considered "family" without necessarily biological or legal recognition (Hull & Ortyl, 2019). TGE youth with strong support networks not only are less likely to experience victimization, but the support may also decrease symptoms of depression and anxiety (Button et al., 2012).

For social work, when evaluating strengths and resilience of a TGE client, it is essential to understand the sociocultural protective factors of diverse family and community structures. In knowing how the client defines family/community, how they relate themselves to the larger environment through or without these networks, and their activities within those structures will allow social workers to assess the systems influencing the client and possible appropriate interventions to use, depending on the presenting problem(s).

From Systemic to Interpersonal: The Therapeutic Process with TGE Youth

By recognizing the disparities in social access, the historical inequalities of the profession, and personal power within sociocultural structures, social workers can connect systematic barriers to TGE individual or communal experiences, bearing witness to the history of subjection with sincerity. In grasping how gender, race, ethnicity, class, ability, and sexuality congregate and reinforce marginalization, social workers can apply appropriate interventions that question normative directives of gender and wellbeing (McLaughlin, 2011). Through an examination of the communal environment, relationships (family, friends, and peers), individual development, and medical history, social workers can conduct comprehensive trauma-informed and trans-centered MH care (Austin, 2017).

Infusing Macro-Understanding of Barriers to Care and Identity Complexities

We have outlined that TGE communities disproportionately face multidimensional oppression – socioeconomic discrimination, sociocultural stigma, and harassment within and outside mental and physical health care (Snow et al., 2019). In moving from institutions, community, and use of self to more direct practice, we will begin to delineate how to implement trans-centered MH care through the stages of therapy and engagement. Moreover, we will discuss ways to shape your space through a cooperative and client-focused lens.

INTAKE AND INITIAL ASSESSMENT QUESTIONS

The role of social workers in intake sessions often falls into probing clients to detail some of the most personal, and sometimes traumatic, moments of their lives. During an initial assessment, forms require data gathering of basic characteristics and presenting issues. Conducting an intake assessment provides another opportunity to acknowledge and examine the structures of power we have as social workers and medical professionals. We should consider the entire journey of the client that preceded the intake session. We have to keep in mind other intersecting forms of oppression, which may include race, class, and ability. As explained in *Reducing Stigma and Pathologization,* social workers should be curious about how both clinician and client identities affect the therapeutic relationship.

CONFIDENTIALITY

Confidential care is one of the most important service qualities indicated by TGE youth (Hoffman, Freeman, & Swann, 2009). It is essential that social workers provide information related to confidentiality (and limits of) at the start of care. TGE youth may feel reticent to engage in care if the bounds of confidentiality are not explained or if they are not assured a safe therapeutic space.

ENGAGEMENT

While the information outlined in the *Early, Middle, and Later Sessions* sections is critical, it is only impactful if TGE youth continue to come and participate fully and genuinely in sessions. As such, there are several strategies that social workers can incorporate into initial sessions that might enhance TGE youth's participation in their MH care.

Assess Care-Seeking Histories   Many TGE individuals have negative experiences within the health/MH systems that can inform inhibitions in client-clinician communication and trust (Bradford, Reisner, Honnold, & Xavier, 2013). Social workers should elicit detailed care-seeking histories and gain an understanding of how past experiences may have shaped beliefs, attitudes, and expectancies around MH and MH treatment (Romanelli & Hudson, 2017; Romanelli & Lindsey, 2020; Romanelli, Lu, & Lindsey, 2018). This practice might improve connections to treatment by signaling to clients that we are dedicated to understanding and unwilling to replicate past harmful treatment experiences.

Assess Barriers to Care   TGE youth can experience both perceptual and actual barriers that might influence treatment decisions. An assessment of logistical barriers, for example, might bring to light issues related transportation (Romanelli & Hudson, 2017), need for parental consent, or insurance benefits (Hoffman et al., 2009) that might preclude continued participation in care. Social workers might elicit this information by asking, "What do you think will be the biggest obstacle to participating in sessions?" and importantly, offer practical assistance or problem-solve through further inquiry (e.g., "How can I help you address some of these concerns?"). Psychoeducation can be employed to reduce perceptual barriers to care if the TGE youth does not believe MH treatment is relevant to their needs or if they are experiencing fear, shame, or stigma related to treatment participation, for example.

Shaping Your Space As another way to promote engagement, office environments can signal trans-inclusivity. It is important that TGE youth feel that they are in a safe space where they can present authentically, as this allows them to participate in carefully (Hendricks & Testa, 2012; Redfern & Sinclair, 2014). "How can I signal to my client that this is a trans-inclusive space?" This is an everchanging question that operates in tandem with self-awareness and agency evaluation. Above specific techniques, the therapeutic process with TGE youth must aim to craft a space that acknowledges potentially harmful, isolating, or coercive prior experiences with authority figures and MH care services. The space we co-create with our TGE youth and with other colleagues is the foundation for ensuring a gender affirming environment.

One of the ways that social workers can increase trans-inclusivity in our personal practice is through physical and verbal signs. We can model a culture shift by adding pronouns to our email signatures and stating our pronouns when initially introducing ourselves to all clients regardless of gender identity. Through this normalization, social workers can begin to undo the reliance on binary and heteronormative language. This practice aims to reduce trans discrimination and microaggressions, e.g., mis-gendering and dead name usage. Social workers should also use intake forms and display materials representative of TGE youths' experiences (Bauer et al. 2009) and ensure that their non-discrimination policies and patients' bill of rights include language surrounding gender identity. This information should be distributed to TGE youth care-seekers and visibly posted in the office (Romanelli et al., 2018).

Questions to Consider
- What type of message does this organization send to TGE youth?
- How do you outreach to TGE youth?
- Where do I advertise my services?
- Are my services accessible to TGE youth? (e.g., Do I offer sliding scale payments? Do I accept insurance? Do I require parental consent?)
- What is the mission statement?
- How are bathrooms structured?
- How are non-trans staff introduced?
- What are ways that social workers can signal in their office/in their space that you are trans-inclusive?
- Are my non-discrimination policies posted and given to clients?
- How can you practice allyship as an accomplice?
- Is ally/allyship a noun or a verb?

Early Sessions

Try beginning your early sessions by asking clients what they would like you to know about their identity. Instead of asking direct, close-ended questions about gender identity, sexual orientation, or any other portion of who they are, it is crucial that social workers ask open-ended questions. This gives control to the client. They will have the agency to disclose information as they feel comfortable. Invitational language and choice-making options foster self-determination and active and collaborative participation (Larson, 2008). The engagement phase during these early sessions is paramount in inaugurating trust. A question to begin some of these sessions might look like, "What would you like me to know about your identity as it relates to your gender and/or sexuality?"

Middle Sessions

During the middle phase of MH treatment, central issues are faced, coping skills are practiced in session or in-vivo, and clients often experience significant symptom improvement (Gelso & Carter, 1994; Howard, Lueger, Maling, & Martinovich, 1993; Woody & Adessky, 2002). During this important phase of the therapeutic process, creative and collaborative techniques, and those outside of the traditional treatment framework, should be considered when working with TGE youth.

Narrative Creation

This tool is a trauma-informed storytelling process that recounts relationships, cultural backgrounds, and identities over the entire life-course. It is a process of defining the self from and within a community and a society at large. Narratives situate context and reality (Burack-Weiss, Lawrence, Mijangos, & Charon, 2017). Within narrative creation, social workers and clients discover who, what, where, and how of lived experiences and the relation to the present. Through self-determination in an environment of connection and collaboration with radical and continuous gender affirmation, MH care will be attuned to the individual(s) (Hick, 2005). Agency – the ability to dictate individual or community narratives – is a central and motivating theme of trauma-informed care.

The foremost application of narrative creation is asking the client what they need/want. In frontloading any therapeutic process with this simple set of questions, clients are able to set boundaries and expectations for MH services. Mapping identity, discussing community participation, and observing family or intimate relationships will allow social workers to pinpoint assets and sociocultural systematic gaps for a client (White, 2007). Moreover, these details can provide a tailored service plan for working alongside clients to gain personal autonomy, community connections, and maintain/develop short-term and long-term coping mechanisms to buffer risk and minimize adversity (Brown & Augusta-Scott, 2007; Strong & Pare, 2003).

A primary narrative positioning example for TGE youth can be their ongoing stories of "coming-out" (internally or externally). Coming-out is not a one-time occurrence that magically solves all the sociocultural pressure placed on the trans+ community (Klein, Holtby, Cook, & Travers, 2015). Coming-out is a prime model to address the diversity within the gender identity and relationships to individuals and self. To live openly or "out" does not automatically remove shame and stigma that TGE youth may or may not have internalized (Austin, 2017). As social workers, we must hold the complexity of learning and unlearning gender essentialism and create room for clients to share and detail their evolving relationship with their identity. In order to live a full life, clients do not need to come out to everyone. Social workers must be aware of safety, desire, and protection. In decentering our professional and identity-based power, we need to remove the pressure to disclose information. What is best for us or one situation does not directly apply to everyone. Instead, open the conversation around gender identity development and "coming-out" as a process of letting someone into the story of the client (Brumbaugh-Johnson & Hull, 2019). The client does not owe anyone more information and intimacy than they want to give. It may take weeks, years, or never in some cases. We should take the role of aiding in navigating barriers within interpersonal relationships and systematic institutions.

Creativity

Detailed earlier in *Traditional MH Care: Institutional Psychotherapy*, traditional care does not always capture the vast array of outlets for coping and expression, such as creativity. For TGE youth, concepts discussed in traditional talk therapy may be limited due to heteronormative language, stigma, or internalized anti-transness. If we believe another form of care would be beneficial, social workers should advocate for additional types of treatment.

TGE youth may benefit from creative avenues where they can delve into gender, sexuality, shame, familial conflict, and identity. An example of an activity used to explore gender identity in a therapeutic setting is an "Inside Me, Outside Me" exercise. The client is asked to create two portraits of themselves: one is how they present to the public, and the other is how they view themselves (Pelton-Sweet & Sherry, 2008). In addition, clients may draw, sculpt, or move their bodies as a way to uncover and reflect without speaking. Through creativity, a client may be supported in their ability to externalize feelings without solely depending on speaking, providing them with supplementary tools to unearth their full identity.

Spirituality

There are entangled and difficult linkages between transness and institutionalized religion. Regardless of this, spirituality can be viewed through the prism of finding meaning and relating yourself to the world around you (Senreich, 2013). Not exclusive to TGE youth, religiosity or spirituality may be a tether to examine the texture of identity and the meaning-making outlook of a client. Especially in understanding our sense of self, our bodies, and emotional regulation, figuring out how the client views spirituality is an effective tool in building client-clinician alliances and investigating coping mechanisms and grounding tools. Even if not directly labeled spirituality or a "spiritual" practice, be open and curious about the perspective of the client and their participation/interest in meditation, breathing, prayer, and trans-inclusive religious engagement (Erickson-Schroth, 2014).

Later Sessions

The length of time in MH care may vary based on type of intervention, program, and setting, but later sessions typically detail implementation, goal evaluation, termination. After a relationship is established with clear, but flexible goals, later sessions revolve around continuous check-ins about experiences in and out of therapy. It is critical to be able to accurately and authentically reflect back the experiences of the client, as well as affirm the fluidity of gender through supporting and reassuring that identity shifts and changes over time. Trans-centered care requires clinicians to create a holding space for TGE youth to explore the evolving state of gender regardless of medical and/or social transition (Austin, Craig, & Alessi, 2017). Beyond affirming care, clinicians must guarantee that TGE youth are able to partake in programming (within housing, school, community, or at the agency in support groups) based on gender rather than SAB (Austin, 2017). The groundwork for establishing ongoing support through strength-based, trauma-informed, and anti-oppressive practices that match the goals and needs of the client, taking into account intersectional identities and lived experiences, is a driving force in partnering with TGE youth.

Case Study

This case study will present information related to the initial outreach and assessments completed with Jay (pronouns: he/his) by a school social worker. Through these early contacts, the social worker not only collects information traditionally evaluated during biopsychosocial assessments, but seeks context for Jay's beliefs towards MH and MH treatment and identifies barriers to care in order to build an understanding around what might prevent Jay from coming back or from uninhibited participation in sessions. The social worker also leaves space in beginning sessions for Jay to name his community/informal care networks.

Jay is a 15-year-old, first-generation Pakistani American, trans male who attends 10th grade at a large, urban public high school. He self-referred to the school-based MH clinic after the school social worker gave an outreach presentation to the Gender and Sexuality Alliance (GSA). During the presentation many of the students in attendance had questions related to confidentiality and what information would be disclosed to parents. Jay was concerned that if he wanted to go to therapy, the social worker would have to give his mother – with whom he lives alone – information related to his gender identity. The social worker provided the group with psychoeducation around the ethical responsibilities of social workers with respect to confidentiality, noting its limits in a situation of danger to self or others.

After the presentation Jay told the social worker he was interested in services; however, he was worried about receiving consent – a clinic requirement – from his mother who "doesn't believe in therapy." The social worker explained to Jay that there are several paths that students take to receive care at the school's MH clinic. Some parents call and ask that their child is seen for counseling, other students are referred by teachers and guidance counselors, and some students come of their own volition, like Jay. In the latter two instances, the social worker sends home written materials that describe the general benefits of counseling as they relate to supporting students navigate the school environment, particularly emphasizing how counseling can support academic success, relationships, and overall wellness. With the broad framing that Jay would see the social worker to receive support to help improve his functioning in the school environment, Jay was able to gain consent from his mother and returned the required signed documentation to the MH clinic.

While Jay presents with depressive symptoms and has previously taken medication for depression, Jay asserts that he does not believe that he has depression or a mood disorder. Instead, Jay states that his mood fluctuates with specific triggers related to gender. For example, when his hair grows longer, he can become more depressed; when he is misgendered in school by teachers, students, or staff, this triggers feelings of sadness, hopelessness, isolation, and anxiety. Jay relays that sometimes he corrects pronoun usage by teachers and peers, but his decisions around identity disclosure and correction are usually based on the closeness of the relationship and feelings of safety. Navigating his gender with teachers and peers frequently contributes to mood lability. For example, in a single day, Jay can move from one class where he is completely out to a teacher, feels safe, and never experiences misgendering, to the next class where he has told the teacher his pronouns, is misgendered, but feels safe to correct, to another class where he has told the teacher his pronouns, is misgendered, but does not feel safe to correct, to a different class where he has not come out. Jay also reports being given a hard time by school security because the name and picture on his school ID do not match his current gender expression (Jay cuts his hair short – though sometimes it grows longer because his mother does not like it short – and often wears tracksuits, sweatpants, or athletic attire). His school has separate security lines for male and female students, and some security guards will not let him go through the line with other male students, while others ask him a lot of questions before letting him go through. Jay is anxious each morning, anticipating these security checks. At home, Jay notes that he has started to feel distant from his mother. Jay feels that he cannot discuss his gender or MH with her. Though Jay's mother has verbally expressed her dislike for his short hair, any direct discussions around gender and sexuality are avoided in the household.

Before delving more into specific triggers and symptoms, the social worker wanted to understand more about Jay's beliefs around depression, MH, and MH treatment. Ultimately, this might help shape the treatment plan and also elucidate the relationship between Jay and his mother, as Jay noted that he could not talk about MH with her. When beginning to explore this, Jay states that he thinks MH is all situational; mood is connected to what is happening around you, and without negative experiences, people would feel fine. Here, the social worker notes Jay's initial viewpoint of depression and mood revolves around the external environment, rather than internal or balanced influences on MH. This outlook also matches his statement that he does not have depression, despite his symptom expression. With this perspective, the social worker does not just have a list of Jay's symptoms, but a more holistic appreciation for how his standpoint may shape his participation in treatment.

Moreover, Jay explains that his mother thinks that there are only a few legitimate reasons to seek MH care. When asked to expand, Jay reflects that a few years ago his maternal aunt, who lived with him and his mother, passed away. Afterward, Jay began to experience his first depressive symptoms. Jay began counseling and seeing a psychiatrist in response, but his mother attended all sessions. Therefore, Jay was never honest in sessions, denied symptoms, and did not want to continue treatment. Jay underscores that he never had the opportunity – his own space or freedom – to explore his gender in therapy.

The social worker acknowledges these experiences, assuring Jay that sessions were confidential and a time to explore his gender, MH, relationships, experiences at school, or anything else; Jay could share as much or as little as he felt comfortable with in each session. Jay indicates that he immediately felt that he could talk about being trans with the social worker based on the content of the outreach presentation and what he observed about the physical space of the social worker's office when he walked in, noting the rainbow and trans flags, safe space stickers, and flyers from the GSA. Jay tells the social worker he was relieved to see this representation in the office – especially the GSA flyers since, to date, he had been relying on two older trans members of the group for support and guidance.

Before ending, the social worker asks Jay if there might be anything that would keep him from coming back to the next sessions. School-based social work breaks down many typical barriers to care (e.g., transportation problems; lack of insurance), yet, given Jay's history with MH treatment, it is important to assess and problem-solve around barriers. Jay identifies two potential concerns. If Jay were to continue working with the social worker he does not want the social worker to: (1) call him out of classes, or; (2) call his mother or if absolutely necessary, not use he/him pronouns or the name Jay as he is not out as trans to her yet. In response to Jay's first concern, the social worker and Jay agree to schedule sessions during an elective or lunch period so that he can walk himself to the social worker's office. Jay further explains that being pulled from class signals to classmates that he has MH problems, and he does not want to experience double stigma from his peers related to both his trans identity and MH. After thanking Jay for communicating the second barrier, the social worker attempts to normalize his concerns by informing Jay that fear of identity disclosure is a frequently identified barrier to care for many TGE youth. The social worker also re-iterates that they can continue to work together without a need to disclose Jay's trans identity to his mother and reassures Jay that they would work together on a plan that felt safe if there were ever a need to call his mother. Ultimately, working collaboratively with Jay to gather all of these details early will inform a tailored treatment plan and environment where Jay feels supported and safe to fully engage in the therapeutic process and re-lationship.

Additional Resources

The Trevor Project

Crisis intervention and MH services for those ages 13–24
  https://www.thetrevorproject.org/
  24-Hour Hotline (phone or text): 1-866-488-7386

GLSEN

K–12 educational resources, policy guidelines, recommendations for service providers
  https://www.glsen.org/

CenterLink

Database of LGBTQ community centers by location
  https://www.lgbtcenters.org/LGBTCenters

RAD Remedy

Community-sourced list of trans-affirming healthcare providers
  https://www.radremedy.org/

Out2Enroll

Insurance resources and guidelines for trans physical and MH care
https://out2enroll.org/

National Alliance on Mental Illness (NAMI)

National network of MH care providers, as well as a provider database
http://www.nami.org/Find-Support/LGBTQ
Help-Line: 1-800-9506264

References

Agass, D. (2002). Countertransference, supervision and the reflection process. *Journal of Social Work Practice, 16*(2), 125–133.

American Psychiatric Association. (2017). *Diagnostic and statistical manual of mental disorders: DSM-5.* Arlington: American Psychiatric Association.

Austin, A. (2016). "There I am": A grounded theory study of young adults navigating a transgender or gender nonconforming identity within a context of oppression and invisibility. *Sex Roles, 75*(5–6), 215–230.

Austin, A. (2017). Practice with transgender and gender non-conforming client. In M. P. Dentato (Ed.), *Social work practice with the LGBTQ community: The intersection of history, health, MH, and policy factors.* New York: Oxford University Press.

Austin, A., Craig, S. L., & Alessi, E. J. (2017). Affirmative cognitive behavior therapy with transgender and gender nonconforming adults. *Psychiatric Clinics of North America, 40*(1), 141–156.

Balestrery, J. E. (2017). Marching toward LGBTQ equality. In M. P. Dentato (Ed.), *Social work practice with the LGBTQ community: The intersection of history, health, MH, and policy factors.* New York: Oxford University Press.

Bauer, G. R., Hammond, R., Travers, R., Kaay, M., Hohenadel, K. M., & Boyce, M. (2009). "I don't think this is theoretical; this is our lives": How erasure impacts health care for transgender people. *Journal of the Association of Nurses in AIDS Care, 20*(5), 348–361.

Becerra-Culqui, T. A., Liu, Y., Nash, R., Cromwell, L., Flanders, W. D., Getahun, D., … Quinn, V. P. (2018). MH of transgender and gender non-conforming youth compared with their peers. *Pediatrics, 141*(5), 1–11.

Bockting, W. O., Miner, M. H., Swinburne Romine, R. E., Hamilton, A., & Coleman, E. (2013). Stigma, mental health, and resilience in an online sample of the US transgender population. *American Journal of Public Health, 103*, 943–951.

Boyd, K. K. (1996). Power imbalances and therapy. *Focus, 11*(9), 1–4.

Bradford, J., Reisner, S. L., Honnold, J. A., & Xavier, J. (2013). Experiences of transgender related discrimination and implications for health: Results from the Virginia Transgender Health Initiative Study. *American Journal of Public Health, 103*(10), 1820–1829.

Brown, C., & Augusta-Scott, T. (2007). *Narrative therapy. Making meaning, making lives.* Thousand Oaks: Sage.

Brown, T. N. T., Herman, J. L., & Park, A. S. (2017). *Exploring international priorities and best practices for the collection of data about gender minorities, report of meeting.* Los Angeles: The Williams Institute.

Brumbaugh-Johnson, S. M., & Hull, K. E. (2019). Coming out as transgender: Navigating the social implications of a transgender identity. *Journal of Homosexuality, 66*(8), 1148–1177.

Budge, S. L., Adelson, J. L., & Howard, K. A. S. (2013). Anxiety and depression in transgender individuals: The roles of transition status, loss, social support, and coping. *Journal of Consulting and Clinical Psychology, 81*(3), 545–557.

Burack-Weiss, A., Lawrence, L. S., Mijangos, L. B., & Charon, R. (2017). *Narrative in social work practice: The power and possibility of story.* New York: Columbia University Press.

Burgess, D., Tran, A., Lee, R., & van Ryn, M. (2007). Effects of perceived discrimination on MH and MH services utilization among gay, lesbian, bisexual and transgender persons. *Journal of LGBT Health Research, 3*(4), 1–14.

Busa, S., Janssen, A., & Lakshman, M. (2018). A review of evidence-based treatments for transgender youth diagnosed with Social Anxiety Disorder. *Transgender Health, 3*(1), 27–33.

Butler, A., Elliott, T., & Stopard, N. (2003). Living up to the standards we set: A critical account of the development of anti-racist standards. *Social Work Education, 22*(3), 271–282.

Butler, J. (1999). *Gender trouble: Feminism and the subversion of identity.* New York, NY: Routledge.

Button, D. M., O'Connell, D. J., & Gealt, R. (2012). Sexual minority youth victimization and social support: The intersection of sexuality, gender, race, and victimization. *Journal of Homosexuality, 59*(1), 18–43.

Chodzen, G., Hidalgo, M. A., Chen, D., & Garofalo, R. (2019). Minority stress factors associated with depression and anxiety among transgender and gender-nonconforming youth. *Journal of Adolescent Health, 64*(4), 467–471.

Coleman, E., Bockting, W., Botzer, M., Cohen-Kettenis, P., DeCuypere, G., Feldman, J., … Zucker, K. (2012). Standards of care for the health of transsexual, transgender, and gender-nonconforming people, version 7. *International Journal of Transgenderism, 13*(4), 165–232.

Coleman, E., Wylie, K., Coates, R., Rubio-Aurioles, E., Hernandez-Serrano, R., Wabrek, A., … Forleo, R. (2017). Commentary: Revising the International Classification of Diseases (ICD-11) and improving global sexual health: Time for an integrated approach that moves beyond the mind-body divide. *International Journal of Sexual Health, 29*(2), 113–114. doi:10.1080/19317611.2017.1311126.

Constance-Huggins, M. (2012). Critical race theory in social work education: A framework for addressing racial disparities. *Critical Social Work, 13*, 1–16.

Craig, S. L., & Austin, A. (2016). The AFFIRM open pilot feasibility study: A brief affirmative cognitive behavioral coping skills group intervention for sexual and gender minority youth. *Children and Youth Services Review, 64*, 136–144.

Davy, Z., & Toze, M. (2018). What is gender dysphoria? A critical systematic narrative review. *Transgender Health, 3*(1), 159–169.

Dewane, C. J. (2006). Use of self: A premier revisited. *Clinical Social Work Journal, 34*(4), 543–558.

Dietert, M., & Dentice, D. (2013). Growing up trans: Socialization and the gender binary. *Journal of GLBT Family Studies, 9*(1), 24–42.

di Giacomo, E., Krausz, M., Colmegna, F., Aspesi, F., & Clerici, M. (2018). Estimating the risk of attempted suicide among sexual minority youths: A systematic review and meta-analysis. *JAMA Pediatrics, 172*(12), 1145–1152.

Drescher, J. (2010). Queer diagnoses: Parallels and contrasts in the history of homosexuality, gender variance, and the diagnostic and statistical manual. *Archives of Sexual Behavior, 39*(2), 427–460.

Edwards-Leeper, L., Leibowitz, S., & Sangganjanavanich, V. F. (2016). Affirmative practice with transgender and gender nonconforming youth: Expanding the model. *Psychology of Sexual Orientation and Gender Diversity, 3*(2), 165–172.

Erickson-Schroth, L. (2014). *Trans bodies, trans selves: A resource for the transgender community.* New York: Oxford University Press.

Fisher-Borne, M., Cain, J. M., & Martin, S. L. (2015). From mastery to accountability: Cultural humility as an alternative to cultural competence. *Social Work Education, 34*(2), 165–181.

Gelso, C. J., & Carter, J. A. (1994). Components of the psychotherapy relationship: Their interaction and unfolding during treatment. *Journal of Counseling Psychology, 41*(3), 296–306.

Gridley, S. J., Crouch, J. M., Evans, Y., Eng, W., Antoon, E., Lyapustina, M., … McCarty, C. (2016). Youth and caregiver perspectives on barriers to gender-affirming health care for transgender youth. *Journal of Adolescent Health, 59*(3), 254–261.

Hardy, S., & Monypenny, J. (2019). Queering queer spaces: Journey of a creative arts program for trans, non-binary, and gender creative youth. *Voices: A World Forum for Music Therapy, 19*(3), 1–15.

Hatchel, T., Polanin, J. R., & Espelage, D. L. (2019). Suicidal thoughts and behaviors among LGBTQ youth: meta-analyses and a systematic review. *Archives of Suicide Research, 25*, 1–37.

Heck, N. C. (2015). The potential to promote resilience: Piloting a minority stress-informed, GSA-based, MH promotion program for LGBTQ youth. *Psychology of Sexual Orientation and Gender Diversity, 2*(3), 225–231.

Hendricks, M. L., & Testa, R. J. (2012). A conceptual framework for clinical work with transgender and gender nonconforming clients: An adaptation of the Minority Stress Model. *Professional Psychology: Research and Practice, 43*(5), 460–467.

Herman, J. L., Flores, A. R., Brown, T. N. T., Wilson, B. D. M., & Conron, K. J. (2017). *Age of individuals who identify as trans in the United States.* Los Angeles, CA: The Williams Institute.

Hernández, P., & McDowell, T. (2010). Intersectionality, power, and relational safety in context: Key concepts in clinical supervision. *Training and Education in Professional Psychology, 4*(1), 29–35.

Hick, S. (2005). Reconceptualizing critical social work. In S. Hick, J. Fook, & R. Pozutto (Eds.), *Social work. A critical turn.* Toronto: Thompson Educational Publishing.

Higa, D., Hoppe, M. J., Lindhorst, T., Mincer, S., Beadnell, B., Morrison, D. M., … Mountz, S. (2014). Negative and positive factors associated with the wellbeing of LGBTQ youth. *Youth & Society, 46*(5), 663–687.

Hoffman, N. D., Freeman, K., & Swann, S. (2009). Healthcare preferences of lesbian, gay, bisexual, transgender and questioning youth. *Journal of Adolescent Health, 45*(3), 222–229.

Howard, K. I., Lueger, R. J., Maling, M. S., & Martinovich, Z. (1993). A phase model of psychotherapy outcome: Causal mediation of change. *Journal of Consulting and Clinical Psychology, 61*(4), 678–685.

Hudson, K. D., & Romanelli, M. (2019). "We are powerful people:" Health-promoting strengths of LGBTQ communities of color. *Qualitative Health Research, 30*(8),1156–1170.

Hull, K. E., & Ortyl, T. A. (2019). Conventional and cutting-edge: Definitions of family in LGBT communities. *Sexuality Research and Social Policy, 16*(1), 31–43.

Ivey-Stephenson, A. Z., Demissie, Z., Crosby, A. E., Stone, D. M., Gaylor, E., Wilkins, N., … Brown, M. (2020), Suicidal ideation and behaviors among high school students—Youth Risk Behavior Survey, United States, 2019. *MMWR Surveillance Summaries, 69*(1), 47–55.

Johns, M. M., Lowry, R., Andrzejewski, J., Barrios, L. C., Demissie, Z., McManus, T., … Underwood, J. M. (2019). Transgender identity and experiences of violence victimization, substance use, suicide risk, and sexual risk behaviors among high school students—19 states and large urban school districts, 2017. *Morbidity and Mortality Weekly Report, 68*(3), 67.

Kattari, S. K., Bakko, M., Hecht, H. K., & Kattari, L. (2020). Correlations between healthcare provider interactions and MH among trans and nonbinary adults. *SSM-Population Health, 10*, e100525.

Kattari, S. K., Bakko, M., Hecht, H. K., & Kinney, M. K. (2020). Intersecting experiences of healthcare denials among transgender and nonbinary patients. *American Journal of Preventive Medicine, 58*(4), 506–513.

Kattari, S. K., Walls, N. E., Speer, S. R., & Kattari, L. (2016). Exploring the relationship between transgender-inclusive providers and MH outcomes among transgender/gender variant people. *Social Work in Health Care, 55*(8), 635–650.

Katz-Wise, S. L., Budge, S. L., Fugate, E., Flanagan, K., Touloumtzis, C., Rood, B., … Leibowitz, S. (2017). Transactional pathways of transgender identity development in transgender and gender nonconforming youth and caregivers from the Trans Youth Family Study. *The International Journal of Transgenderism, 18*(3), 243–263.

Klein, K., Holtby, A., Cook, K., & Travers, R. (2015). Complicating the coming out narrative: Becoming oneself in a heterosexist and cissexist world. *Journal of Homosexuality, 62*(3), 297–326.

Kuff, R. M., Greytak, E. A., Kosciw, J. G., Gay, Lesbian and Straight Education Network (GLSEN), & American School Counselor Association (ASCA). (2019). *Supporting safe and healthy schools for lesbian, gay, bisexual, transgender, and queer students: A national survey of school counselors, social workers, and psychologists.* New York: GLSEN.

Kuper, L. E., Wright, L., & Mustanski, B. (2018). Gender identity development among transgender and gender nonconforming emerging adults: An intersectional approach. *International Journal of Transgenderism, 19*(4), 436–455.

Larson, G. (2008). Anti-oppressive practice in MH. *Journal of Progressive Human Services, 19*(1), 39–54.

Lev, A. I. (2009). The ten tasks of the MH provider: Recommendations for revision of the World Professional Association of Transgender Health's Standards of Care. *International Journal of Transgenderism, 11*, 76–101.

Levitt, H. M. (2019). A psychosocial genealogy of LGBTQ+ gender: An empirically based theory of gender and gender identity cultures. *Psychology of Women Quarterly*, *43*(3), 275–297.

McLaughlin, A. (2011). Exploring social justice for clinical social work practice. *Smith College Studies in Social Work*, *81*, 234–251.

Mizock, L., & Lundquist, C. (2016). Missteps in psychotherapy with Transgender clients: Promoting gender sensitivity in counseling and psychological practice. *Psychology of Sexual Orientation and Gender Diversity*, *3*(2), 148–155.

Movement Advancement Project. (2020). *Equality maps: Identity document laws and policies*. Retrieved from https://www.lgbtmap.org/equality-maps/identity_document_laws

National Association of Social Workers. (2017). *Code of ethics*. Washington, DC: National Association of Social Workers.

Noltemeyer, A. L., & Bush, K. R. (2013). Adversity and resilience: A synthesis of international research. *School Psychology International*, *34*(5), 474–487.

Pelton-Sweet, L., & Sherry, A. (2008). Coming out through art: A review of art therapy with LGBT clients. *Art Therapy*, *25*(4), 170–176.

Pflum, S. R., Testa, R. J., Balsam, K. F., Goldblum, P. B., & Bongar, B. (2015). Social support, trans community connectedness, and MH symptoms among transgender and gender nonconforming adults. *Psychology of Sexual Orientation and Gender Diversity*, *2*(3), 281–286.

Pryor, R. E., & Vickroy, W. (2019). "In a perfect world, you wouldn't have to work the system to get the things you need to survive:" A pilot study about trans health care possibilities. *Transgender Health*, *4*(1), 18–23.

Redfern, J. S., & Sinclair, B. (2014). Improving health care encounters and communication with transgender patients. *Journal of Communication in Healthcare*, *7*(1), 25–40.

Reisner, S. L., Deutsch, M. B., Bhasin, S., Bockting, W., Brown, G. R., Feldman, J., … Goodman, M. (2016). Advancing methods for U.S. transgender health research. *Current Opinion in Endocrinology, Diabetes, and Obesity*, *23*(2), 198–207.

Romanelli, M., & Hudson, K. D. (2017). Individual and systemic barriers to health care: Perspectives of lesbian, gay, bisexual, and transgender adults. *American Journal of Orthopsychiatry*, *87*(6), 714–728.

Romanelli, M., & Lindsey, M. A. (2020). Patterns of healthcare discrimination among transgender help-seekers. *American Journal of Preventive Medicine*, *58*(4), e123–e131.

Romanelli, M., Lu, W., & Lindsey, M. A. (2018). Examining mechanisms and moderators of the relationship between discriminatory health care encounters and attempted suicide among US transgender help-seekers. *Administration and Policy in MH and MH Services Research*, *45*(6), 831–849.

Russell, S. T., & Fish, J. N. (2016). MH in lesbian, gay, bisexual, and transgender (LGBT) youth. *Annual Review of Clinical Psychology*, *12*(1), 465–487.

Russell, S. T., Pollitt, A. M., Li, G., & Grossman, A. H. (2018). Chosen name use is linked to reduced depressive symptoms, suicidal ideation, and suicidal behavior among transgender youth. *Journal of Adolescent Health*, *63*(4), 503–505.

Senreich, E. (2013). An inclusive definition of spirituality for social work education and practice. *Journal of Social Work Education*, *49*(4), 548–563.

Shipherd, J. C., Green, K. E., & Abramovitz, S. (2010). Transgender clients: Identifying and minimizing barriers to MH treatment. *Journal of Gay & Lesbian MH*, *14*(2), 94–108.

Singh, A. A., & Dickey, L. M. (2017). *Affirmative counseling and psychological practice with transgender and gender nonconforming clients.* Washington, DC: American Psychological Association.

Snow, A., Cerel, J., Loeffler, D. N., & Flaherty, C. (2019). Barriers to MH care for transgender and gender-nonconforming adults: A systematic literature review. *Health & Social Work, 44*(3), 149–155.

Sperber, J., Landers, S., & Lawrence, S. (2005). Access to health care for transgendered persons: Results of a needs assessment in Boston. *International Journal of Transgenderism, 8*(2–3), 75–91.

Stotzer, R. L., Silverschanz, P., & Wilson, A. (2013). Gender identity and social services: Barriers to care. *Journal of Social Service Research, 39*(1), 63–77.

Strauss, P., Cook, A., Winter, S., Watson, V., Wright Toussaint, D., & Lin, A. (2017). Trans *Pathways: the MH experiences and care pathways of trans young people: Summary of results.* Perth, Australia: Telethon Kids Institute.

Strong, T., & Pare, D. (2003). *Furthering talk: Advancing in the discursive therapies.* Boston: L-Kluwer.

Substance Abuse and MH Services Administration (SAMHSA). (2012). *Top health issues for LGBT populations information & resource kit.* Rockville, MD: HHS.

Sullivan, N. (2003). *A critical introduction to queer theory.* New York: NYU Press.

Tan, K. K., Treharne, G. J., Ellis, S. J., Schmidt, J. M., & Veale, J. F. (2019). Gender minority stress: A critical review. *Journal of Homosexuality, 67*(10), 1471–1489.

Tervalon, M., & Murray-García, J. (1998). Cultural humility versus cultural competence: A critical distinction in defining physician training outcomes in multicultural education. *Journal of Health Care for the Poor and Underserved, 9*(2), 117–125.

Turner, S. G., & Maschi, T. M. (2015). Feminist and empowerment theory and social work practice. *Journal of Social Work Practice, 29*(2), 151–162.

White, M. (2007). *Maps of narrative practice.* New York: W. W. Norton.

Wilkerson, J. M., Schick, V. R., Bauldry, J., Butame, S. A., Romijnders, K. A., & Montrose Center. (2017). Social support, depression, self-esteem, and coping among LGBTQ adolescents participating in Hatch Youth. *Health Promotion Practice, 18*(3), 358–365.

Woody, S. R., & Adessky, R. S. (2002). Therapeutic alliance, group cohesion, and homework compliance during cognitive-behavioral group treatment of social phobia. *Behavior Therapy, 33*(1), 5–27.

14 Trans and Gender Expansive Youth and Fertility

Hez Wollin

Introduction

It is rare that teenagers want to talk about their (future) reproductive health. A renowned reproductive endocrinologist, whom I interviewed for the purpose of writing this chapter, said "When I meet with families about fertility preservation, many of the teens are so embarrassed, they don't even want to look at me." Most teenagers are not thinking about their future fertility. They are more likely trying to prevent pregnancy or prevent getting someone else pregnant. Trans and gender expansive (TGE) adolescents are even less likely to be thinking about their fertility, because they may be focused on accessing gender-affirming medical care, or learning how to establish their gender identities. Even though they might not be actively thinking about pregnancy or fertility, TGE adolescents have similar pregnancy rates to their cisgender peers (Veale et al., 2016). They also engage in sexual activity at similar rates as their cisgender peers, demonstrating a need for medical and mental health providers to talk in depth with their adolescent trans clients about emotional and physical safety around sex and reproductive health.

Not all TGE adolescents want to take hormones or have surgeries that can impact their future fertility but the question of fertility can be a barrier for adolescents who want to access gender-affirming medical care. This is often because of parental or caregiver concern that their children might never be able to reproduce. However, some adolescents may want to keep their options open and decide to pursue discussions of fertility preservation on their own without parental suggestion. TGE fertility, pregnancy, and conception is an emerging area in the reproductive healthcare field. There is limited research on this topic, and there are many unknowns about how gender-affirming hormone therapy and surgery impact fertility. The research is even more limited for young people, and new options for fertility preservation for TGE adolescents are emerging as I write this. There are few studies that have examined fertility and parenting intentions in TGE youth. The two studies that have indicate that the percentage of TGE youth and adolescents who undergo fertility preservation is between 3–5 (Chen & Simons, 2018; Nahata et al., 2017), noting that there are many barriers to fertility preservation

DOI: 10.4324/9780429297687-14

among this population. Social workers and other mental health providers can assist TGE youth and families in sorting through important questions about fertility. However, there is a large gap around mental health providers' knowledge of medical options for gender care, which highlights the need for more education and understanding among social workers around how to serve TGE youth.

This chapter explores ways in which the possibility of future fertility and gender-affirming care can co-exist for TGE youth. It outlines some of the historical discourse on fertility for TGE people. This chapter also discusses current options for fertility preservation for TGE youth. Finally, the chapter offers recommendations for social workers and other mental health providers to discuss fertility options with TGE youth and their families.

Disparities in Health Care for Transgender and Gender Expansive Clients

TGE people face discrimination in many areas of life, and reproductive health is no exception. Historically, physicians have cited ethical considerations to avoid offering assisted reproductive services to trans people (Cheng et al., 2019, Jones, 2000), stating that trans people were "unfit" to be parents due to "mental health concerns" (read: transphobia). Many people who transitioned believed that the possibilities of accessing gender-affirming care and the possibilities of becoming biological parents were mutually exclusive. As recently as 2017, 20 European countries enforced a sterilization requirement for transgender people (Dunne, 2017), and when the mandate was reviewed in 2015, both Poland and Finland upheld it, among others. In these countries, in order for trans people to change their legal gender with the state, they must have had genital surgery and additionally prove that they cannot reproduce. These coercive practices create state-endorsed violence against transgender people and uphold eugenic practices of forced sterilization (Nixon, 2013). Additionally, they reproduce gender binaries that limit embodiment for TGE people and are rooted in white supremacy.

In the United States there is a long history of reproductive oppression levied primarily against Black and Brown bodies. Some of these atrocities include forced sterilization of Black, Brown, and indigenous women, requiring the use of long-acting hormonal contraceptives in order to obtain food stamps, welfare family caps (Nixon, 2013), the inherent eugenics of anti-miscegenation laws, and laws requiring sterilization of people deemed "unfit" to have children. Strangio states "[i]f we establish in law and social discourse that bodies must be coherently sexed to be legitimate, we make spaces for the harassment and violence levied upon those whose bodies transgress those expectations." TGE people often disrupt expectations around what is means to be "coherently sexed," particularly if they actively inhabit reproductive bodies. Medicolegal gatekeeping, which acts as a barrier to care for TGE people in all forms, is a form of state-sanctioned violence. Today in the United States, there is no universal standard of care across medical and social establishments for TGE people who want to change their legal documents or access gender-affirming care. Polices are widely different from state to state and from medical provider to medical provider. For example, in California, one can change their name and gender marker by going to court, without a letter from a medical provider. In Ohio, however, people who want to change their names must publish their request three times in a newspaper. TGE people are often denied full bodily autonomy over reproductive and other medical choices, and the reproductive healthcare needs of TGE communities are overshadowed by both mainstream issues in LGBTQ communities and issues in mainstream reproductive justice considerations (National Latina Institute for Reproductive Health; Nixon, 2013).

TGE people face disproportionate barriers to care at any and all stages of the reproductive healthcare process. The journey towards family making is incredibly gendered, as evidenced by the amount of pink splashed across all fertility products, the discussion boards where the word "ladies" is prolific, and even the "Mother and Baby Unit" at many hospitals. Many TGE people can feel isolated, alone, and completely erased by such practices. Although fertility clinics sometimes have more inclusive policies that relate to their TGE patients, they are not necessarily implemented clinic-wide, disempowering TGE patients before they even enter the clinic.

A Personal Journey

As a transgender, queer clinical social worker who has been on a reproductive health journey myself, I found myself somewhat shocked at the lack of competence and ignorance I have faced along the way. I spoke with a gynecologist who said "we can just take you up the back stairs to our clinic so you don't have to sit in the waiting room." I have been misgendered with equal frequency as I have been gendered correctly. My doctor knows my pronouns, but not all of the staff do. I can't be assured that the weekend on-call doctor will have looked at my chart and noted that I am trans. All of the intake forms cater to heterosexual cisgender patients. When I made my initial appointment and told the receptionist I was trans, they said "are you sure you're here for fertility?" When I asked if the person who I had been assigned to work with was trans competent, the person I spoke with said "let me check" and then told me they would need to postpone my appointment because the only trans competent provider at a major research hospital in a large West Coast city did not have any open appointments. I filled out the "transgender intake form" after I had already filled out the standard intake form. My partner and I were required to meet with a psychologist to make sure we had fully thought through the plan to have a known donor. We have paid an unthinkable amount of money to purchase and ship sperm. These practices are not only discriminatory to trans people, they also exclude single parents by choice and queer parents. I am privileged enough to have access to excellent insurance, without which I would not be able to afford treatment, and as a white, middle-class person, I have never experienced discrimination based on my race when I have tried to access medical care. And yet, the hoops I have jumped through to gain access are much higher and more numerous than those that my straight cisgender peers have navigated. While this is anecdotal, I am fairly certain that I am not alone in having this experience.

Transgender Fertility and Options for Fertility Preservation for TGE Youth

Recent research indicates that transgender men/transmasculine people have the same or similar odds of getting pregnant as cisgender people, even if they have taken masculinizing hormones (Boston IVF, 2020). When fertility preservation and in-vitro fertilization have been studied for transgender men, they had the same number of follicles as their cisgender control group (Adeleye, Reid, Kao, Mok-Lin, & Smith 2019) whether or not they had been on testosterone. When some transgender women stopped taking hormones to try to get their partners pregnant or banked their sperm, the sperm samples showed conflicting results ranging from atrophy and lack of mature sperm (Levey et al., 2017; Nahata et al., 2019) to completely normal spermatogenic activity (Nahata et al., 2019). Therefore, we know it is possible for TGE people to both contribute sperm to have biological children and to achieve pregnancy, even though the research is lacking and we are not yet able to track the exact number of biological children born to TGE people. Reproductive medicine providers cannot definitively say what kind of impact, if any, taking testosterone and estradiol has on future fertility. There is no comparison around infertility rates among TGE populations and cisgender populations. But we know that is it possible for TGE people to reproduce.

Up until very recently, the most common route for adolescents to preserve their fertility was to go through the puberty of their sex assigned at birth, complete an egg retrieval or sperm banking, and then start hormones (if desired). For TGE adults who want to get pregnant or contribute sperm to build a family, the most common way to do this is to stop taking hormones (if they are taking them), either become pregnant or contribute sperm, and then resume hormones if and when ready. For adults, the process can be protracted if it takes a long time to conceive. The longer a person is off of their hormones, the more likely they are to experience greater levels of gender dysphoria. Even if someone is not taking hormones, becoming pregnant or banking sperm to conceive a child can bring up complex emotions, not to mention that TGE people are attempting parenthood in a transphobic and ciscentric society. For some TGE people who wanted to be biological parents, the dysphoria can be overwhelming, and many decide to stop the process altogether or pursue other routes towards parenthood.

New technologies and advancements in fertility, have pushed mainstream healthcare to become more inclusive. The field of reproductive health is expanding around what it knows to be possible. By the time today's adolescents reach reproductive age, it is likely that widespread changes in technology and societal shifts will mean that they will not have to endure as many feelings of fear, awkwardness, and a lack of understanding if they are considering family building. Furthermore, emerging research on fertility outcomes among TGE people suggests that the landscape of fertility preservation will change dramatically in the future.

Trans men and transmasculine people can still opt to have a hysterectomy but keep their ovaries if they would like to donate eggs for reproduction. Semen can be extracted from the testes without ejaculation through electro-ejaculation or surgical sperm removal, possibly leading to decreased dysphoria for some trans women. Emerging reproductive techniques suggest that sometimes people do not need to discontinue testosterone in order to do an egg retrieval. There is not enough research to know if these gametes will be viable to create a child, but they do suggest that there are many more possibilities for TGE youth who are considering biological parenthood. These new practices, coupled with what we know about TGE people's ability to get pregnant and become biological parents, mean that TGE adolescents may not need to engage in a process of fertility preservation prior to beginning hormones if they know that they have reproductive options in the future.

For TGE youth who are on puberty blockers prior to initiating hormone therapy, it was, until very recently, unknown if fertility would be possible (Nahata et al., 2019). However, new technologies have been developed that preserve ovaries and ovarian tissue so that the youth does not have to come off their blockers if they do not wish to do so. Sperm has been less widely studied than eggs, but it is also possible to extract sperm from the testes without ejaculation. There is no guarantee that these gametes will be viable, but it is possible to obtain them. Youth who have taken puberty blockers can cease taking them in order to undergo fertility preservation and undergo some form of endogenous puberty, but this may cause a great deal of distress and dysphoria. The research on fertility and TGE youth who take blockers is scant, and there have been no confirmed pregnancies with cryopreserved ovarian or testicular tissue for youth who have taken blockers.

The cost of fertility treatment is extremely prohibitive for many people. Most insurance policies have a specific exclusion in their policy against covering in-vitro fertilization, of which an egg retrieval is a part. Additionally, very few, if any, insurance companies will cover these procedures for people under eighteen. Medicaid and CHIP (Children's Health Insurance Plan), do not cover them either (Kyweluk et al., 2018), which means that families at lower income brackets cannot access these services.

The out-of-pocket cost for egg retrieval, including medications, can range from $8,000–$35,000 (Nahata et al., 2019). Families have to pay to store these gametes, which can add thousands of dollars to an already expensive process. The cost of banking and storing sperm, on average, starts at about $2,500 and then participants have to pay a yearly storage fee. If a 15 year old stores her sperm for 20 years, she could be paying $10,000 over time (Nahata et al., 2019). These expenses and the lack of access to equitable health care means that only TGE youth from the most wealthy families are able to access this option. Most likely, given the correlation between socioeconomic status and race in this country, they are white families. These costs act as barriers for TGE people of color to access reproductive options available to them.

The Role of Social Workers in Providing Affirming Care

As medical providers and mental health providers become more competent in working with TGE clients in general, they can bring up broader conversations about fertility for TGE adolescents. Unfortunately, there is a large gap in social workers' and other mental health providers' knowledge about gender-affirming medical interventions, particularly when they become more specialized. There are no mandated trainings for mental health providers about providing gender-affirming mental health care, let alone learning about medical interventions for TGE people. National Association of Social Workers' most recent training about trans people that is accessible online is from 2010, and uses woefully outdated and language that is similarly outdated (National Association of Social Workers, 2006, https://www.socialworkers.org/assets/secured/documents/da/da2008/reffered/Transgender.pdf).

Most social workers leave their master's programs without ever having taken a course regarding trans and gender considerations in clinical practice (Austin, Craig, & McInroy, 2016), resulting in mental health providers who are often ill-equipped to provide affirmative mental health care. Research has shown that social workers and other mental health providers lack specific knowledge about how to work with TGE children and adolescents (Austin, 2018). Furthermore, while "understanding social context and humility are part of social work training and values, using sensitive language around gender identity is not always intuitive" (Mallon, 2009) which leaves TGE clients feeling misheard, potentially harmed by practitioner ignorance, misunderstood, and less likely to engage in care. If social workers are not being trained in their academic programs, the onus is on them to pursue their own training. The intersections around learning about fertility options for trans adolescents are narrow, and will attract a self-selecting group of social workers.

However, a social worker may be one of the first points of contact for TGE adolescents considering accessing hormones or surgery. If a social worker has an ongoing relationship with a client, they may be one of the only people with whom the client feels comfortable discussing their gender. It is critical that social workers maintain a truly affirming lens by using the client's chosen name and pronouns, having visible materials in their office that affirm and celebrate TGE people, and including options for chosen name and pronouns on intake forms. Social workers should also advocate for all-gender restrooms in office spaces if none exist in their place of work. Social workers are in a unique position to help TGE youth and families to sort through significant questions about if and when to access puberty blockers, hormones, or surgery. They are also in a unique position to discuss fertility considerations with clients and families, underscoring the importance of social worker training and knowledge about affirmative care.

Best practices for social workers working with TGE adolescents around the topic of fertility are still being developed. Below are some recommendations for social workers to provide affirming care around questions of fertility.

1. Social workers should examine their implicit and explicit biases and reframe their beliefs about what becoming a parent looks like. While there are many stereotypes about "pregnant men," these are outdated and problematic. Since Thomas Beattie became famous in mainstream media in 2008 for being a "pregnant man," there have been several recent examples of transmasculine people who have become gestational parents that have expanded the cultural discussion around pregnancy and parenting (https://www.nytimes.com/2018/04/24/opinion/transgender-fertility-preservation.html and https://www.nytimes.com/2020/04/16/parenting/fertility/transgender-pregnancy.html). Social workers should also be aware of the history of forced sterilization in TGE communities and communities of color and the ways that these practices are still in effect today.

2. Social workers who work with TGE families should be familiar with the medical aspects of gender-affirming care. This should include hormones, surgeries, and the impact of both on future fertility. For example, an 18-year-old trans woman who opts to have orchiectomy (removal of testes) will have different considerations around possible future fertility than an 18 year old who decides not to pursue this option. Medical providers may not have had in-depth conversations around fertility with their adolescent clients. Health literacy depends on a myriad of factors including age, learning differences, literacy rates, developmental disabilities, language barriers, family support, and cultural considerations. Social workers should not assume that their clients have a robust understanding of the impact of hormones and surgery on future fertility, even if they have talked with their medical provider about it. Social workers can help clients process through the emotional impact of these questions in a way that a medical provider or a parent cannot.

3. When working with children, adolescents, and families, social workers should consider the developmental stages of adolescence that their clients are in and how that might impact fertility. TGE clients who opt to take puberty blockers before hormone replacement therapy will have different considerations than those who have gone through puberty. However it is possible to extract eggs from clients who have not gone through menarche, although there is no guarantee that they will be viable or mature (Nahata et al., 2019).

4. A TGE adolescent who has undergone the puberty of their sex assigned at birth and now wants to start hormones has more options. When faced with parental concern that their child will not be able to have a child someday, it is critical that social workers talk openly with parents about options. They should also and encourage parents to talk with their medical providers about these concerns.

5. The reproductive endocrinologist I mention in the beginning of this article noted that the teenagers she sees for fertility preservation view the meeting as another barrier to beginning hormones. Social workers should be aware of this and familiarize themselves with mental health outcomes among children and adolescents who are not accepted in their gender identities (Allen et al., 2019; de Vries et al., 2014; Olson et al., 2016; Turban et al., 2020). The decision to use gametes to create a future family should not ever come at the cost of accessing gender-affirming medical care, especially given the negative mental health outcomes for adolescents who delay transition because of parental resistance. Often families feel that if they do not opt into fertility preservation at this point, it will be too late for their child. Social workers can provide needed psychoeducation around the consequences of delaying hormones, including the emotional and physical impact going through an unwanted puberty and/or having to take hormones associated with their sex assigned at birth to go through fertility preservation. Social workers should be aware of the ways that dysphoria can impact their clients if they have to come off of their hormones to go through fertility treatments and come up with a plan to minimize distress, even if it means waiting until adulthood to address the question of fertility.

6. From a family systems perspective, a parent who is initially supportive of a TGE youth wanting to take hormones and who then places emphasis on fertility can make waves within the system. Teens often see this approach as unsupportive, and the levels of tension between a young person and their parent may dramatically increase because of this. Social workers should be ready to bridge the gap between the teen and their parent(s) and again, provide needed psychoeducation around the benefits of initiating hormone therapy sooner rather than later. Social workers should also help parents to understand the emotional impact on the TGE teen of this type of approach to accessing gender-affirming care: namely that it can serve as a barrier and may cause their child to withdraw their trust at a time when parental and caregiver support is greatly needed (Olson et al., 2016; Ryan et al., 2009; Ryan, Huebner, Diaz, & Sanchez, 2009). For parents who are grieving the loss of potentially becoming a grandparent, the social worker will want to encourage the parent not to express this grief to the TGE youth, as this may further contribute to barriers in the perception of support in the parent–child relationship.

7. TGE teens may be experiencing pressure to preserve gametes from parents and/or from medical providers. In these cases, social workers

should listen closely for discrepancies between what a young person is saying and what their family is saying. Social workers will want to center the needs of their adolescent client around reproductive and bodily autonomy and let their client know that they are never under any obligation to pursue fertility preservation, even if their family wants them to.

8. Social workers may also want to explore the meaning of future parenthood for TGE adolescents. Research has shown that an important theme for TGE adolescents considering parenthood is the process of decoupling their social role as a parent from their reproductive biology (Kyweluk, Sajwani, & Chen, 2018) and that the gender identities of future partners also play an important role in envisioning their reproductive options (Kyweluk, Sajwani, & Chen, 2018). Research has also shown that today's TGE youth are also excited about the possibility of new reproductive technologies.

Case Example

Alex (he/him/his) is a 15-year-old multiracial (Asian and White) transgender boy. He first began to identify as trans when he was 13, and came out to his family one year ago. Although they were not supportive of him at first, they have slowly opened to the idea that they have a trans son, and they have mostly been able to use his name and pronouns (with a few slips here and there). With his parents' support, he was able to start the school year using a new name and his pronouns. When he first came out to them, they told him he could not initiate taking testosterone until he turned eighteen. Last fall, Alex went through a period where he was more depressed, dysphoric, and anxious. He started withdrawing from family and friends, and his grades began to slip. His parents were concerned about his mental health and sent him to speak with Anya (she/her), a clinical social worker who specializes in working with trans youth. Alex is very excited about beginning testosterone, and he and Anya have been talking more about taking hormones. Alex believes that it would help his mood immensely. Anya is in agreement that Alex would be much happier if he were able to start hormones. She believes that delaying Alex's access to hormones would have a negative impact on his mental health, particularly because some of his trans friends have been allowed to start hormones, and because he wants to go through puberty with his peers. Starting his period was difficult for Alex, and the thought of going through puberty again as an adult is terrifying to him. Alex asks Anya to have a family session so that he can address the topic with his parents.

During the family session, Alex's parents are surprisingly more open to the idea of Alex starting hormones than either Alex or Anya believed they would be. However, his mother says "I have always wanted to be a grandmother, and I am really concerned that Alex won't be able to have children if he starts hormones now." Alex's parents struggled to conceive him, and went through a long and emotional journey before they eventually conceived Alex with in-vitro fertilization. Alex's mother shares that she does not want this for Alex and is concerned that testosterone will act as a barrier to conception in the future. Alex's father is in agreement and suggests setting up a family meeting at a reproductive health clinic so that the family can learn more about their options before Alex starts testosterone. At this statement, Alex rolls his eyes and says "What are you talking about? I don't ever want to have kids. I don't want to meet with a doctor about this stuff." Anya provides Alex's parents with some psychoeducation about the risks for Alex's mental health of delaying hormones, and facilitates a conversation between Alex and his parents about this new information. She validates both Alex's and his parents' concerns. The family agrees to think through their options and meet again as a group in a few weeks.

During their next meeting, the family reports that things have been very tense around the house since their last session. Alex says to his parents "you are creating a barrier to me starting testosterone because you don't want me to take it. This whole kid thing is a ploy—they are going to pump me full of female hormones and it's going to make it worse for me." Alex then storms out of the room. His parents look to Anya for guidance and she helps the family to think through the complexities of the situation and what they are asking Alex to do. She asks them to see the situation from his perspective, and his mom says, "When I was 15, I wasn't thinking about kids, either. It is unfair to him that he has to consider this now when who knows what will happen in the future." Alex's father still remains adamant about meeting with a reproductive endocrinologist, but Anya recommends a different clinic where the doctor is known to be more trans affirming. She also suggests that the parents meet with the doctor without Alex so that he does not have to go undergo the embarrassment of meeting with a doctor and considering these questions. Alex's parents agree to take these next steps and come back to therapy to discuss their options. Anya also suggests that they talk with Alex's primary care doctor to share their feelings and concerns about starting testosterone. She suggests that having a conversation with his PCP about moving forward will help him to feel more supported and affirmed, no matter what the family decides to do about fertility.

At the next session, Alex is remarkably more upbeat and says that he feels his parents are finally taking him seriously regarding hormones. When Anya asks him how he feels about the fertility discussions, he says "you know, I still don't think it's for me, but I'm learning that if I do decide to be a parent in the future, that I have some options." Alex shares that his parents met with the doctor Anya suggested to discuss reproductive health options and fertility preservation. The doctor outlined that Alex could go through the process of having an egg retrieval before starting testosterone. She also suggested that he could start testosterone now, and come off it if he felt ready to do an egg retrieval at some point. The doctor shared with the family the statistics around transmasculine people conceiving children and noted that if Alex ever wanted that, he could come off testosterone at that time, noting that there are no current studies about the long-term effects of testosterone on egg quality or conception. This particular clinic does not have the technology or expertise to freeze ovarian tissue or do an egg retrieval with patients who are currently on testosterone, ruling out this option. Alex and his parents mutually decided that given the cost of the egg retrieval, the storage, and the distress it would cause Alex to go through this process, it did not make sense to proceed with fertility preservation at this time. The family agreed that they would revisit this topic if and when Alex feels ready in the future. Alex's parents continue to state a desire for a grandchild, but they also feel comfortable with the options that were presented to them, many of which they did not know about before talking with Anya and meeting with the doctor. Alex maintains that he does not ever want to have children, but he does feel more open to it given what he now knows about the process. Three months later, Alex is able to start testosterone.

In this example, Anya affirms Alex's gender identity and provides important psychoeducation to family members about both the impact of delaying hormones and the fertility preservation process. Anya listens closely to both Alex and his parents' concerns, and reflects back what the other is saying to encourage dialogue and understanding. Anya also provides the family with referrals to providers in the community who are more knowledgeable about reproductive healthcare with TGE youth. Through Anya's advocacy on behalf of Alex, all members of the family are better informed and feel more comfortable with their options. Clearly, Alex's parents are very supportive of his identity as a trans boy and his desire to start hormones. They are also well informed about the options and are privileged enough to have excellent access to care. Anya's knowledge about fertility preservation among TGE youth, comfort with openly discussing these considerations, and help in thinking through the complexities of this situation is an important starting point for Alex's family as they navigate the landscape of his transition.

Conclusion

This chapter outlines several aspects of fertility preservation for TGE adolescents. It looks at the history of TGE people being denied bodily autonomy over access to gender-affirming care and reproduction, rooted in a context of racism and transphobia. The chapter also discusses fertility preservation options for TGE adolescents and the ways in which options for creating a future family can co-exist alongside the desire and need for accessing gender-affirming care. The chapter highlights barriers to fertility preservation among TGE adolescents, both structurally, medically, and emotionally. The role of social workers is highlighted in helping TGE youth and their families to process some of these considerations and discuss best practices with this population. As shown in the case study, the role of a knowledgeable and thoughtful social worker can be paramount in helping TGE youth to process the emotional and physical impact of accessing hormones, and future fertility concerns. As social workers, we are often not trained around the medical aspects of gender-affirming care, and therefore may lack important knowledge that can be crucial to our clients' decision making. It is paramount that we educate ourselves about the medical aspects of transgender health and collaborate with medical providers to ensure that our clients have been able to discuss future fertility options.

Some of us are trans therapists who have our own lived experiences of this very topic, which places us in a unique position to consider the complexities of this issue. We bridge systems and help advocate for our clients amidst a sociomedical system that is often disempowering to them. We also help to advocate for our clients' needs within their own families, especially if they are at odds with what their parents are hoping for. We are walking with our clients towards a future in which TGE youth can resist harmful practices of medical gatekeeping and work towards full bodily autonomy.

References

Adeleye, A. J., Reid, G., Kao, C. N., Mok-Lin, E., & Smith, J. F. (2019). Semen parameters among transgender women with a history of hormonal treatment. *Urology*, *124*, 136–141. doi:10.1016/j.urology.2018.10.005

Allen, L. R., Watson, L. B., Egan, A. M., & Moser, C. N. (2019). Well-being and suicidality among transgender youth after gender-affirming hormones. *Clinical Practice in Pediatric Psychology*, *7*(3), 302–311.

Austin, A., Craig, S. L., & McInroy, L. B. (2016). Toward transgender affirmative social work education. *Journal of Social Work Education*, *52*, 297–310. doi:10.1080/1 0437797.2016.1174637.

Austin, A. (2018). Transgender and gender diverse children: Considerations for affirmative social work practice. *Child and Adolescent Social Work Journal*, *35*, 73–84. doi:https://doi.org/10.1007/s10560-017-0507-3

Boston IVF. (2020). Fertility advice. https://www.bostonivf.com/

Chen, D., Kyweluk, M. A., Sajwani, A., Gordon, E. J., Johnson, E. J., Finlayson, C. A. & Woodruff, T. K. (2019). Factors affecting fertility decision-making among transgender adolescents and young adults. *LGBT Health*, *6*(3), 107–115. doi:10.1 089/lgbt.2018.0250

Chen, D., & Simons, L. (2018). Ethical considerations in fertility preservation for transgender youth: A case illustration. *Clinical Practice in Pediatric Psychology*, *6*(1), 93–100. doi:https://doi.org/10.1037/cpp0000230

Cheng, P. J., Pastuszak, A. W., Myers, J. B., Goodwin, I. A., & Hotaling, J. M. (2019). Fertility concerns of the transgender patient. *Translational Andrology and Urology*, *8*(3), 209–218. 10.21037/tau.2019.05.09

de Vries A. L., McGuire J. K., Steensma T. D., Wagenaar E. C., Doreleijers T. A., & Cohen-Kettenis P. T. (2014). Young adult psychological outcome after puberty suppression and gender reassignment. *Pediatrics*, *134*, 696–704.

Dunne, P. (2017). Transgender sterilisation requirements in Europe. *Medical Law Review*, *25*(4), 554–581. 10.1093/medlaw/fwx028

Jones, H. W. (2000). Gender reassignment and assisted reproduction: Evaluation of multiple aspects. *Human Reproduction, 15*(5, May): 987, 10.1093/humrep/15.5.987.

Kyweluk, M. A., Sajwani, A. & Chen, D. (2018) Freezing for the future: Transgender youth respond to medical fertility preservation. *International Journal of Transgenderism, 19*(4), 401–416. doi: 10.1080/15532739.2018.1505575

Levey, M., Trottman, M., Liedl, B., Reese, S., Stief, C., Freitag, B., Baugh, J., Spagnoli, G., & Kölle, S. (2017). Effects of elevated β-estradiol levels on the functional morphology of the testis – New insights. *Scientific Reports, 7*, 39931.

Mallon, G. P.(Ed.) (2009). *Social work practice with transgender and gender variant youth.* New York: Routledge.

Nahata, L., Chen, D., Quiinn, G. P., Travis, M., Grannis, C., Nelson, E. Tishelman, A. C. (2019). Reproductive attitudes and behaviors among transgender/nonbinary adolescents. *Journal of Adolescent Health, 66*(3), 372–374.

Nahata, L., Tishelman, A. C., Caltabellotta, N. M., & Quinn, G. P. (2017). Low fertility preservation utilization among transgender youth. *Journal of Adolescent Health, 61*(1), 40–44.

National Association of Social Workers. (2006). Transgender and gender identity issues. https://www.socialworkers.org/assets/secured/documents/da/da2008/reffered/Transgender.pdf

National Center for Transgender Equality. (2016). Transgender survey. https://transequality.org/issues/us-trans-survey

Nixon, L. (2013). The right to (Trans) parent: A reproductive justice approach to reproductive rights, fertility, and family-building issues facing transgender people. *William & Mary Journal of Race, Gender, and Social Justice, 20*(1–5), 72–103. https://scholarship.law.wm.edu/wmjowl/vol20/iss1/5

Obedin-Maliver, J., & Makadon, H. J. (2015). Transgender men and pregnancy. *Obstetric Medicine,* 10.1177/1753495X15612658

Olson, K. R., Durwood, L., & McLaughlin, K. A. (2016). Mental health of transgender children who are supported in their identities. *Pediatrics, 137*(3), e20153223.

Planned Parenthood. (2020). What do I need to know about transitioning? https://www.plannedparenthood.org/learn/gender-identity/transgender/what-do-i-need-know-about-transitioning

Ryan C., Huebner D., Diaz R. M., & Sanchez J. (2009). Family rejection as a predictor of negative health outcomes in white and Latino lesbian, gay, and bisexual young adults. *Pediatrics, 123*(1), 346–352.

Turban, J. L., King, D., Carswell J. M., & Keuroghlian, A. S. (2020). Pubertal suppression for transgender youth and risk of suicidal ideation. *Pediatrics, 145*(2), e20191725.

Veale, J., Watson, R. J., Adjei, J., Saewyc, E. (2016). Prevalence of pregnancy involvement among Canadian transgender youth and its relation to mental health, sexual health, and gender identity. *International Journal of Transgenderism, 17* (3–4), 107–113. doi: 10.1080/15532739.2016.1216345.

15 Medical Care for Trans and Gender Expansive Youth

Finn Brigham

Introduction

Health care is one of the most complicated aspects of a trans or gender expansive (TGE) person's life. For some it can be a supportive gateway to feeling more at peace with their body and a portal into taking better care of themselves. For others it is a journey fraught with discrimination, misinformation, and shame. Current philosophy is shifting away from identifying TGE identity as a mental health concern and towards conceptualizing TGE identities as a treatable medical condition, *if* that is in alignment with the interests and goals of the individual. Finding a team of healthcare providers that are supportive, competent and affordable for TGE youth is often difficult, even in large American cities. It is important for social workers to understand the landscape of TGE health care so they can support their clients in navigating this system and utilizing it to assist them in aligning their bodies with their internal gender identities. Social workers are imperative brokers to complicated and bureaucratic systems that leave many TGE youth (and cis youth for that matter) overwhelmed and hopeless, so it is crucial that they are knowledgeable about how to navigate often complex healthcare systems and services.

Why Is Trans-Competent Health Care Necessary?

It is important first to examine why trans-competent health care is so critical for TGE youth and young adults. The majority of TGE youth are perfectly healthy and may not, if at all, utilize the healthcare system. For TGE youth, finding and maintaining qualified providers can greatly improve their healthcare journey and permit them to medically transition safely and affordably, if that is their goal. Even very knowledgeable TGE youth and their parents may find many barriers to locating a team of trans-competent healthcare providers. In some cases, if a TGE youth or their family can identify and access a local healthcare provider who is willing to provide care to their TGE youth, they often do not have the knowledge needed to adequately provide the care that a young person may need.

DOI: 10.4324/9780429297687-15

While a range of hormone therapies are becoming more accessible and surgery may be more affordable than in previous years, there are complicated factors that providers must understand in order to competently care for TGE youth. The following are a few examples of the kinds of nuanced considerations it is important for medical providers to understand:

- If a primary care physician is willing to provide hormone therapy or hormone (puberty) blockers (see more on hormone blockers below) for a TGE youth, will they be able to understand the preventative health care screenings necessary for a TGE youth?
- Does a TGE young woman who is on hormones have the same breast cancer risk as a cisgender young woman?
- Is it necessary for a TGE young man that has been on hormones for five years to get a hysterectomy?

This type of trans competency-based care is not taught in medical and nursing schools. Most medical professionals do not get trans-related training at all and if they do, it is usually focused solely on HIV risk.

A 2009 study by Lambda Legal asked 4,900 lesbian, gay, bisexual, and transgender (LGBT) people their barriers to health care and then compared the lesbian, gay, and bisexual (LGB) identified respondents to TGE-identified respondents. Findings showed that TGE people have a much harder time accessing competent medical care. Over 65% of TGE respondents reported that providers were unaware of their healthcare needs compared to 44% of LGB responders. Almost 30% of TGE participants reported being refused care because of their gender identity comparted to 7.7% of LGB participants (Figure 15.1).

How to Determine Trans Competence

When looking to determine if a provider or clinic are TGE affirming it is not simply about training in TGE care (although that is important). There are many ways a clinic can show competency in tandem with the training of the providers. For example, all gender bathrooms are one way for a clinic/hospital to show publicly that the healthcare entity supports TGE people. Hiring of TGE staff and appointing TGE people to the board of directors is another way to demonstrate competency. Ensuring the health clinic you attend accepts Medicaid is another way to ensure competency, as trans people in general are less likely to have private health insurance. Another way to ascertain competency is by reviewing the clinic's intake forms. When reviewing intake forms, do they:

- Ask for legal name AND chosen name?
- Ask what personal pronouns to use?
- Include "partnered" as an option for marital status?

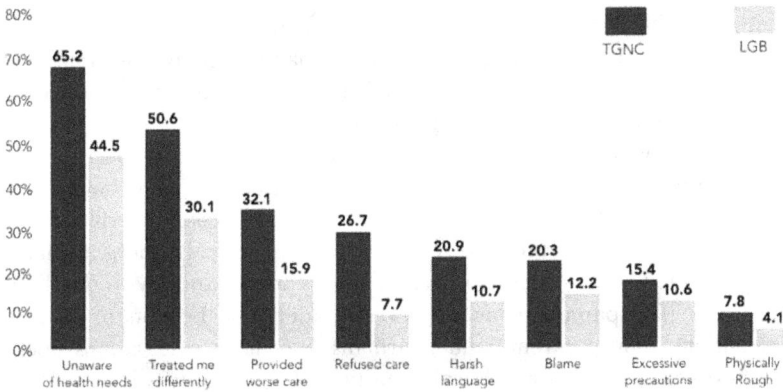

Figure 15.1 Experiences of Discrimination and Substandard Care: Transgender or Gender-Nonconforming Compared to Lesbian, Gay, and Bisexual.

- Ask for sexual orientation and gender identity and have the appropriate options of those identities listed?
- Ask the sex that is listed on a person's health insurance to ensure billing is done accurately?

Assuming one can find such a clinic and set of providers, why is it important that a healthy, young TGE person start accessing care? After all, if they are not seeking transition-related care is their care that different than a cis youth? The answer is yes. There are many reasons that TGE youth should engage with a trans competent provider even before they make decisions about starting medical transition. First, every young person deserves to receive competent health care from a provider that is knowledgeable about and affirming of their identities. Additionally, if starting hormone care, a competent provider will monitor a TGE person's lab work including things like hormone levels and liver functioning. Although this can be done at the start of a medical transition, it is very helpful to have baseline data prior to the start of a transition. In addition, many medical transition decisions are based on the stage of puberty a TGE youth is in. Tracking the various stages of puberty (known as Tanner Stages) are important indicators of when medical intervention may be necessary.

Another reason to start as early as possible is that many parents/guardians (as well as the youth themselves) may need time to understand the nuances of TGE care. They will have questions and anxieties that are important to work though before starting a transition, if transitioning is what the young person desires. If a TGE youth has been receiving primary care from a trans competent provider this work can begin before any medical transition is necessary or desired. Many times a TGE youth won't ask a parent/guardian about a medical transition until they feel ready (or have felt ready for a long time) for this step. It can take parents/guardians months or even years to "catch up" and feel comfortable taking the next steps. Not having to start at the step of finding a competent provider can save years of difficult work while the youth considers their options regarding possible medical transition. Similarly, even though TGE youth may have done meticulous research about their transition options, most parents will want to hear directly from a healthcare provider about the medical options available to their child. The provider can become a very important ally to the TGE youth in helping parents to understand the safety and benefits of medical interventions. Many parents and guardians may have reservations about a TGE youth beginning a medical transition. That said, it is important to note that gender-affirming models of care have been recommended by nearly every major American medical association including the American Academy of Pediatrics, the American Medical Association, the American Psychological Association, the Endocrine Society, the World Professional Association for Transgender Health, and the American College of Obstetricians and Gynecologists (Rafferty, 2018). These are the types of things a competent provider can help a parent to understand so they will be more comfortable with the idea of a physical transition, if that is what the young person chooses to pursue.

In addition, research demonstrates that physical outcomes of a transition are improved when a youth starts hormone therapy and/or puberty blockers at younger ages, for example it might eliminate the need for some surgeries in the future. If a medical transition can occur before a youth progresses very far into puberty it is likely their physical transition will be more successful, for example trans masculine youth who begin hormones or blockers at a young age may be less likely to need top surgery as breasts are less likely to develop. Finally, when contemplating a TGE youth's eventual ability to have biological children if that is a goal, a youth must freeze their eggs or sperm prior to a medical transition starting. This can delay a start of a medical transition so getting accurate information about fertility as early as possible is important.

It is important to note that not all TGE youth are interested in a medical transition. There are many factors that go into decisions about medical transition including but not limited to costs, potential outcomes, physical transition goals, insurance status, medical conditions, family acceptance, career impacts, mental health concerns, and many more (White Hughto, Rose, Pachankis, & Reisner, 2017). Some youth may want to access surgery but cannot afford it. Some youth may have surgery covered by their insurance but are not interested in it. Some youth may want a medical intervention at a later point in their lives but not currently. Some may want some of the surgeries available to them but not all. It is important not to assume all TGE youth will someday want a medical transition. For some youth this is a goal and for some it is not and never will be. That said, as a social worker it is important to understand the options for medical transition so you can discuss them with your clients.

Hormone Therapy

There are variety of hormone therapy options for TGE youth depending on age, health, and goals. These can be adjusted for each person. When given under the care of a trans competent medical provider, hormones are considered largely safe. There are few known health issues associated with hormones and most people's quality of life when taking hormones largely outweighs any potential health issues. It can be important to monitor some patient's liver functions as well as bone density, but the overall health risks are minimal (Lambrese, 2010). This section will give an overview of hormone effects and the timing of those effects. For more information on dosage and health risks visit the website of the World Professional Association of Transgender Health (https://wpath.org/).

For trans feminine youth who decide to take hormones, both estrogen and hormone blockers are traditionally taken. There are a variety of modalities to administer these hormones (again, see WPATH). The effects of estrogen on a typical trans feminine person include:

* redistribution of the body fat, from the waist/stomach to the thighs and buttocks
* softening of the skin
* decrease of muscle mass and strength
* decreased libido and erections
* breast growth
* decreased sperm production

These effects will typically start between 1 and 3 months of starting hormones and there will be minimal additional changes after 2–3 years on hormones. Typically a trans feminine person on estrogen will not experience changes to their voice. It is important to note that once a TGE person begins taking hormones, they will have to take hormones for their rest of their life if they want the effects to be maintained.

Trans masculine people may decide to take testosterone (estrogen blockers are not necessary). Typical effects of testosterone include:

* increased skin oiliness and acne
* facial and body hair growth
* scalp hair loss
* increased muscle mass/strength
* fat distribution (from buttocks/thighs to waist/stomach)
* cessation of menses
* clitoral enlargement
* deepening of voice

These effects will typically take place between 3 and 6 months after beginning testosterone and there will be minimal additional changes after 2–5 years of taking testosterone. As with trans feminine people, trans masculine people will need to take testosterone for the rest of their lives for effects to stay in place. It is also worth noting that taking higher doses of hormones than prescribed will not increase the speed of a transition but could lead to negative health outcomes.

Hormone Blockers

Hormone blockers are another important option for TGE youth. Hormone blockers (or suppressors) are medicines that block the release of hormones. This then stops testosterone from being released from the testes, and estrogen being released from the ovaries. Without exposure to these hormones, the body does not go through the changes typically associated with the production of these hormones. In TGE youth, puberty blockers are used to suppress the changes that can increase the youth's gender dysphoria. The age at which hormone blockers should be started will differ between youth. Medical providers use what are known as Tanner Stages to track puberty in youth. These stages are measured by things such as pubic hair growth, the size of breasts, and genitals. Hormone blockers are typically begun in Tanner Stage 2 (Mahfouda, Moore, Siafarikas, Zeph, & Lin 2017). Hormone blockers are an important tool for medical providers, TGE youth, and their families. It can be difficult for family members and caregivers to discern if a youth will want to live their entire lives in gender identity different than that typically associated with their assigned birth sex. It can also be anxiety producing for both TGE youth and their families/caregivers to commit to some of the effects of hormones that may not be reversible. Hormone blockers effectively put a "pause" on puberty, but the pause is temporary. If a TGE youth decides that they do not want to take hormones and they go off blockers their puberty will proceed as normal (Olsen-Kennedy, Rosenthal, Hastings, & Wesp, 2016).

Surgical Options

There are many options for surgical interventions for TGE youth. Again, it is important to note that some TGE youth and adults will opt for all the surgical interventions available to them and some will never pursue surgery. The decision to pursue surgery is an individual choice, that can also be constrained by structural challenges such as access to trans competent providers, insurance coverage, and lack of financial resources. Surgical options are provided in this chapter in an effort to educate social workers about current available options. Society at large often places unnecessary and invasive attention on the bodies of trans people. Do not question trans people about their bodies or about surgeries. In the context of therapeutic work, discussions about a TGE youth's body will likely arise. Therefore, it is important for social workers to be educated about surgical interventions. This section will outline the most common surgical options available to TGE youth and adults. It is also important to note that surgical options are progressing at a rapid pace and new and more advanced options are being made available every day.

Examples of surgical options for transmasculine individuals include chest masculinizing surgery (also commonly referred to as top surgery), metoidioplasty (or meta), and phalloplasty. Examples of surgical options for transfeminine people include chest/breast augmentation, orchiectomy, vaginoplasty, and facial feminization surgery. For detailed information about these surgeries, visit callen-lorde.org or another trusted trans-affirming medical center.

How to Assist a Client Thinking about Surgery

As a social worker you may be working with a client that is contemplating hormones or surgery. They may be working through various issues that come up when contemplating these medical interventions. There are a lot considerations, including but not limited to, figuring out how to pay for it, fear of doctors/surgeons/hospital stays, the pain associated with the surgery, how family/friends/coworkers will react to physical changes, feeling ambivalence or loss about one's body parts, concerns about sexual functioning and pleasure, and many more.

These decisions can be difficult. They can greatly affect someone's finances, physical appearance, and in some cases their physical safety. Even clients that are very "sure" of their decisions are likely to second-guess these decisions at some point. That is a completely normal part of the decision making process and should not lead social workers to assume the TGE person is not a good candidate for medical intervention. For the past few decades when TGE people needed to get letters from therapists in order to obtain surgery or hormones they had to be very careful with their wording when requesting such letters. If therapists thought an individual was expressing any doubt or if there were any co-occurring mental health issues these letters would not be written, and the client could not obtain surgery. Because of this, TGE people have been trained to tell therapists that they are "trapped in the wrong body" and they simply cannot go on living in their current body. While this is true for some, it is not true for everyone. The result, unfortunately, is that TGE people may not feel they can be honest with their therapists about the understandable questions they may be having. They may be afraid if a therapist senses any doubt about their decisions, then they won't receive the needed documentation. It is good practice to assume that an individual possesses the knowledge needed to make decisions about their own bodies. The role of the therapist here is to simply help an individual figure out what is best for them at this point in their lives. Examples of questions a social worker might ask, after developing rapport, include:

- What are your goals?
- How do you want your body to change?

- What do you think your life will be like if you move forward with this medical intervention and what will it be like if you do not?
- Do you have the resources and support to recover from surgery safely?
- Have you discussed with a surgeon the realities of the surgery and what can reasonably be accomplished?
- Do you fully understand the risks of the procedures and have you thought about what it might be like if the final outcome of surgery isn't what you expected?

It is imperative that these questions do not come from, and are not perceived as coming from, a place of judgment or doubt in an individual's ability to make informed decisions about their bodies. These are questions for both the social worker and the TGE person to be curious about and to discuss openly, so that an individual can make a more informed decision for themselves.

Finding a Trans Competent Surgeon

Finding a trans competent surgeon can be a difficult process. There are few TGE surgeons in the United States. The ones that do exist are mostly in large cities and can have long waitlists. For the most sought-after surgeons in the country, a patient may wait several years to even get a consultation. Another barrier to accessing surgery is insurance coverage. While in some states insurances do cover hormones and surgery, an individual will often have to obtain the surgeries in the state where they live, which can keep them from accessing most of the best surgeons in the country. Even if insurance covers surgery, that is no guarantee that the desired surgeon will take that specific insurance. In some states like New York, the state Medicaid program will pay for TGE surgery, but not all surgeons take Medicaid. If a person is able to pay out of pocket for these surgeries, they may have to travel several states over to obtain surgery which adds to the total cost because of travel and accommodations. For genital surgeries, an individual will often have to stay near the surgeon for several weeks, which can mean additional housing costs.

When choosing a question, there are some important questions an individual should ask their potential surgeon. For instance, an individual should be informed of all costs associated with the surgery. They should ask about the recovery time, any potential complications, and realistic outcomes including sexual functioning and pleasure. An individual may also want to know what screenings a surgeon will require before the surgery. For example, different surgeons will have different rules about what body mass index (BMI) a patient can have to be eligible for surgery. Virtually all surgeons will ask that an individual not smoke tobacco products for a certain time before surgery, but those timelines vary. Some surgeons will even require a patient to take a nicotine screening test within days of the surgery.

An individual should also ask about the support they can expect to receive after the surgery. Examples of these questions include:

- How long will they stay in the hospital?
- How often will they see the surgeon after their surgery?
- Who can they call with questions after the surgery?
- What should they do should complications arise?
- What is the complication rate of the surgeon?
- Will the patient be expected to pay up front and be reimbursed by their insurance company or will the surgeon deal directly with the insurance company?
- What letters does the surgeon require prior to surgery?

Gatekeeping

Social workers often find themselves in the role of gatekeeper when working with TGE individuals, because it is the responsibility of a mental health professional to make recommendations for gender-affirming medical interventions. This dynamic can challenge the relationship between a TGE person and a social worker (Nealy, 2019). Some have criticized the role of social worker as gatekeeper, arguing that it forces individuals to prove and then defend their gender identities and limits an individual's bodily autonomy. The letter from a social worker is meant to ensure the surgeon and the insurance company that the individual is "ready" for surgery. The process directly places another individual in control of the TGE person's body, questioning their own expertise about their own bodies and identities and upholding the idea of trans as pathology (Shelton, Kroehle, & Andia, 2019). While a reader might believe such a process is necessary when an individual wants to alter their body, consider the fact that cisgender individuals who access plastic surgery need no such letter. A therapist should get clarity from the surgeon/insurance company as to exactly what information is needed in the letter. Most trans affirming health centers can provide social workers with a template for the letter. The social worker should give as little information about the patient as necessary while still ensuring the letter includes information required by the surgeon and insurance company. Typically a surgeon will need the letter to include the length of time the social work has worked with the patient, that the patient has been diagnosed with gender dysphoria, how long the patient has been on hormones (if they are on hormones), and the social worker's assessment of the patient's understanding of the risks and benefits of the surgery. Though this chapter is focused on medical interventions, it is important to note that much controversy exists about the DSM-V including "gender dysphoria" as a diagnostic category. Some advocates argue that in our current medical system it is important to have a medical diagnosis in order to be able to get access care and have that care covered by insurance. Other advocates argue that to continue to include gender dysphoria as a diagnostic category in the DSM perpetuates the notion of trans as pathology and should be removed from the DSM altogether (like homosexuality was).

As Arlene Istar Lev states in *Gender Dysphoria: Two Steps Forward, One Step Back*:

> I have always taken a definitive position that removal of the diagnosis would be the best way to depathologize transgender people. Trans people deserve access to medical care, not because they are mentally ill and fit the criteria within a diagnostic manual, but rather precisely because they are sane and actualizing their authentic gender is their civil right. Having said that, I think that the change in nomenclature from the DSM-IV to the DSM-5 is a step forward, that is, removing the concept of gender as the site of the disorder and placing the focus on issues of distress and dysphoria. The placement of the gender dysphoria diagnosis within its own section in the DSM-5 helps to separate it from sexual dysfunctions and paraphilias. The new nomenclature is significantly less sexist, somewhat less cisgenderist, and helps to distinguish between gender nonconformity and gender dysphoria (p. 295).

Preventative Care

When discussing TGE care it is also important to note that, like all people, TGE people need to engage in preventative care. Regardless of a patient's gender identity, if they have certain body parts, they need regular screenings. It is understandable that if, for example, a transman has breasts that he hates, he may not want to get preventative breast cancer screenings. However, it is just as important, if not more important, that all TGE people get the screenings needed for the body parts they have. If TGE people have breasts, cervixes, or prostates they should get them screened on the timeline recommend by their primary care physician. There are steps a medical provider can take to make these exams as easy as possible. Asking a patient what words they use for their body and then using those words can be helpful. For example, if a transman would prefer the word "chest exam" to "breast exam" there is no reason to not utilize this terminology. Telling a TGE patient exactly what the provider is going to do can be helpful. Being trauma informed is also helpful. Many TGE people have histories of trauma, violence, or abuse that can make these screenings even more difficult (Shipherd, Maguen, Skidmore, & Abramovitz, 2011). Being sensitive to these needs is important to help ensure a patient is as comfortable with the screenings as possible.

Fertility

Another important part of TGE medical care for youth are the options around fertility. Chapter 14 in this book will cover fertility in depth but it is important to note two things. The first is that in most cases hormones and genital surgery will result in infertility for both transmasculine and transfeminine people. Although it can be hard for a TGE youth to answer questions around if they will want to have biological children many years into their future, it is important to at least have these discussions before starting a medical transition so the youth can be given the option to freeze sperm or eggs. Although most medical transitions will result in infertility, it is important to note that it is not exactly clear how long it will take for a TGE youth to become infertile after starting hormones. This is important as hormones are NOT meant to be used as birth control. It is possible for a TGE youth to become pregnant or impregnate someone else in the months after they begin hormones. It is also possible to go off of hormones and become fertile again. All of these options should be discussed with a TGE competent medical provider before beginning hormones or getting surgery (Cheng, Pastuszak, Myers, Goodwin, & Hotaling, 2019).

Nonbinary Care

Many TGE youth identify as nonbinary (or genderqueer, gender expansive, genderfluid, etc.). Medical care for nonbinary people is very much evolving in real time but it is important to note they ways in which it is similar to transgender care and the ways in which it is not. Just as the path for all transgender people does not always involve medical transition (such as hormones and affirming surgery), the same is true for nonbinary youth. Some nonbinary youth may want to obtain hormones/blockers and some many not. Some may pursue surgery and some never will. When working with a nonbinary youth the best thing to do is to discuss with them their goals regarding their physical body and ask how they can be supported in reaching these goals. For instance, does the nonbinary youth want a flat chest? A higher voice? Facial hair? A more feminine body with curves? Some of these goals can be achieved through hormones and surgery but there are other ways as well. For example, for many TGE youth, menstruating can be very triggering. A youth may not be ready for blockers or hormones but might really struggle with the dysphoria associated with a monthly period. Getting an IUD can be a way for a youth to stop getting their period without hormones. If a nonbinary youth does not want any medical interventions but expresses that their deep voice is a source of anxiety for them, they can take voice lessons to learn to speak in a higher register that might make them feel more confident and comfortable. In some spaces, nonbinary identities are becoming more embraced and in other spaces they are still very misunderstood. A social worker's role is not to try to convince a nonbinary youth of any identity but to simply support them in their self-discovery and in being more comfortable with themselves.

Case Study

Jace is an 8 year old. From a young age most people would refer to Jace as a "tomboy," although Jace didn't use this word. Jace wanted to wear clothes with Spiderman and Black Panther on them and preferred swim trunks to the bikini Jace's parents bought. Although Jace was a happy kid, things started to change around age 11 when Jace started to go through puberty. As Jace started to grow breasts, Jace's parent's felt it was important that Jace wear a shirt when playing outside. This threw Jace into tantrums and tears that Jace's parents didn't understand. Jace became sad and withdrawn. Jace insisted his parents use "he" pronouns and pushed back against anything feminine. Jace's parents spoke to their pediatrician who assured them it was just a phase and all kids tried on different roles as they grew older. Despite this reassurance, Jace seemed more upset than ever. He stopped playing with his friends and refused to use the girl's bathroom. After Jace's teachers told him he had to use the girl's room, he was given detention for urinating outside the school on the football field. By the time Jace was 13 he was cutting his arms and seemed to have few friends. In desperation Jace's parents went to an LGBTQ-focused health center to seek advice. After speaking with Jace and his family the medical provider gave Jace's parents information on puberty blockers and encouraged them to embrace his masculinity. After further research, much to Jace's happiness, his parents agreed to let him take the blockers. Jace's parents spoke to his school and reminded them that by law in their state Jace had a right to use the boy's bathroom and be called by he/him pronouns. They also had Jace join the LBGTQ ally group at his school. In addition they found Jace an LGBTQ competent child therapist. Things began to get better for Jace as the people around him started to embrace the fact that he was a boy. He was happier, stopped cutting, and started dating a girl that knew about his gender identity. Before going to college, he asked his parents if he could start testosterone and have top surgery so he could go to college with a body that more accurately reflected his gender. Given the happiness he had found living as a young man, they agreed. The testosterone gave him a more muscular physique and he grew facial hair. With each physical change he seemed more himself and his parents started to wonder how they ever thought of him as a girl. He had top surgery the summer before his freshman year at Connecticut College and was able to room with another young man. He was grateful to his parents for giving him what he needed when he was young and knew things could have gone much worse for him had they not found an LGBTQ-competent medical provider.

Reflection Questions

1. Did any aspects of the case study make you feel uncomfortable? What were they? Can you identify the source of your discomfort?
2. Do you know what the policies are in your local school district regarding bathroom use and name/pronoun changes?
3. How can you imagine working with the healthcare provider if they did not support hormone blockers for Jace?

References

Chen, D., Abrams, M., Clark, L., Ehrensaft, D., Tishelman, A. C., Chan, Y. M., … Hidalgo, M. A. (2020). Psychosocial characteristics of transgender youth seeking gender-affirming medical treatment: Baseline findings from the trans youth care study. *The Journal of Adolescent Health: Official Publication of the Society for Adolescent Medicine*, S1054-139X(20)30453-5. doi:10.1016/j.jadohealth.2020.07.033

Cheng, P. J., Pastuszak, A. W., Myers, J. B., Goodwin, I. A., & Hotaling, J. M. (2019). Fertility concerns of the transgender patient. *Translational Andrology and Urology, 8*(3), 209–218. Doi:10.21037/tau.2019.05.09

Lambrese, J. (2010). *Virtual Mentor, 12*(8), 645–649. doi:10.1001/virtualmentor.201 0.12.8.jdsc1-1008. Retrieved from https://journalofethics.ama-assn.org/article/ suppression-puberty-transgender-children/2010-08

Mahfouda, S., Moore, J., Siafarikas, A., Zeph, F., & Lin, A. (2017). Puberty suppression in transgender children and adolescents. *The Lancent Diabetes & Endocrinology, 5*(10), 816–826.

Nealy, E. (2019). *Trans kids and teens: Pride, joy, and families in transition.* New York: W. W. Norton & Company.

Olsen-Kennedy, J., Rosenthal, S., Hastings, J., & Wesp, L. (2016). Health considerations for gender non-conforming children and transgender adolescents. *UCSF Transgender Care & Treatment Guidelines*. Retrieved from https://transcare.ucsf.edu/ guidelines/youth

Shelton, J., Kroehle, K., & Andia, M. (2019). The trans person is not the problem: Brave spaces and structural competence as educative tools for trans justice in social work. *Journal of Sociology and Social Welfare, 46*(4), 97–123.

Rafferty, J (2018). AAP COMMITTEE ON PSYCHOSOCIAL ASPECTS OF CHILD AND FAMILY HEALTH, AAP COMMITTEE ON ADOLESCENCE, AAP SECTION ON LESBIAN, GAY, BISEXUAL, AND TRANSGENDER HEALTH AND WELLNESS. Ensuring Comprehensive Care and Support for Transgender and GenderDiverse Children and Adolescents. *Pediatrics, 142*, e20182162.

Shipherd, J. C., Maguen, S., Skidmore, W. C., & Abramovitz, S. M. (2011). Potentially traumatic events in a transgender sample: Frequency and associated symptoms. *Traumatology, 17*(2), 56–67. doi: 10.1177/1534765610395614

White Hughto, J., Rose, A., Pachankis, J., & Reisner, S. (2017). Barriers to gender transition-related healthcare: Identifying underserved transgender adults in Massachusetts. *Transgender Health, 2*(1), 107–118, doi: 10.1089/trgh.2017.0014

16 Social Work Practice with Trans and Gender Expansive Youth in Child Welfare Systems

Gerald P. Mallon, Ryan Karnoski, Oliver Stabbe, Liam Waller, and Valentin Sierra

Introduction

Child welfare professionals have repeatedly documented their observations of disproportional overrepresentation of transgender and gender expansive (TGE) youth in the U.S. public child welfare systems (Mallon, 1999, 2008; Paul, 2018). The few methodologically rigorous studies conducted provide empirical evidence of this phenomenon suggest that TGE youth may be overrepresented in public child welfare systems at nearly three times the rate of their non-TGE peers (Fish, Baams, Wojciak, & Russell, 2019). Information about a youth's gender identity is not typically collected at the time of their initial entry into the child welfare system (in fact, the majority of states never track this information at all), contributing to lack of understanding regarding the underlying causes of this overrepresentation.

The first part of this chapter provides an overview of the unique experiences of marginalization that TGE youth face within the child welfare system. Transgender youth are particularly vulnerable to caregiver rejection; a lack of permanency and social challenges related to frequent placement changes; identity-based legal barriers; accessing appropriate healthcare; and other forms of disparate treatment. For transgender youth in U.S. child welfare systems, disparities are particularly evident in disparately higher rates of mental illness and/or engagement in risky behaviors.

The second part of this chapter discusses best practices and guidance on how social workers and in particular how child welfare professionals can help provide appropriate care for TGE youth in the child welfare system. Based on recommendations from national organizations and research groups, and scholars, these best practices highlight the importance of safety in living arrangements and outline how to provide gender-affirming care and social service delivery in a child welfare setting. The best practices discussed here include directly asking all child welfare system-involved youth about their gender identity (or from a caregiver or parent only if necessary). This section also prepares child welfare social workers to identify the individual needs of each child welfare system involved TGE youth and to advocate for the youth across service settings. Additionally, readers will be given tips on how to

DOI: 10.4324/9780429297687-16

identify and connect with local organizations and community-based child welfare resources in their area that may have support groups or other services tailored to meet the needs of TGE youth in care.

The third section of this chapter presents a case study that demonstrates some of the needs, challenges, and sources of support for child welfare system-involved TGE youth. The case study offers alternate scenarios that challenge the reader to consider how these experiences may vary for youth at different stages of development. Following the case study, questions are presented that allow a reader to reflect on how different placement settings, permanency plans, and other factors may impact a TGE youth's experience in the child welfare system. The chapter concludes with the identification of additional resources for social workers in both direct clinical practice and academic or other professional settings to strengthen their knowledge of existing sources of information on TGE youth in child welfare systems.

Background

The child welfare system is a distinct area of practice for social workers and is governed by both state and federal laws, which are enforced through local, state-level, and tribal governments. Governmental child welfare systems frequently partner with non-governmental family service organizations, many of which are affiliated with religious or other community-based organizations. All children and youth who enter the child welfare system have unique social, emotional, educational, and familial circumstances which must be considered when doing case planning. Transgender and gender expansive youth have been noted to be overrepresented in child welfare systems at rates 1.5–2 times higher than expected based on overall population proportion (Fish et al., 2019). For this reason, it is particularly important that social workers who work with transgender and gender expansive (TGE) youth develop a foundational understanding of issues effecting TGE in public child welfare systems (Mallon, 2021).

Most TGE young people are not placed in child welfare systems. In fact, the majority of TGE youth live with their families and never rely on a foster home, a group home, a shelter, or a child welfare setting at all. Those TGE youth who do come to the attention of the child welfare system are young people who have experienced difficulties within their family system to such a degree that they cannot or should not continue to live at home.

Although some TGE youth are thrown out of their homes when they disclose their gender orientation or gender identity expression or when they are "found out" by their families, not all of them enter child welfare systems because of issues directly related to their gender identity. Like their lesbian, gay, bisexual, or cisgender counterparts, the majority of TGE young people were placed in these systems before or during the onset of adolescence (DeCrescenzo & Mallon, 2000). Some were placed for the same reasons that other young people are placed: Family disintegration; divorce, death, or physical or mental illness of a parent; parental substance abuse or alcoholism; physical abuse or neglect.

Child welfare systems (foster homes, group homes, congregate care settings, and shelters) have long been and continue to be an integral part of youth services systems (see Bullard, Owens, Richmond, & Alwon, 2010). The structure of the different types of out-of-home programs varies widely and can take many forms. They range from family-based foster homes to small community-based group homes and short-term respite care or shelter facilities to large congregate care institutions that provide short-term therapeutic or longer-term custodial care. Some facilities have a juvenile justice component to them (Irvine, 2010; Irvine & Canfield, 2015; Mallon & Perez, 2020) some are family foster care programs (Clements & Rosenwald, 2007), and others still are programs designed for runaway and homeless youth (Maccio & Ferguson, 2016; Shelton, 2015, 2016). All of these different types of services share one common feature, however: They provide care for youth on a 24-hour-a-day basis, which is very different from other youth services that are not residential in nature.

Generally, most group homes, juvenile justice facilities, and shelters are staffed by individual youth care workers or counselors who are employed by an agency to work in shifts to cover the facility and provide care for a youth 24 hours a day. The youth care workers who work in group care settings play a very important role in the lives of the TGE young people in their care. Nevertheless, they are generally the lowest paid – and in many cases, have obtained the least education and training – in the youth services system. The daily stress of working with youth in these settings, combined with the poor pay, can make it difficult for some staff to be empathetic and compassionate in their dealings with the young people, and these factors also account for a high staff turnover.

Most child welfare care settings for adolescents focus on preparing these young people for the transition to adulthood – on or before their 18th birthday, or 21st birthday in some states. Some foster homes, group homes, and congregate care settings are warm, loving, and accepting of diversity and others are cold, poorly maintained, and rigid. TGE young people live in and speak about both.

In 2011, the U.S. Administration for Children, Youth, and Families Commissioner, Bryan Samuels, issued a memorandum encouraging protection and support of lesbian, gay, bisexual, transgender, and questioning (LGBTQ) youth in foster care. These recommended practices elaborate on the provision of services to LGBTQ youth in the areas of foster care, child protection, family preservation, adoption, and youth development. They aimed to assist state child welfare agencies to meet the needs of this particularly vulnerable and underserved population by promoting safe, competent and supportive settings for LGBTQ youth and were significant in that the Administration for Children Youth and Families (ACYF) had never before issued a written policy or offered guidance to supports states in working with

LGBTQ youth. Despite some changes in policies from the subsequent more conservative administration, this memorandum stands as the official guidance from the U.S. Department of Health and Human Services (United States Department of Health and Human Services, 2011).

Key areas of understanding for social work practitioners who serve child welfare system-involved youth include an overview of contemporary research and legal policy related to this population, best practices for serving this population, and resources offering additional support and information. For TGE child welfare system–involved youth, it is imperative that families of origin, foster parents, and/or relative caregivers provide gender-affirming interactions, homes, and access to healthcare and social supports.

A child welfare social worker may find themselves in a position where it is necessary to act as an advocate for these needs to be met. In this case, social workers should ask themselves the following questions:

- Has this youth entered the child welfare system due to experiences of maltreatment, discrimination, or marginalization based on their identity?
- How has the system worked with the family to preserve their connection to this young person?
- What/who are the natural supports within this youth's community that can provide a gender-affirming space (living environment, social environment, medical center, school, faith community)
- Which of these supports may be able to offer guidance to parents, caregivers, or other individuals who may need additional assistance in creating a safe and affirming environment for a child welfare system–involved TGE youth?
- What can be done within the present and future living environments to create a safe and supportive living environment with respect to gender identity?
- Are there particular individuals or environments that introduce specific risks or supports to a TGE youth? How can these risks be mitigated or resolved?

Risks and Opportunities

Social workers should be aware of the risks and opportunities to which the child welfare system can expose TGE youth. In child welfare settings, TGE youth face specific risks of maltreatment, discrimination, and marginalization based on actual or perceived gender identity (Mallon, Paul, & López López, 2021; Paul & Monahan, 2019). These risk factors can occur prior to entry into the child welfare system in a youth's family of origin, during child welfare system placement, or post–child welfare system exposure. Areas of risk include identity-based abuse or maltreatment within a family of origin or by relatives or caregivers in an "out of home" placement. Bullying by other youth in the home, school, or community, and social isolation or an absence of social support from gender-affirming peers or adults also pose risks to the health and safety of child welfare system involved youth. There are also increased rates of mental health issues and risky behaviors associated with youth in these populations (Russell & Fish, 2016).

On a positive note, TGE youth may also cultivate and develop additional sources of strength and resilience through supportive interactions with the child welfare system. For TGE youth, supportive interactions with child welfare social workers and appropriate placements and gender-affirming care facilitated through the child welfare system may provide transgender and gender expansive youth with protection from abuse or maltreatment, a safe and supportive living environment, and gender-affirming parenting. Finally, in states with anti-discrimination laws that include such protections, child welfare system involvement can mandate equitable access to gender-affirming healthcare, educational support services, and other culturally oriented supports to preserve peer relationships and community ties (Mallon, 2021).

Transgender and Gender Expansive Youth in Child Welfare Systems, Past and Present

Current understanding of the issues faced by TGE youth have been informed by firsthand accounts of social workers and researchers of these youth and their experiences (DeCrescenzo & Mallon, 2000; Mallon & DeCrescenzo, 2006; Mallon, 1999; Paul, 2018, 2019) These historical accounts provide insight into the discriminatory attitudes and beliefs of social workers who saw transgender youth as "deviant." The needs of TGE youth in child welfare systems were often not addressed, or worse, were invisible to those who were charged with caring for them. Caregivers who did provide gender-affirming living environments for these youth were often deemed to be enabling of this "deviance," and children and youth were removed from their homes. These stigmatizing beliefs and the subsequent administrative actions punished caregivers for being open about their identities and beliefs. Such practices led to marginalization of this population based on exclusionary placement practices.

Current Issues in the Field

There have always been TGE young people in child welfare systems but it has often been difficult for professionals to recognize their existence for three reasons: (1) Many of these youth are invisible to untrained workers; (2) for safety reasons, TGE young people are socialized to hide; and (3) many residential youth services professionals are contemptuous of a TGE orientation (Mallon, 1999; Paul, 2018). In addition, most professionals are completely lacking in knowledge about normative TGE adolescent development. Additionally, some administrators of child welfare service agencies are fearful that acknowledging a self-identified TGE young person in their program might be seen as "encouraging" or "promoting" a TGE identity.

The end result is that TGE youth often remain hidden and invisible in residential systems, and if they do come out, they are often not provided with the same quality of care that is extended to their cisgender counterparts (Gallegos et al., 2011).

TGE youth, whose circumstances and needs are particularly misunderstood, often suffer especially poor treatment in child welfare systems. They are regularly targeted for harassment and assault, denied necessary medical treatment for their gender dysphoria, given sex-segregated rooming assignments inconsistent with their gender identities, called by their names and personal gender pronoun or names and forced to dress in ways that allow no room for their gender expression (Mallon & Perez, 2020). TGE young people in child welfare systems interviewed for this publication reported both positive and negative responses to their gender identity expression, though the negative stories outnumber the positive. Several themes emerge from the above vignette and from data collected from narratives provided by other TGE youth. These themes, discussed below, are useful in understanding the experiences of TGE youth in residential settings.

Invisibility and Hiding

TGE young people in child welfare systems are frequently an invisible population. This allows administrators and staff to convince themselves that there are no TGE young people in their care. The majority of TGE young people are silent and hidden witnesses to the negative attitudes of staff, administrators, and peers toward those who workers believe to be TGE identified. Most TGE young people in child welfare systems receive – from multiple sources – the message: "Stay in the closet! We do not want to deal with this!"

Stress and Isolation

Living in silence, as so many TGE young people in foster care are forced to do, is the source of a high level of stress and isolation in their lives. The comments of Sawyer exemplify this:

> I tried to hide it 'cause I saw how they treated those kids who they thought were trans. I mean, they were treated terribly – just because the others thought they were trans. I knew that I was trans, so imagine how they would treat me if they ever found out. I felt so alone, so isolated, like no one ever knew the real me. I couldn't talk to anybody about who I was. It was a horrible experience. Trying to hide who you really are is very difficult and exhausting. Sometimes I felt so bad I just wanted to kill myself. (Mallon, 2021, p. 129).

Multiple Placements

Moving from one's family to a child welfare setting is, in and of itself, a stressful and traumatic experience. Subsequent moves from one placement to another have been identified as a major difficulty for youth in residential settings. The constant challenge of adapting to a new environment is unsettling, provokes anxiety, and undermines one's sense of permanence. Unlike other cisgender adolescents in residential settings who move from setting to setting because of individual behavioral problems, TGE youth report that their gender identity expression itself led to multiple and unstable placements, not their behavior.

Young people report experiencing unstable placements for four reasons: (1) They are not accepted because staff has difficulties dealing with their gender identity expression; (2) they felt unsafe due to their gender identity expression and either "AWOL" (run away) from the placement for their own safety or requested new placements; (3) they were perceived as a management problem by staff because they were open about their gender identity expression; or (4) they were not accepted by peers due to their gender identity expression.

Tracy provided this narrative which captured their experience of living in a child welfare system:

> I left home at 16 when it was clear that I was TGE and my family just couldn't support me. They said you can be trans, but you can't live here. They had their own problems with drugs, abuse, and all that mess but somehow, I became the punching bag for everyone's issues when I came out as trans. I went to one foster home and that was terrible, because they were worse than my family about my identity; I then went to another foster home and stayed there for a year – it wasn't so bad, because the foster mother just didn't even pay attention to us (there were four other foster kids in that home) and then the agency winded up closing her home and we had to move again. I then went to a group home and that place was just disgusting – the place was filthy; the staff were plain ignorant about TGE people and almost everything else. I asked to leave there and I went to another group home – it wasn't so bad and I stayed there for about two years until I aged out. Now, I am on my own – in five years I was in four different places and I guess I was lucky, lots of TGE kids that I know were in like ten or fifteen different places.

These case examples exemplify the ways in which TGE young people are continuously faced with having to negotiate new environments, many of which are inhospitable and lacking in the conditions necessary for healthy psychological development.

Many agencies simply get rid of TGE youth because staff cannot deal with the youths' gender identity expression. Many of these youth have been in multiple placements or re-placements by agencies at all levels of care. One young person provides this account:

> I have had so many different placements, I can't even remember. Too many to remember ... a lot of places. I was 15 when I went to my first one, I've been to lots of them, but I kept running away because I just couldn't live there – the staff just couldn't seem to deal with me they never called me by my chosen name and they never used the pronoun I asked them to use. They just kept saying – "you're gay right?" and I tried to explain that I was TGE and not gay, but they just couldn't understand or didn't want to.

These case examples exemplify the ways in which TGE young people are continuously faced with having to negotiate new environments, many of which are inhospitable and lacking in the conditions necessary for healthy psychological development.

Replacement and Feelings of Rejection

The majority of TGE young people sense that they are not welcome in many of the residential settings where they have been placed. They perceive that they are reluctantly accepted into some placements and consequently feel isolated and have negative reactions to their placement. Many young people are impassioned about their maltreatment in these settings, as this quotation from Carter illustrates:

> How was I treated? Oh, God, it was terrible, and it started as soon as I walked into the group home. This staff member, I think she was the supervisor, just pulled me aside and said – I heard you are gay or TGE or whatever, and I just want to tell you that you are not gonna go any of that stuff here in this group home. I mean I wasn't even in the door and they were giving me shit.

When young people were met with acceptance and provided with care that suggested staff were competent in dealing with TGE youth, they remained in the setting, as Dane noted in this narrative:

> Many things fade from my memory as I get older, but the lessons that I learned at GC and the kindness the staff there showed me, the care that they imparted in the most professional way, while still showing that they were human, will never fade. When we lacked a father and a mother our staff were our parents. I can say now that I love myself, I know my self-worth, I value myself and that I can have a healthy relationship despite all I went through because the staff in that agency guided me through this time of my life. Thanks to them I learned to not

be afraid of social workers and while there are good and bad ones, having now seen some good ones, I know there are many more out there that are good than there are bad ones. Thanks to their goodness I was able to feel like a whole person. Today, I am a whole person, if a little cracked in some spots.

Conversely, however, other young people reported that they left their placement once they realized that they were not welcomed. Tracy recalls this experience vividly:

I tried to be what they wanted me to be, but I just couldn't. I was who I was and after six months in that place I thought if I have to stay here I will kill myself. One day, I had just had enough and I thought, living in the streets would be better than living in that hell-hole and I just took my stuff and left. No one even tried to convince me to stay and no one ever came to look for me. I lived with friends, I sofa surfed and then I found this shelter programs that was pretty good and accepted me as I was.

Frequently, young people who leave placements become lost in the system, and their multiple placements create a sense of impermanence and drift.

Verbal Harassment and Physical Violence

Many young people enter foster care because, at its best, it offers sanctuary from abusive family relationships and violence in their homes. However, with the constant threat of harassment and violence within the system, TGE youth report being unable to feel completely secure or confident (see Mottet & Ohle, 2006). Although violence and harassment may be an unfortunate component of residential care from time to time for all youth, TGE young people, unlike their cisgender counterparts, are targeted for attack specifically because of their gender identity expression. Petra recalled the nightmare of verbal harassment and physical violence:

I was coming home to the shelter one night from my job and I was just minding my own business when these three boys from the shelter started to yell at me – "Hey, you she-male, what are you anyway, a guy or a girl?" I tried to ignore them and walked a bit faster to get to the shelter, but they kept following me – taunting me, embarrassing me in front of all of these people on the street. I felt so humiliated, so bad, so low. Finally, one of them jumped me from behind, pulled up my skirt and tried to sexually assault me with his fingers. That's when someone stopped their car and yelled from them to stop. They ran, and this guy got out of his car and asked if I was all right – I said I was because I was embarrassed and humiliated – but I was hurt, inside more than outside.

I didn't go back to the shelter that night or any other night. I had some money so I rented a cheap room for the night and then I went to stay with friends. It was a terrible experience, but I never reported it – I figured no one would do anything about it.

The Importance of Policy

Child welfare policies provide an administrative backbone for how a child welfare system involved youth should be treated by their caregivers. While all youth should be affirmed in their gender identity, TGE youth in the child welfare system may have identity-specific needs related to safe and equitable living environments, access to gender-affirming healthcare, appropriate educational environments, and social supports. Thus, it is important that the needs of these youth are ratified in handbooks, policies, and guides used by organizations that serve this population. In the absence of written policies prohibiting discrimination and protecting equitable care for transgender and gender expansive youth, caseworkers, administrators, and caregivers with a limited understanding of the necessity of gender-affirming care may approach their interactions with the youth in ways that are consciously or unconsciously discriminatory or marginalizing.

Gender-affirming policies and practices on organizational and individual provider levels are particularly important in a child welfare setting. For example, denying the importance of gender identity, denying healthcare until 18 years, youth will systemically be maltreated, resulting in abuse. In addition to defending youth from harm through discrimination, explicitly naming TGE youth within the policies mandates training opportunities for case managers. Social Workers should be aware of what policies (if any) exist within their organization regarding TGE youth and critically examine the impact that translating these policies into praxis would have.

A handful of states have passed gender-based or LGBTQ-specific protections for youth in child welfare systems (downloaded 11/25/2020, https://www.lambdalegal.org/child-welfare-analysis). In several states, policy makers have passed religious-based exemptions to intentionally discriminate against TGE youth in their care. Due to the inconsistent and evolving climate of policy discrimination protections on a state level without a current federal mandate regarding the issue, service providers should take the steps to prohibit TGE discrimination within their organization, regardless of federal or statewide climate.

Supporting TGE Youth in Child Welfare Systems

In order to competently serve and safeguard TGE youth, child welfare staff should understand what it means for a youth to be TGE and should be familiar with and use appropriate terminology. In addition:

- Child welfare staff should receive mandatory cultural humility training on gender identity and expression, including education regarding social and medical transition issues for TGE youth.
- Child welfare staff have a legal duty to protect the physical and emotional safety of TGE youth. Child welfare staff should take immediate action to end any form of harassment or bullying against TGE youth, whether perpetrated by staff, foster parents, or peers.
- Child welfare staff should maintain confidentiality regarding the gender identity of TGE youth in their care and be aware of legal obligations to treat such information confidentially. Staff should not disclose information about a youth's gender identity without first obtaining the youth's permission.
- Child welfare staff should respect a TGE youth's name and personal gender pronouns that best affirm the young person's gender identity.
- Child welfare staff should allow TGE youth to express their gender identity through chosen attire, grooming and mannerisms without punishment or ridicule.
- Child welfare staff should not assume that TGE youth are "acting out" inappropriately when expressing their gender identity.
- Child welfare staff should not consider or classify youth as sexually aggressive simply because they are TGE. These youth are no more likely than any others to be sexually aggressive.
- Child welfare staff should avoid making assumptions about the sexual orientation of TGE. TGE and gender-diverse youth may identify as gay, lesbian, bisexual, questioning, queer, non-binary, asexual, or cisgender.
- Child welfare staff should be aware of health care protocols for medical treatment for TGE individuals and should ensure that TGE youth have access to competent and trans-affirming mental and medical health services, including access to competent mental health and medical care to support their identity. Mental health treatment should be focused on providing support, not changing a person's gender identity, and may include services such as individual and family counseling, and, with a physician's care, hormone therapy and surgery to align the physical body with the gender identity of the youth. Staff should ensure that existing social and medical transition-related treatment is provided after a youth arrives at an agency or facility.

In sex-segregated facilities, TGE youth should not be designated to the girls' or boys' units strictly based on the sex designated to them at birth. Instead, child welfare staff should make individualized decisions based on the physical and emotional well-being of the youth, considering the young person's wishes, the level of comfort and safety, the degree of privacy afforded, the types of housing available and the recommendations of mental health and medical professionals. The safety of TGE and gender-diverse youth should be protected without resorting to isolating or segregating the youth from the general population. However, single occupancy rooms, if available in units that correspond with the young person's gender identity, are often appropriate for TGE youth in sex-segregated facilities.

TGE youth should be permitted use of bathrooms that correspond to their gender identity. The facility should counsel others that the youth is entitled to use the bathroom corresponding to the youth's gender identity, and can make available private single-person bathrooms as an option. TGE youth should not be singled out as the only people allowed to use or routed to private single-person bathrooms.

Child welfare staff should support the academic achievements of TGE and gender-diverse youth and ensure that they are safe in schools. The gender expressions of TGE youth can make them more visible, and therefore more vulnerable, to harassment and violence at school. Some school dress policies make it more difficult for youth to dress consistently with their gender identities.

Child welfare staff should take immediate action to protect TGE youth facing harassment or discrimination at school, either on-site or off-site, including protection from being disciplined for expressing their gender identity or being denied access to locker rooms, showers, and bathrooms that match their gender identity.

Child welfare staff should locate and develop resources to help TGE youth with their legal issues. TGE youth may need assistance and advocacy to obtain proper legal identity documents reflecting gender identification and chosen names, such as birth certificates, state identification cards, driver's licenses, health insurance cards, Social Security cards, passports, and school identification cards.

Best Practices

Educate Yourself and Commit to Addressing Your Biases

There is a lot of harmful misinformation about gender identity and expression. This information is conveyed through both explicit messaging (e.g., laws criminalizing TGE youth from using public bathrooms) and implicit (e.g., misbeliefs that being transgender is "just a phase"). Take the time to evaluate your own biases and understandings of TGE youth and make meaningful connections with TGE adults in your life.

Assume There Are TGE Youth in Your Care

Given the overrepresentation of TGE youth within child welfare systems, in all likelihood, child welfare social workers have already or will eventually have a TGE youth within their care. While some of these youth identify their gender identity, many choose not to due to fear of retaliation, hostility, or affirming environments, associated with a poorer mental health and quality of life. Rather than waiting for youth to come out and subsequently adopting TGE affirming practices, embrace proactive planning to implement affirmative, evidence-based policies and practices to support and mandate competency trainings led by TGE adults to educate about TGE youth.

Guiding Principles

No two TGE youths' experiences with gender are identical. Approaches should be custom tailored to each youth's preferences. TGE youth are experts in their own experiences and can best speak to their own needs. Listen to these youth, their stories, preferences, and strengths to better understand how to support them.

Names and Pronouns

Child Welfare social workers should use TGE youths' chosen names and pronouns with the consent of the youth within chosen contexts. Research has shown that more contexts or settings (e.g., schools, medical institutions, homes) where youth are able to use their chosen name, the stronger their mental health will be (Pollitt, Ioverno, Russell, Li, & Grossman, 2021). In private, ask the youth if you may document their name and pronouns and in which contexts you may refer to them accordingly, including with other caseworkers. Some youth may decline to use their name and pronoun within some or all contexts such as with their family of origin or schools out of fear of harassment or discrimination. Work with the youth to identify areas in their lives in which they feel safe and comfortable using the correct name and pronouns.

Consider Gender Identity When Determining Placement

Ask all youth coming into the system about gender identity as it pertains to a child/youth's overall culture with respect to your work in a child welfare setting, e.g., placement suitability or connection/referral to other services. Make it a regular part of the intake process to ask all youth how they identifies with respect to their gender and sexual orientation.

Seek Support as Needed

Seek support around mandated reporting as needed, seeking supervision/consultation with agencies that specialize in working with and caring for TGE youth.

Develop Gender-Affirming Policies

Non-Discrimination Policies

Advocate for non-discrimination policies that explicitly protect sex, gender identity, gender expression, intersex traits, and genetic makeup (i.e., inclusive of intersex individuals). Due to evolving social under-standings of the transgender community, it is necessary for policy to address all aspects of potential grounds for discrimination. For example, in lieu of the previously named protections, some may view TGE as protected as under sex discrimination, while others may view TGE youth as not protected as all.

Mandate TGE Competency Training

While TGE youth are should be treated with the same respect as all other youth in care, the TGE population can face additional barriers by uninformed cisgender case managers who are unaware of their shortfalls in understanding TGE youth and their treatment is not in the best interest of the youth/con-stitutes unintentional disrespect. Mandating that caseworkers understand this community, their needs, and addressing their own biases and combats the systemic issues that these youth face.

Consult TGE Alumni When Developing New Practices

No one understands what TGE youth need better than those who were once in their same position. Alumni of child welfare systems or those who have utilized their services have unparalleled expertise in TGE youth needs. When constructing and reviewing proposed practices and policies, it is recommended to hire a TGE child welfare system alumni to collaborate.

"Show and Tell" Your Status as an Advocate or Ally

As a professional, introduce yourself with your pronouns. Clearly convey ally ship (pride flags, know your rights posters, create a trans-affirming environment). Show that you are knowledgeable about social support/support groups/competent medical providers/resources, maintain up to date list of referrals. Demonstrate that you know how TGE youth get information in other ways (i.e., word of mouth, community info).

Case Study 2

Kassidy (she/her/hers) is a 12 year old who identifies as a demi-girl (a gender identity describing someone who partially, but not wholly, identifies as a woman, girl or otherwise feminine, whatever their assigned gender at birth; they may or may not identify as another gender in addition to feeling partially a girl or woman). Kassidy is currently in a relative guardianship with her grand-parents, who do not respect her pronouns in her home environment.

Her grandmother called a local LGBTQ+ youth center and spoke with the center's executive director, a heterosexual, cisgender woman, earlier in the day to seek advice. During the phone call, Kassidy's grandmother expressed that her grandchild, who wanted to be called Kassidy, expressed suicidal ideations at home. Kassidy's grandmother noted that she had kept her out of school that day due to the severity of her suicidal ideations and agreed to potentially bring Kassidy to the center that night.

Andrea (she/her/hers) is a 25-year-old transgender woman who is working as social worker at the LGBTQ+ youth center. As she came in to facilitate a group of LGBTQ+ youth ages 12 to 18 years old that afternoon, Andrea was informed about Kassidy's grandmother's call and that she may be joining the group. Thirty minutes into the group that night, Andrea noticed a car pull up outside the center; she went to the door and greeted an older man and a young person. The elderly man did not introduce himself and stated that he was dropping this youth off for the group. In front of the older man, the child identified themselves as Max and expressed their pronouns as he/him/his. Once they entered the center and the older man left, the child corrected themselves and told Andrea that their name is Kassidy and that she would like to use she/her/hers pronouns if that was okay.

Reflection Questions

1. How might Andrea "show and tell" her status as an advocate to Kassidy?
2. If you were a state social worker working with Kassidy, what additional information would be helpful for you to know to best support her? What recommendations and resources would you offer her?
3. If you were an in-school social worker working with Kassidy at her new school, what additional information would be helpful for you to know to best support her? What recommendations and resources would you offer her?
4. Identify the risk factors and areas for opportunities in Kassidy's current situation. How might the risks be addressed? How might the opportunities be acted on?
5. In addition to the support group at the LGBTQ+ youth center, what resources would you recommend to Kassidy if you were working with her? What resources would you recommend to Kassidy's grandparents?

Case Studies

You are a social worker at Child Protective Services and have been assigned Dom's case. Dom (they/them/theirs) is a Black 8-year-old child who was assigned female at birth and identifies as non-binary. Dom has recently been placed into a relative guardianship with their paternal aunt and uncle, living also with their two older twin cousins, Malik and Terrance. Previously, Dom had been living with their mother, Jada, who could not provide stable housing or a safe living environment because of her drug and alcohol addiction. Dom's father has been incarcerated for drug possession since Dom was 4. Jada encouraged Dom's gender expression and had recently started to refer to Dom by they/them pronouns consistently. After their placement with their aunt and uncle, Dom transferred schools to begin 4th grade at the same majority-white school with Malik and Terrance.

At their new school, Dom is struggling to make friends and is getting bullied about their pronouns, clothes, and family history. Malik and Terrance are both in 6th grade and rarely see Dom at school; when they do, they share that Dom is "shy and quiet." At home, Dom is having conflict with their aunt and uncle about their insistence that they should "try fitting in." Dom's aunt and uncle were frequently involved in Dom's early childhood, and they report having been worried about Dom's "rejection of things for normal girls ever since it started." Dom has also been arguing with their aunt and uncle about having access to the internet; Dom had unsupervised access to the internet while living with their mom and thinks that their aunt and uncle are deliberately keeping them from their online friends. Dom's aunt and uncle think that Dom is too young to be using the Internet as much as they had while living with Jada.

Reflection Questions

1. What additional information would be helpful for you to know in order to best support Dom?
2. What safety risks can you identify that are unique to Dom's case? How would you work to address these risks?
3. As Dom's social worker, what are the first questions you would ask when meeting Dom and their family? What are the recommendations you would make?
4. While working with Dom and their family, how can you remain strength-based while building and maintaining rapport?
5. What are some supports in the community that you would recommend to Dom and their family?

Conclusion

The issues encountered by TGE adolescents and their families are frequently ignored and largely unrecognized by the majority of child welfare professionals – analogous to the ways in which the child welfare system has been deficient in addressing the specific needs of diverse ethnic and racial minorities. An understanding of the impact of societal stigmatization of TGE individuals and their families is crucial to the recognition of, and response to, the needs of this population.

In addition, child welfare professionals and the systems they work in should consider moving away from residential-type programs and focusing more energy on keeping young people at home, preserving connections with their families of origin, when it is safe to do that, and creating kinship or family-based foster homes for TGE youth who cannot reside with their families of origin (McCormick, Scheyd, & Terrazas, 2017; Salazar et al., 2018).

Effecting changes in attitudes and beliefs in pursuit of competent practice with TGE adolescents and their families requires education, training, and self-exploration on both the individual and institutional level (see Mallon, 2009). The development of competence in this area holds promise for preserving and supporting families and for the establishment of appropriate trans-affirmative child welfare services for these young people and their families.

References

Bullard, L., Owens, L. W., Richmond, L., & Alwon, F. (Eds.). (2010). Residential issues in child welfare. *Child Welfare, 89*(2), 11–14.

Clements, J. A., & Rosenwald, M. (2007). Foster parents' perspectives on LGB youth in the child welfare system. *Journal of Gay & Lesbian Social Services: Issues in Practice, Policy & Research, 19*(1), 57–69.

DeCrescenzo, T., & Mallon, G. P. (2000). *Serving transgender youth: The role of child welfare systems – Proceedings of a colloquium – September 2000.* Washington, DC: Child Welfare League of America.

Fish, J. N., Baams, L., Wojciak, A. S., & Russell, S. T. (2019). Are sexual minority youth overrepresented in foster care, child welfare, and out-of-home placement? Findings from nationally representative data. *Child Abuse and Neglect, 89*, 203–211.

Gallegos, A., White, C., Ryan, C., O'Brien, K., Pecora, P., & Thomas, P. (2011). Exploring the experiences of lesbian, gay, bisexual, and questioning adolescents in foster care. *Journal of Family Social Work, 14*, 226–236.

Irvine, A. (2010). "We've Had Three of Them": Addressing the invisibility of lesbian, gay, bisexual, and gender nonconforming youths in the juvenile justice system. *Columbia Journal of Gender and Law, 19*(3), 675–701.

Irvine, A., & Canfield, A. (2015). The overrepresentation of lesbian, gay, bisexual, questioning, gender nonconforming and transgender youth within the child welfare to juvenile justice crossover population. *Journal of Gender, Social Policy, & the Law, 24*(2), 243–261.

Maccio, E., & Ferguson, K. (2016). Services to LGBTQ runaway and homeless youth: Gaps and recommendations. *Children and Youth Services Review, 63*, 47–57.

Mallon, G. P. (Ed.). (1999). *Social services with transgendered youth*. New York: Haworth Press.

Mallon, G. P. (Ed.). (2008). *Social work practice with transgender and gender variant youth*. New York: Routledge.

Mallon, G.P. (Ed.). (2009). *Social work practice with transgender and gender variant youth* (2nd ed.). New York: Routledge.

Mallon, G. P. (2021). *Strategies for child welfare professionals working with transgender and gender expansive youth*. London: Jessica Kingsley.

Mallon, G. P., & DeCrescenzo, T. (2006). Transgender children and youth: A child welfare practice perspective. *Child Welfare, 85*(2), 215–241.

Mallon, G. P., Paul, J., & López López, M. (2021). Protecting LGBTQ+ children & youth. In R. Krugman & Korbin (Eds.), *Handbook of child maltreatment* (2nd ed.). New York: Springer Press.

Mallon, G. P., & Perez, J. (2020). The experiences of transgender and gender expansive youth in juvenile justice systems. *Journal of Criminological Research, Policy and Practice, 25*(5), 217–229.

McCormick, A., Scheyd, K., & Terrazas, S. (2017). Policy essay: Fostering the acceptance and inclusion of LGBTQ youth in the child welfare system: Considerations for advancing trauma informed responses for LGBTQ youth in care. *Journal of Family Strengths, 17*(2), 21–26.

Mottet, L., & Ohle, J. (2006). Transitioning our shelters: Making homeless shelters safe for transgender people. *Journal of Poverty, 10*, 77–101. doi:10.1300/j134v10n02_05

Paul, J. (2020). Exploring support for LGBTQ youth transitioning from foster care to emerging adulthood. *Children & Youth Services Review, 119*(4), 105–118.

Paul, J. C. (2018). *Under the radar: Exploring support for lesbian, gay, bisexual transgender, queer and questioning (LGBTQ) young people transitioning from foster care to emerging adulthood*. Doctoral dissertation, University of Wisconsin-Madison, Madison, WI.

Paul, J. C., & Monahan, E. K. (2019). Sexual minority status and child maltreatment: How do health outcomes among sexual minority young adults differ due to child maltreatment exposure? *Child Abuse & Neglect, 96*, 104099.

Pollitt, A. M., Ioverno, S., Russell, S. T., Li, G., & Grossman, A. H. (2021). Predictors and mental health benefits of chosen name use among transgender youth. *Youth & Society, 53*(2), 320–341. https://doi.org/10.1177/0044118x19855898

Russell, S. T., & Fish, J. N. (2016). Mental health in lesbian, gay, bisexual and transgender (LGBT) youth. *Annual Review of Clinical Psychology, 12*(1), 465–487.

Russell, S. T., Pollitt, A. M., Li, G., & Grossman, A. H. (2018). Chosen name use is linked to reduced depressive symptoms, suicidal ideation, and suicidal behavior among transgender youth. *Journal of Adolescent Health, 63*, 503–505.

Salazar, A. M., McCowan, K. J., Cole, J. J., Skinner, M. L., Noell, B. R., Colito, J. M., … Barkan, S. E. (2018). Developing relationship-building tools for foster families caring for teens who are LGBTQ2S. *Child Welfare, 96*, 75–97.

Shelton, J. (2015). Transgender youth homelessness: Understanding programmatic barriers through the lens of cisgenderism. *Children and Youth Services Review, 59*, 10–18.

Shelton, J. (2016). Reframing risk for transgender and gender-expansive young people experiencing homelessness. *Journal of Gay & Lesbian Social Services, 28*(4), 277–291.

U.S. Department of Health & Human Services, Admin. on Children, Youth & Families, Information Memorandum ACYF-CB-IM-11-03, Lesbian, Gay, Bisexual, Transgender and Questioning Youth in Foster Care (2011, April 6).

17 More than a Shelter Bed: Working Towards Housing Justice for TGE YYA Experiencing Homelessness

Jama Shelton

Introduction

In a country as resourced as the United States, no one should be without a home. Homelessness is intricately connected to poverty and racism, and is a form of discrimination and social exclusion. People experiencing homelessness not only lack secure and stable housing, they are also often lumped into the socially constructed identity category of "the homeless" and as a group face criminalization, victimization, and discrimination (Canada Without Poverty, 2016). Unless an individual specifically claims the identity label "homeless," it is important for social workers to see homelessness as an experience an individual has, and to understand that the experience of homelessness does not define the entirety of the individual experiencing it. Groups that are marginalized in society are often overrepresented in the population of people experiencing homelessness. And, once homeless, they are then further marginalized as a result of their experience. This is true for trans and gender expansive (TGE) youth and young adults (YYA).

Historical Context

In order to understand TGE YYA homelessness, we must first understand the social deviant status that has historically been assigned to TGE YYA as well as to YYA experiencing homelessness. Housing instability among TGE YYA is a relatively recently acknowledged issue, however the concept of "runaway" youth is a documented concept in the U.S. dating back to the 1600s. At that time, the response was centered on the delinquency of the "unproductive" young person resulting in punitive legal consequences. Industrialization and urbanization led to the development of state control over YYA, as expectations of YYA began to change during the 1800s and social and legal distinctions between adults and youth began to emerge. These distinctions were reinforced through reform measures regulating child labor and proposing mandatory education. Importantly, state interventions for runaway youth marked the beginning of state control over the family. Further formalizing state power over family matters, the juvenile

DOI: 10.4324/9780429297687-17

court system was developed in the early part of the twentieth century (Libertoff, 1980). The perception of unhoused youth during this time remained one of delinquency, and the reform measures centered on control, due to the historic responsibility of court officials and police officers for controlling "delinquent" youth (Libertoff, 1980). YYA homelessness was considered a criminal matter in the United States until recent decades (Ray, 2006; Varney & van Vliet, 2008). Though experiencing homelessness is not in and of itself considered a criminal matter today, people experiencing homelessness are routinely criminalized for engaging in activities that are necessary for daily living and survival. For instance, laws restrict where individuals can sleep, obtain food, ask for money, and even sit down (National Law Center on Homelessness and Poverty, 2016).

Just as YYA were historically criminalized for their housing status, TGE identities have also been considered deviant, pathologized, and criminalized. The historical criminalization of gender expression dates back to 1848 when laws were passed in multiple American cities outlawing cross-dressing and finding individuals appearing in public "in a dress not belonging to his or her sex" (Stryker, 2008, p. 32). Though these kinds of laws do not formally exist in the United States today, the genders and bodies of TGE people are routinely policed by individuals and within institutions that are premised on a binary classification and static understanding of sex and gender.

Western medical discourses have informed the ways society thinks of TGE identities and have shaped the frameworks made available to society at large (Sanger, 2008). This is not to minimize the positive impact that medical intervention has had for individual people. Medical intervention has certainly been crucial for the survival of many TGE people. However, the discourse of disorder that is central to the historical treatment of TGE people has contributed to the oppression and stigmatization of TGE individuals and communities. Central to western medical models is a focus on a binary construction of gender, a binary construction of sex, and a binary construction of trans identity. The historical focus of medical intervention has been on "correcting" gender deviance through reassignment to the "appropriate" gender (Shelley, 2009, p. 30). This inherently oppressive framework perpetuates the binary gender system and reflects the systemic rejection and denial of TGE identities and experiences (Shelley, 2009).

Though not all professions subscribe to the medical model of correction and reassignment mentioned above, TGE YYA frequently interact with macro- and micro-systems that are rooted in pathologically based conceptualizations of TGE identities. In fact, the very social systems that should provide support to TGE YYA experiencing homelessness are often built upon these pathological (mis)understandings. Consequently, the systems TGE YYA experiencing homelessness engage in either deny their existence (Bauer et al., 2009) or are not equipped to provide affirming care (Abramovich, 2016; Shelton, 2015). When social systems do not provide TGE competent and affirming care, and when family and community are not accepting, TGE

YYA may find themselves on their own, without stable residence. Once on their own, TGE YYA face the increased likelihood of coming into contact with the previously described systems founded on the premise of controlling YYA, especially YYA without housing, through a deviance-oriented and pathological lens. Consequently, TGE YYA, especially TGE YYA of color, are disproportionately involved in the U.S. carceral systems (Hunt & Moodie-Mills, 2012).

Though we have seen some progress in the past decade related to protections for TGE people, advances are not guaranteed and are consistently threatened by a conservative backlash, enacted through hetero/ciscentric policies and hetero/cissexist practices (Mertus, 2007). This leads to a lack of security and confidence in the protections that do exist, and can result in TGE YYA being hypervigilant and presuming rejection from social workers and others that could potentially be sources of support. The resulting threats to the overall well-being of TGE YYA experiencing homelessness cannot be overstated, as they exist on every level of U.S. society. They are codified into law, institutionalized into systems, and enacted upon individual TGE people through both interpersonal and structural experiences of violence (Butler, 2004). They are perpetuated by oppressive narratives about who TGE expansive YYA experiencing homelessness are, and who they can become.

Why Do TGE YYA Experience Homelessness?

There is no singular cause of homelessness for any population. A variety of factors often impact one's housing stability and must be considered when conceptualizing the problem of homelessness among TGE YYA. Systemic factors include racism, cisgenderism, heterosexism, and poverty. Family conflict is often reported to be a reason for homelessness. Additional pathways into homelessness for TGE YYA may include child welfare or juvenile justice system involvement, mental health challenges, and family homelessness (Choi, Wilson, Shelton, & Gates, 2015; Ecker, Aubry, & Sylvestre, 2019; Shelton et al., 2018). Pervasive discrimination and anti-transbias within an individual's home of origin, as well as in their broader community, within the housing sector, in school settings, and in the workplace make TGE YYA more susceptible to poverty and housing instability (Mottet & Ohle, 2006).

The dominant narrative around homelessness among TGE YYA is identity-based family rejection (Choi et al., 2015; Shelton & Bond, 2017). Being rejected by one's family because of a TGE identity and being ejected from one's home seriously impacts TGE YYA during adolescence and throughout their adult lives. Experiencing identity-based family rejection increases the risk of homelessness and suicidality (James et al., 2016). When family rejection results in a TGE YYA being kicked out of their homes, TGE YYA may negative outcomes related to housing stability, educational attainment, financial stability, physical, and mental health (James et al., 2016). Literature documents the role of identity-based family rejection as a contributing factor to homelessness among TGE YYA, however it is not always the only factor at play. When the focus is solely on family level characteristics and individual risk, systematic oppression and structural barriers are often ignored. It is important for social workers to consider the broader context within which an individual experiences homelessness. Additional contributing factors to homelessness for TGE YYA noted in the literature include family violence, parental substance use, child welfare system involvement, and a lack of affordable housing (Choi et al., 2015; Gangamma, Slesnick, Toviessi, & Serovich, 2008; Shelton et al., 2018).

In addition to the above pathways into homelessness for TGE YYA, the role of poverty in must be examined. TGE people are more likely than the general population to live in poverty and to be underemployed. Anti-trans bias in the workplace and employment discrimination contribute to high rates of poverty among TGE people (James et al., 2016). Finding stable employment can be difficult for TGE YYA who may lack formal training or work experience. Without employment, or with limited employment, obtaining and maintaining housing can be incredibly difficult for TGE people, who may also be targets of discrimination by landlords.

Addressing TGE YYA Homelessness

Homelessness among TGE YYA cannot be solved with the provision of services alone. Addressing the overrepresentation of TGE YYA in the population of YYA experiencing homelessness requires intervention on the micro and macro level. Micro level interventions geared towards meeting the basic needs of TGE YYA experiencing homelessness must be inclusive and affirming of TGE YYA. Macro interventions are needed to alleviate the oppressive conditions that perpetuate stigma and marginalization of TGE YYA. Structural competence provides social workers with a framework for focusing on both the micro and macro level. A key component of structural competence is the identification, examination, and action toward the causes of oppression (George & Marlowe, 2005). To adequately and effectively address homelessness among any population, we must also reimagine the way we think about services, housing, and homelessness in this country. One of the most important ideological shifts to make is to see housing as a basic human right.

Housing Is a Human Right

Homelessness is often thought about as an individual failure to secure and maintain housing, rather than what is actually is – a structural failure and political problem (Canada Without Poverty, 2016). This is evident in the ways people experiencing homelessness are criminalized, resulting in further social exclusion and increasing the barriers people may face in exiting homelessness. From a human rights perspective, homelessness is seen as the product of structural inequity and the failure of states to ensure the human rights of all.

As per the United Nations Committee on Economic, Social and Cultural Rights, the human right to adequate housing includes the following seven components:

1. "Security of tenure: housing is not adequate if its occupants do not have a degree of tenure security, which guarantees legal protection against forced evictions, harassment, and other threats.
2. Availability of services, materials, and infrastructure: housing is not adequate if its occupants do not have safe drinking water, adequate sanitation, energy for cooking, heating, lighting, food storage, or refuse disposal.
3. Affordability: housing is not adequate if its cost threatens or compromises the occupants' enjoyment of other human rights.
4. Habitability: housing is not adequate if it does not guarantee physical safety or provide adequate space, as well as protection against the cold, damp, heat, rain, wind, other threats to health, and structural hazards.
5. Accessibility: housing is not adequate if the specific needs of disadvantaged and marginalized groups are not taken into account.
6. Location: housing is not adequate if it is cut off from employment opportunities, health-care services, schools, childcare centers, and other social facilities, or if located in polluted or dangerous areas.
7. Cultural adequacy: housing is not adequate if it does not respect and take into account the expression of cultural identity" (UN Habitat, n.d., p. 4)

For every right within the human rights framework, a corresponding duty exists for the government to respect, protect, and fulfill the right.

What Does the Right to Housing Mean?

While the right to housing does place responsibility on the government to actualize the right to adequate housing, it does not mean that the it is the government's responsibility to build a house for every individual and provide it to them for free. Ways in which the government may actualize the right to adequate housing include creating incentives for private developers to create affordable housing, allocating resources to housing vouchers and public housing units, regulating the market (rent control), ensuring habitability through housing codes, or providing legal protections around foreclosure and evictions. The right to housing framework is in direct contrast to the way we currently view housing in the United States. At present, housing is treated as a market-driven commodity (Tars, 2018).

Homeless Services in Context

TGE YYA experiencing homelessness exist within and are impacted by social systems and institutions that may or may not be inclusive of them, much less affirm and celebrate their identities. When examining service delivery for TGE YYA experiencing homelessness it is imperative to keep the broader social context in mind – remembering that oppressive societal structures produce and maintain the marginalization of TGE YYA in society at large, within their families and communities, and within the housing market and homeless serving systems. And that having to navigate these oppressive societal structures day in and day out may lead TGE YYA to experience a range of mental and behavioral health disparities and challenges engaging in traditional service models, most of which were created with the cisgender service user in mind. Consequently, homeless systems in the United States are not designed to accommodate TGE people and organizational policies and practices may not apply to or include TGE people (Abramovich, 2016; Mallon, 2009; Pyne, 2011; Shelton, 2015).

Service Barriers

Understanding of service delivery in context helps deepen the understanding of barriers TGE YYA may experience when attempting to access homelessness and housing related assistance. Anti-transbias shapes the interactions of TGE YYA interpersonally, within communities and systems such that rejection and discrimination often become the anticipated norm. TGE YYA experiencing homelessness often find themselves having to find their way within oppressive systems that frequently disregard or denies their self-designated genders. Examples of disregarding or denying one's gender can be experienced in a variety of settings, showing up in the form of binary gender bathrooms, sex-segregated facilities, frequent questioning about one's identity and/or body parts, inaccurate documentation, misgendering, victimization, harassment, and even service denial (James et al., 2016; Shelton, 2015). When faced with only binary gendered options within service settings, TGE YYA often experience marked distress (Herman, 2013). The impact of this systematic failure to recognize and respect how people would like to be classified within the gendered space results in many TGE YYA either opting out of critical services and support, or using survival strategies that may be classified as behavioral problems or viewed as non-compliance.

Re-Envisioning Services: House of Tulip

House of Tulip is a nonprofit collective, led by TGE people, creating housing solutions for TGE people in Louisiana. Their initial goal includes purchasing and renovating a property in New Orleans that would provide zero-barrier housing for up to nine TGE people. Importantly, this property (and any future properties the group purchases) will be operated under a Community Land Trust. This means that the House of Tulip Founders Circle will maintain the property and make sure that the rent remains affordable and free from the impact of gentrification. They plan to prioritize community members who are among the most vulnerable, including TGE people of color, young people, sex workers, elders, disabled people, undocumented immigrants, and immunocompromised people.

House of Tulip is not an emergency shelter or a transitional living program. It is about a long-term investment in housing solutions for TGE people in Louisiana. The ultimate goal is to move residents from homelessness to home ownership. See houseoftulip.org.

Reflection Questions:
1. What are the ways in which House of Tulip is an innovative solution to TGE homelessness?
2. What challenges do you anticipate the collective may face?
3. What are other examples of outside the system housing solutions that you can imagine might be effective for TGE YYA?

Conclusion

Housing is a human right, not a privilege. A human rights approach to housing and homelessness shifts the locus of the problem from the individual to structural inequities and the failure of states to ensure the human rights of all. The oppressive structural dynamics of cis/heterosexism and racism that permeate the daily experiences of TGE YYA experiencing homelessness are also a violation of human rights. The overrepresentation of TGE YYA in the population of YYA experiencing homelessness is a product of these oppressive structural dynamics.

It is absolutely necessary that YYA services are inclusive and affirming for TGE YYA, however, creating TGE-inclusive and affirming services is simply not enough to adequately address TGE YYA homelessness and to achieve housing justice. A paradigm shift must occur such that housing is not viewed as a privilege to be earned, but rather is considered a human right. It is the responsibility of social workers, policy makers, elected officials, housing advocates, and organizational leadership to adopt a human rights approach to housing and homelessness and to extend their work beyond supporting individual TGE YYA and also include efforts to dismantle the systems that produce and maintain housing inequities.

References

Abramovich, A. (2016). Understanding how policy and culture create oppressive conditions for LGBTQ2S youth in the shelter system. *Journal of Homosexuality, 64*(11), 1484–1501.

Bauer, G., Hammond, R., Travers, R., Kaay, M., Hohenadel, K., & Boyce, M. (2009). "I don't think this is theoretical; this is our lives": How erasure impacts health care for transgender people. *Journal of the Association of Nurses in AIDS Care, 20*(5), 348–361.

Butler, J. (2004). *Undoing gender*. New York, NY: Routledge.

Canada Without Poverty. (2016). *Youth rights! Right now! Ending youth homelessness: A human rights guide.* Retrieved from https://www.homelesshub.ca/sites/default/files/attachments/YouthRightsRightNow-final.pdf

Choi, S. K., Wilson, B. D. M., Shelton, J., & Gates, G. (2015). *Serving our youth 2015: The needs and experiences of lesbian, gay, bisexual, transgender, and questioning youth experiencing homelessness.* Los Angeles: The Williams Institute with the True Colors Fund.

Ecker, J., Aubry, T., & Sylvestre, J. (2019). A review of the literature on LGBTQ adults who experience homelessness. *Journal of Homosexuality, 66*(3), 297–323.

Gangamma, R., Slesnick, N., Toviessi, P., & Serovich, J. (2008). Comparison of HIV risks among gay, lesbian, bisexual and heterosexual homeless youth. *Journal of Youth and Adolescence, 37,* 456–464.

George, P., & Marlowe, S. (2005). Structural social work in action: Experiences from rural India. *Journal of Progressive Human Services, 16*(1), 5–24.

Herman, J. (2013). Gendered restrooms and minority stress: The public regulation of gender and its impact on transgender people's lives. *Journal of Public Management and Social Policy, 19*(1), 65–80.

Hunt, J., & Moodie-Mills, A. (2012). *The unfair criminalization of gay and transgender youth: An overview of the experiences of LGBT youth in the juvenile justice system.* Washington, DC: Center for American Progress.

James, S., Herman, J., Rankin, S., Keisling, M., Mottet, L., & Anafi, M. (2016). *The report of the 2015 U.S. transgender survey.* Washington, DC: National Center for Transgender Equality.

Libertoff, K. (1980). The runaway child in America: A social history. *Journal of Family Issues, 1*(2), 151–164.

Mallon, G. (2009). Knowledge for practice with transgender and gender variant youth. In G. Mallon (Ed.), *Social work practice with transgender and gender variant youth* (pp. 22–37). London and New York: Routledge.

Mottet, L., & Ohle, J. (2006). Transitioning our shelters: Making homeless shelters safe for transgender people. *Journal of Poverty, 10*(2), 77–101.

Mertus, J. (2007). The rejection of human rights framings: The case of LGBT advocacy in the US. *Human Rights Quarterly, 29,* 1036–1064. doi:10.1353/hrq.2007.0045

National Law Center on Homelessness and Poverty. (2016). *Housing not handcuffs: Ending the criminalization of homelessness in U.S. cities.* Washington, DC: National Homelessness Law Center.

Pyne, J. (2011). Unsuitable bodies: Trans people and cisnormativity in shelter services. *Canadian Social Work Journal, 28*(1), 129–138.

Ray, N. (2006). *Lesbian, gay, bisexual and transgender youth: An epidemic of homelessness.* New York, NY: National Gay and Lesbian Task Force Policy Institute and the National Coalition for the Homeless.

Sanger, T. (2008). Queer(y)ing gender and sexuality: Transpeople's lived experiences and intimate partnerships. In L. Moon (Ed.), *Feeling queer or queer feelings? Radical approaches to counseling sex, sexualities and genders* (pp. 72–88). London, UK, and New York, NY: Routledge.

Shelley, C. (2009). Trans people and social justice. *The Journal of Individual Psychology, 65*(4), 386–396.

Shelton, J. (2015). Transgender youth homelessness: Understanding programmatic barriers through the lens of cisgenderism. *Children and Youth Services Review, 59,* 10–18.

Shelton, J. (2016). Reframing risk for transgender youth experiencing homelessness. *Journal of Gay and Lesbian Social Services*, *28*(4), 277–291.

Shelton, J., & Bond, L. (2017). "It just never worked out": How transgender and gender expansive youth understand their pathways into homelessness. *Families in Society*, *98*(4), 235–242.

Shelton, J., DeChants, J., Bender, K., Hsu, H., Narendorf, S., Ferguson, K., ... Santa Maria, D. (2018). Homelessness and housing experiences among LGBTQ youth and young adults: An intersectional examination across seven U.S. cities. *Cityscape*, *20*(3), 9–33.

Stryker, S. (2008). *Transgender history*. Berkeley, CA: Seal Studies.

Tars, E. (2018). Housing as a human right. National Low Income Housing Coalition 2018 Advocates Guide. Retrieved from https://nlihc.org/sites/default/files/AG-2 018/Ch01-S06_Housing-Human-Right_2018.pdf

UN Habitat. (n.d.). *The right to adequate housing*. Office of the United Nations High Commissioner for Human Rights, Fact Sheet No. 1. Retrieved from https://www.ohchr.org/documents/publications/fs21_rev_1_housing_en.pdf

Varney, D., & van Vliet, W. (2008). Homelessness, children, and youth: research in the United States and Canada. *American Behavioral Scientist*, *51*(6), 715–720.

Glossary

A Note about the Language Used in This Book

It can be challenging to accurately reflect the nuances of language that people use to describe themselves within an edited book such as this one. We have chosen to use the phrase "transgender and gender expansive," abbreviated as TGE, throughout the book, both for the sake of consistency and also in an attempt to capture the ways that youth expand our thinking about and challenge dated frameworks for understanding gender. This phrase is meant to include those who identify as nonbinary, genderqueer, gender fluid, agender, autigender, trans masculine, trans feminine, two spirit, bigender, multigender, genderless, and any additional way of naming one's gender outside of cisgender.

We acknowledge that the words people use to describe themselves may change over time, and that terms vary by region and culture. In fact, by the time this book is published, new terms may emerge that we did not even know about at the time of writing. We do not claim to provide definitions to all of the terms that social workers need to know in relation to working with TGE youth. However, given the resources we have to date, we are including the following glossary to guide your understanding of the multiple terms associated with gender, gender expression, gender identity, and working with TGE youth. The definitions we have provided come from multiple sources, including Trans Student Educational Resources (2020), Human Rights Campaign (2020), Shelton and Dodd (2020), Austin et al. (2016), Serano (2016), and Kattari, Kinney, Kattari, and Walls (2020).

Definitions

Affirmed/Authentic gender: The process of bringing one's gender presentation, expression, and/or roles into alignment with one's gender identity.

Agender: A relatively new term to describe the genders of people who do not have a gender and/or have a gender that they describe as neutral. Many, but not all, agender people identify as transgender.

Assigned sex at birth: The sex given to a child at birth, most often based on the child's external anatomy.

Autigender: A word to describe the relationship an autistic person has between them and their gender, which can only be felt or identified with by an autistic person. Autigender is not autism as a gender, but rather acknowledges that gender is so heavily influenced by autism that one's gender and autism cannot be unlinked.

Autism: A neurological variation encompassing a wide range of presentations and experiences. Common characteristics of autism include repetitive behavior and differences in social interaction, interpersonal relationships, and communication. For some people, their gender identity is significantly tied to their identity as an autistic person. *We use identity-first language instead of person-first language for describing autistic people because for some people, their disability is an important part of who they are (this practice comes from the Autistic Self Advocacy Network). We also acknowledge that language and how people describe their identities can vary for each person and change over time.

Ballroom/The Ballroom Scene: A subculture of Black and Latinx youth and adults, providing many queer youth and adults with a chosen kinship structure (see "house") through which collective impact, resiliency, and vital resources are obtained.

Balls: Balls are competitive events organized by houses in the ballroom community. During balls, houses compete in a variety of categories towards the goals of visibility, artistic, and cultural production.

Bigender: Refers to people who identify as two genders. This term should not be confused with Two-Spirit, which is specifically associated with Native American and First Nations cultures.

Binarism: A set of attitudes and beliefs that classify ideas, objects or systems (such as gender, race, sexuality) into two, often opposing, categories.

Cisgender: A term used to describe a person whose gender identity aligns with the gender that is typically associated with their assigned sex at birth. The prefix cis- means "on this side of" or "not across from."

Cissexism/cisgenderism: The structural privileging of cisgender people.

Drag: A term that refers to the performance of masculinity, femininity or other forms of gender expression. A **drag queen** is someone who performs femininity and a **drag king** is someone who performs masculinity.

Gender binary: The pervasive idea that there are two, rigidly bounded genders (woman/man).

Gender affirming surgery: Surgical procedures that change an individual's body so that it more accurately reflects their gender/gender identity. Not all TGE people want to have surgery, and not all of those who want to have surgery can afford it. An individual's TGE identity is not contingent upon surgical intervention.

Gender expansive: An umbrella term used to encompass a wide range of gender identities/expressions. Some prefer this term to "gender nonconforming," which implies there is a "correct" way to conform to one's gender.

Gender expression: The outward manner in which an individual presents their gender, usually expressed through behavior, clothing, haircut, or voice.

Gender fluid: A person who does not identify with a single gender, expressing their gender in a fluid way.

Gender identity: A person's internal sense of self in relation to gender.

Genderqueer: An inclusive term for individuals who reject the idea of fixed gender categories and whose gender identity and/or expression is outside of traditional gender norms. Someone who is genderqueer may or may not identify as trans or nonbinary.

Heterosexism: The structural privileging of people who are heterosexual.

House: Houses are the central kinship structure in the ballroom community. The members of a house function as a family. They are often social configurations, meaning it is called a house, but it is not necessarily a brick-and-mortar place.

Intersex: A term referring to people who are born with a variety of differences in their sex traits and reproductive anatomy. There is a wide variety of difference among intersex variations, including differences in genitalia, chromosomes, gonads, internal sex organs, hormone production, hormone response, and/or secondary sex traits.

Misgendering: Occurs when someone intentionally or unintentionally refers to a person, relates to a person, or uses language to describe a person that doesn't align with their self-designated or affirmed gender.

Multigender: An umbrella term is used to describe people who experience more than one gender identity.

Neurodiverse: The idea that neurological differences (like autism and ADHD) are the result of normal, natural variation in the human genome. This represents a new and fundamentally different way of looking at conditions that were traditionally pathologized.

Nonbinary: A term used by individuals to describe their experience of gender as outside of the binary categories of man/woman. Some non binary people identify as trans, and some do not.

Personal pronouns: The pronoun or set of pronouns that a person uses, when their proper name is not being used. Examples include they/them/theirs, she/her/hers, or he/him/his. There are a range of pronouns an individual may use. It is always best to ask someone what pronouns you should use when referring to them.

Queer: A term that can refer to an individual's gender identity and/or sexual orientation. Queer is sometimes used to describe a fluid gender identity and/or sexual orientation. Previously considered a derogatory word, many in the LGBTQ community have reclaimed the term and many use it to indicate opposition to assimilation.

Sex binary: A oppressive system of viewing sex as consisting solely of two categories, termed male and female, with two sets of matching chromosomes, hormone levels, reproductive organs, and secondary sex characteristics. The sex binary assumes that sex is an immutable biological fact, that no other possibilities or anatomy are believed to exist, or should be allowed to exist.

They/them/theirs: Pronouns that may be used by nonbinary, genderqueer, genderfluid, or gender expansive people. Webster's Dictionary named "they" as the word of the year in 2019, and the American Psychological Association officially recommended that singular *they* be used in professional writing over "he or she" when the reference is to a person whose gender is unknown or to a person who uses the pronoun *they*.

Trans: Prefix or adjective commonly used as an abbreviation for the word *transgender*.

Trans feminine: A term that refers to an individual who was assigned male at birth and who identifies and expresses their gender in a feminine way. A trans feminine person may or may not identify as a woman or as a trans woman.

Trans man/transman: Typically refers to an individual who was assigned female at birth, and who identifies as a man. Trans men are men.

Trans masculine: A term that refers to an individual who was assigned female at birth and who identifies and expresses their gender in a masculine way. A trans masculine person may or may not identify as a man or as a trans man.

Trans woman/transwoman: Typically refers to an individual who was assigned male at birth, and who identifies as a woman. Trans women are women.

Transgender: An umbrella term referring to a person whose gender differs from societal and cultural expectations of the gender associate with their assigned sex at birth.

Two spirit: An umbrella term referring to various indigenous gender identities in North America.

References

Austin, A., Craig, S. L., Alessi, E. J., Wagaman, M. A., Paceley, M. S., Dziengel, L., & Balestrery, J. E. (2016). *Guidelines for transgender and gender nonconforming (TGNC) affirmative education: Enhancing the climate for TGNC students, staff and faculty in social work education.* Alexandria, VA: Council on Social Work Education.

Human Rights Campaign. (2020). *Glossary of terms.* Retrieved from www.hrc.org/resources/glossary-of-terms

Kattari, S. K., Kinney. M. K., Kattari, L., & Walls, N.E. (Eds.). (2020). *Social work and health care practice with transgender and nonbinary individuals and communities: Voices for equity, inclusion, and resilience.* New York: Routledge.

Serano, J. (2016). *Outspoken: A decade of transgender activism and trans feminism.* Oakland, CA: Switch Hitter Press.

Shelton, J., & Dodd, S. J. (2020). Beyond the binary: Addressing cisnormativity in the social work classroom. *Journal of Social Work Education, 56*(1), 179–185.

Trans Student Educational Resources. (2020). *LGBTQ+ definitions.* Retrieved from www.transstudent.org/definitions

Resources

General
- Family Acceptance Project — www.familyproject.sfsu.edu/family-education-booklet
- Gender Spectrum — www.genderspectrum.org
- PFLAG — www.Pflag.org
- Transgender Advocacy Network — www.transadvocacynetwork.org
- TransBucket — www.Transbucket.com
- Transparent — www.transparentusa.org
- Trans Youth Equality — www.transyouthequality.org

Suicide Prevention Hotlines
- Trans Lifeline — www.Translifeline.org
- The Trevor Project — www.Thetrevorproject.org

Child Welfare System
- Recommended Practices to Promote the Safety and Well-Being of Lesbian, Gay, Bisexual, Transgender and Questioning (LGBTQ) Youth and Youth at Risk of or Living With HIV in Child Welfare Settings — https://www.lambdalegal.org/publications/recommended-practices-youth
- Out of the Margins: A Report on Regional Listening Forums Highlighting the Experiences of Lesbian, Gay, Bisexual, Transgender, and Questioning Youth in Care — https://www.lambdalegal.org/publications/out-of-the-margins
- Moving the Margins: Training Curriculum for Child Welfare Services with LGBTQ Youth in Out-of-Home Care: LGBTQ 101 Training Goals & Objectives (2009) — https://www.lambdalegal.org/publications/pp_moving-the-margins
- Moving the Margins: Curriculum for Child Welfare Services with Lesbian, Gay, Bisexual, Transgender, and Questioning Youth in Out-of-Home Care (Train the Trainer Manual) (2009) — https://www.lambdalegal.org/publications/moving-the-margins

- National Recommended Best Practices for Serving LGBT Homeless Youth (2009) – https://www.lambdalegal.org/publications/national-recommended-best-practices-for-lgbt-homeless-youth

Educational Settings
- Trans Students Educational Resources (TSER) – https://transstudent.org/
- National Center for Transgender Equality School Action Center – www.transequality.org/schoolaction
- Bending the Mold: An Action Kit for Transgender Students (2009) – https://www.lambdalegal.org/publications/bending-the-mold
- A Transgender Advocates Guide to Updating and Amending School Records – https://www.lambdalegal.org/know-your-rights/article/youth-ferpa-faq
- Out, Safe & Respected for Educators and Parents: A Guide to LGBTQ Youth in Schools for Educators and Parents – https://www.lambdalegal.org/publications/out-safe-respected-admin
- Preventing Censorship of LGBT Information in Public School Libraries – https://www.lambdalegal.org/publications/fs_preventing-censorship-of-lgbt-information-in-pubilc-school-libraries
- Consortium of High Education: LGBT Resource Professionals – http://tinyurl.com/bestprac4trans
- GLSEN – glsen.org
- National Center for Transgender Equality/GLSEN Model School District Policy – https://transequality.org/sites/default/files/images/resources/trans_school_district_model_policy_FINAL.pdf
- Schools in Transition: A Guide for Supporting Transgender Students in K-12 Schools – https://www.hrc.org/resources/schools-in-transition-a-guide-for-supporting-transgender-students-in-k-12-s

Healthcare
- Creating Equal Access to Quality Health Care for Transgender Patients: Transgender-Affirming Hospital Policies – https://www.lambdalegal.org/publications/20160524_transgender-affirming-hospital-policies
- Health and Medical Organization Statements on Sexual Orientation, Gender Identity/Expression and "Reparative Therapy" – https://www.lambdalegal.org/publications/fs_health-and-med-orgs-stmts-on-sex-orientation-and-gender-identity
- Health Care Fairness for LGBT People and People Living with HIV: Lambda Legal's Health Care Docket – https://www.lambdalegal.org/publications/fs_health-care-fairness-for-lgbt-people-and-people-living-with-hiv

Legal Systems
- Transgender Rights Toolkit: A Legal Guide for Trans People and Their Advocates (2016) – https://www.lambdalegal.org/publications/trans-toolkit

- Changing Birth Certificate Sex Designations: State-by-State Guidelines – https://www.lambdalegal.org/know-your-rights/article/trans-changing-birth-certificate-sex-designations
- Safe Havens: Closing the Gap Between Recommended Practice and Reality for Transgender and Gender-Expansive Youth in Out-of-Home Care – https://www.lambdalegal.org/publications/safe-havens
- Getting Down to Basics: Tools to Support LGBTQ Youth in Care – https://www.lambdalegal.org/publications/getting-down-to-basics

Social Work

- Social work students speak out! The experiences of lesbian, gay, bisexual, transgender, and queer students in social work programs: A study report from the CSWE Council on Sexual Orientation and Gender Identity and Expression (2015) – https://www.cswe.org/getattachment/Centers-Initiatives/Centers/Center-for-Diversity/About/Stakeholders/Commission-for-Diversity-and-Social-and-Economic-J/Council-on-Sexual-Orientation-and-Gender-Identity/CSOGIE-Resources/4878cswe_SWSSO_final_web_REV1.pdf.aspx
- Sexual Orientation and Gender Expression in Social Work Education: Results From a National Survey (Executive Summary) (2009) – https://www.lambdalegal.org/sites/default/files/publications/downloads/bkl_sexual-orientation-and-gender-expression-in-social-work-education_0.pdf
- Council on Social Work Education–Lambda Legal Study of LGBT Issues in Social Work (2009) – https://www.lambdalegal.org/publications/bkl_study-of-lgbt-issues-in-social-work
- The NAME Steps: How to Name and Address Anti-LGBTQIA2S+ Microaggressions in Social Work Classrooms – https://www.cswe.org/CSWE/media/CSOGIE/6861_cswe_CSOGIE_TheNAMESteps_Guide_WEB72_REV2.pdf
- National Resources for LGBTQ Youth (2019) – https://www.lambdalegal.org/publications/fs_resources-for-lgbtq-youth

TGE Dates

- Trans day of Visibility (TDoV) (March 31) – https://tdov.org/ and https://transstudent.org/tdov/
- Day of Silence (Second Friday of April) – GLSEN's annual day of action to spread awareness about the effects of the bullying and harassment of LGBTQ students. In the United States, students take a day-long vow of silence to represent the silencing of LGBTQ students symbolically. https://www.glsen.org/day-of-silence
- LGBTQ Pride Month (June) – https://www.them.us/story/the-complete-history-of-pride
- International Non-Binary People's Day (July 14) – https://www.hrc.org/news/celebrating-the-diversity-of-the-non-binary-community-for-inter-national-non

- National Coming Out Day (NCOD) (October 11) – https://www.glsen.org/activity/coming-out-resource-lgbtq-students?gclid=Cj0KCQiAqo3-BRDoARIsAE5vnaJUh8EpzRx7sSi2DjgZ4T0VTqhL4X9xjoF5MhoFH-zndYi3AHDJTC4aAqiDEALw_wcB
- Trans Day of Remembrance (TDoR) (November 20) – https://www.glaad.org/tdor

Youth and Family Conferences in the United States and Internationally
- Black Transgender Advocacy
  www.blacktrans.org
- Gender Infinity, Houston
  www.genderinfinity.org
- Gender Odyssey, Seattle
  www.genderodyssey.org
- International Lesbian, Gay, Bisexual, Transgender and Intersex Association
  www.ilga.org
- Sparkle (UK)
  www.sparkle.org.uk
- Trans-Tagung Muenchen (Germany)
  www.transtagung-muechen.com
- True Colors LGBT Conference, Connecticut
  www.ourtruecolors.org

Index

Wilchins, R. 29
witness, social worker as 77–8
World Health Organization 32
World Professional Association of
  Transgender Health (WPATH)
  200, 201
WPATH *see* World Professional

Association of Transgender Health
(WPATH)

xenophobia 5

youth-led community advocacy 125–6
YouTube 84

For Product Safety Concerns and Information please contact our EU
representative GPSR@taylorandfrancis.com
Taylor & Francis Verlag GmbH, Kaufingerstraße 24, 80331 München, Germany

www.ingramcontent.com/pod-product-compliance
Lightning Source LLC
Chambersburg PA
CBHW050344270326
41926CB00016B/3599

9 780367 277482